# MERLEAU-PONTY, INTERIORITY AND EXTERIORITY, PSYCHIC LIFE AND THE WORLD

# MERLEAU-PONTY,

## INTERIORITY AND EXTERIORITY,

## PSYCHIC LIFE AND THE WORLD

DOROTHEA OLKOWSKI

and

JAMES MORLEY

Editors

STATE UNIVERSITY OF NEW YORK PRESS

*Body-Image Intercourse: A Corporeal Dialogue Between Merleau-Ponty and Schilder* Copyright (c) 1998. From *Body Images* by Gail Weiss. Reproduced by permission of Routledge Inc.

Published by
State University of New York Press, Albany

© 1999 State University of New York

For information, address State University of New York Press,
State University Plaza, Albany, NY 12246

Production, Laurie Searl
Marketing, Patrick Durocher

**Library of Congress Cataloging-in-Publication Data**

Merleau-Ponty, interiority and exteriority, psychic life, and the
  world / edited by Dorothea Oklowski and James Morley.
      p.   cm.
  Includes bibliographical references and index
    ISBN 0-7914-4277-2 (alk. paper). — ISBN 0-7914-4278-0 (pbk. :
  alk. paper)
    1. Merleau-Ponty, Maurice, 1908–1961.   I. Oklowski, Dorothea.
  II. Morley, James, 1957–     .
  B2430.M3764M4696     1999
  194—dc21                                          98-49628
                                                        CIP

10   9   8   7   6   5   4   3   2   1

This book is dedicated to the members of the

International Merleau-Ponty Circle

and to the memory of Linda Singer

# Contents

# The Continuum of Interiority and Exteriority in the Thought of Merleau-Ponty

## DOROTHEA OLKOWSKI

The chapters in this volume are motivated by a particular reading of the work of Maurice Merleau-Ponty, a reading that finds its place among a broad spectrum of interpretations and uses of Merleau-Ponty's work. According to this reading, throughout Merleau-Ponty's philosophy there is a concerted effort to create and maintain a relation of continuity between what might be considered the "interior" aspects of the subject and the "exteriority" of the world. As the chapters in this volume will show, the continuity between the interior and the exterior holds throughout Merleau-Ponty's oeuvre, from his earliest inquiries to his final work in progress, *The Visible and the Invisible*.[1] It operates, as well, across a broad spectrum of philosophical issues from perception to politics. One of the earliest and clearest expositions of this thesis can be found in *The Structure of Behavior*, a book dedicated to rethinking the connections between and among the organic, psychological, and social levels through the articulation of a novel account of nature. "By nature," writes Merleau-Ponty, "we understand here a multiplicity of events external to each other and bound together by relations of causality."[2] But the relations of causality among external events must be of a quite particular type since, from the very beginning, Merleau-Ponty rejects the mechanical model. This is the model of an isolated body that causally affects the mind, both of which are situated in a physical universe of purely mechanical relations. In such a universe, the interior or mental world organizes itself in the image of the external, physical world, a second reality added on to the first, but always with the proviso that it can be reduced to the physiochemical world of pure material causation.

It is of importance, with respect both to the chapters of this volume and to Merleau-Ponty's project of rethinking the relations between interiority and exteriority, from *The Structure of Behavior* to his final lectures, that Merleau-Ponty appears to place Freud among those thinkers who more or less embrace the materialist position that psychic interiority is grounded in mere mechanical causality. Freud's materialism is, however, somewhat justified for Merleau-Ponty given the undesirability of the alternative: a transcendentally oriented philosophy that makes the world into an objective unity whose meanings are constituted by consciousness.[3] While tending toward mechanistic thinking in his metapsychological accounts, Freud seems to embrace idealism elsewhere, so that Merleau-Ponty is critical when Freud conceives of the unconscious both as the source of instinctual energies irrevocably causing certain mental states and as a psychical system that predetermines our entire destiny.[4] In spite of his reservations, Merleau-Ponty finds rapport and reconciliation in Freud's pronouncement that all physical facts have a meaning, a statement that Merleau-Ponty clarifies according to his own schema. If all physical facts have a meaning, this is because the manner in which instinct and physiology affect human beings is incommensurate with reducing them to external-physical or internal biological causal stimuli, nor is it a sign of a pure consciousness at work. What is at stake, for Merleau-Ponty, is the meaning inherent in physical facts and the manner in which consciousness is dependent upon biological and physical functions.

Merleau-Ponty's own solution to this dilemma is to argue that the instinctual and impersonal physiological life of human beings fully intertwines with psychical, meaningful, and symbolic life until the two are so thoroughly integrated that no human behaviors can be attributed only to either organic functioning or consciousness, for existence gives meaning to body and psyche while integrating them into human life. With this in mind, the first question that arises is, how does animal instinctual behavior develop into complex human psychic modes? Although the truly instinctual behavior of lower animal forms is always concretely determined by its framework of natural causes and, as such, remains biological, chemical, or physical, yet even such purely instinctual behavior consists of a mode of organization, a form. So the issue is whether or not the formal properties of the situation, what Merleau-Ponty calls the structure *in* behavior, remain submerged in material content or emerge from it to become the theme of activity. If the spider cannot learn and cannot change because its purely instinctive existence is unalterably bound to the biological, chemical, and physical causality of unchanging natural laws, nonetheless, even the behavior of a spider occurs only within the context of a specific structure in behavior involving both the spider and its prey. That instinct is structural and not merely material is significant, since a dead fly in the spider's web is not bait. The spider reacts only to a vibrating object, be it a fly or a tuning fork.[5]

More complex structures of behavior allow a living thing to adapt to an actual environment though not to a potential one. This is because objects within the living creature's universe are no longer merely physical realities imposing objective conditions on an environment, although the extent to which most animals can integrate new elements into their behavior is still quite limited. Merleau-Ponty cites Koehler's experiments with lower monkeys in which the animals are able to make use of a rod or rake as an instrument if it can be arranged ahead of time in an appropriate manner. The limitation of this complex behavior form is that the farther away the rake is from the fruit, the less likely is it that the animal will make use of it.[6] Likewise, among less intelligent chimpanzees, the chimpanzee uses available objects as instruments until the mechanical relations existing de facto in the environment become too complicated. If a chimpanzee fails to distinguish which string is attached to desirable fruit from among a group of strings, or is unable to untie a knot, these failures are due to what Merleau-Ponty calls a "sort of animal physics immanent in behavior."[7] In other words, if a chimpanzee fails to make use of a box as an instrument for reaching fruit because it is being used by another chimpanzee as a seat, this is because the world still possesses too much authority as a mechanical invariant. The chimpanzee still lacks symbolic behavior, the ability to "find an invariant in the external object, under the diversity of its aspects."[8] It is a failure of behavior, Merleau-Ponty insists, that is not attributable to the development of the animal's physiology. Instead, animals remain limited by a world wherein each object has one particular form at a time or even at all; this keeps lower animals subject to the needs of the species, needs that are unvarying and unchanging in relation to their particular environment.

Only on the human level is life fully able to be called existence. For humans can vary their relations to things, not only by moving their own bodies as animals do but also by manipulating objects in the world, thereby giving them multiple relations while recognizing that these are simply different properties of the same thing. Precisely this ability to both vary relations and to recognize unity are characterized by Merleau-Ponty as symbolic behavior. Symbolic behavior includes the ability to imagine the future or remember the past and its importance to human life cannot be overestimated. This complex behavior, the ability to vary a point of view, is the basis of human freedom. For, unlike insects and chimpanzees, humans, by creatively manipulating objects, create a multiplicity of relations between themselves and others and themselves and the world. It is by acting in the world and upon things that humans grow into unique beings. Merleau-Ponty explicitly rejects making use of lower, mechanical reactions to explain higher meaning-giving situations (and vice versa) in order to propose that human behavior is neither a physical event nor a view of the situation from the perspective of the "in-itself" of a reflective consciousness that intends the meaning of every situation. Behavior does not unfold in objective time and space like a series of physical events, nor is it constituted in the intentions of reflective consciousness. Rather, Merleau-Ponty maintains that symbolic psychical behavior is the projection outside of the organism of a possibility internal to the organism, a possibility that presupposes a particular view of the situation.[9] What is crucial in this is that, in addition to presupposing a particular point of view, symbolic, psychical behavior must in some sense adhere to the body and to psychic life, for the view is projected from the organism to the world.

The world, for its part, is likewise transformed to accommodate the symbolic forms of psychic life, for it is less a natural, material plenum of juxtaposed parts than a staging ground for behaviors.[10] Thus, behavior, the outward projection of internal possibilities, indicates something like a being-in-the-world. Moreover, what Merleau-Ponty calls the "true world" is at the level of exchanged speech whence the subject of behavior "de-realizes himself" as a pure psychic being so as to be able to constitute the other person as another "I."[11] This implies that a pure psychic life, a pure consciousness, is an impediment to a shared world. If there is to be room in the world for others as others, there must be some connection between a self and an other that exceeds purely psychic life. That is, there must be both a continuum and a separation between psychic life and the world. Such a form is found in the gestalt, a frequent topic in the chapters in this volume.

In the critique of Pavlov's reflexology, Merleau-Ponty argues that reflexology treats behavior as if it were a thing and reinserts it into a world of stimuli interpreted as events in the physical world. When mechanically causal, physical stimuli are confused with the world of the organism, it becomes impossible to locate what Koffka, in *Principles of Gestalt Psychology*, asserts is the behavioral environment of each species.[12] Every species, Merleau-Ponty concurs, has its own a priori, its own manner of elaborating stimuli, a distinct structural reality. So, he concludes, physics and psychology must rethink themselves. In place of abstract parts perfectly contained in a whole, physics must think in terms of milieus and environments in which stimuli only play a role insofar as they participate in any particular species' a priori, whether it be that of spiders embedded in matter, chimpanzees engaged in immediate circumstances, or humans actively involved in existence. And, as the central chapters in this volume demonstrate, there are numerous implications stemming from this theory for understanding the complex interrelations of physical and psychic. When Merleau-Ponty redistributes these two orders into three, he is developing the very notion of the continuity between interiority and exteriority that unifies his work. No longer restricted by nature-consciousness (or body and mind) dichotomies, the organism is now located among three orders in a philosophy of structure; they are quantity or matter, order or life, and signification or mind. "They must represent different degrees of integration and, finally, must constitute a hierarchy in which individuality is progressively achieved."[13] Not only does each sphere represent a greater degree of integration between matter and mind in the life of the living being, but also, the three orders are integrated in accordance with their related formal structures. In short, from the exteriority of matter, to the in-betweenness of life, to the interiority of mind, a continuum exists such that interior and exterior can no longer be separated into unique spheres. Thus, while the chapters in this volume are divided into sections titled, respectively, "Interiority," "Gestalt Connections and Disconnections," and "Exteriority, Life in the World," this is not in order to redraw the lines between interiority and exteriority but only to reflect the focal point of each group of chapters' venture into this continuity. Given the idea of a continuity between "interior" and "exterior," it is all the more important that, with a philosophy of form, Merleau-Ponty is willing to advance beyond Koffka by renouncing the ultimate authority of the causal, physical universe and to exchange it for the universe of forms according to which physical causality is translated into various multirelational formulae according to which what happens at each point is determined by what happens at every other point. Such an "order" is simply a form.[14] In short, all quantitative measures are transformable into forms and no form has a sufficient cause outside of itself. Even distributions of electricity in a conductor never correspond point for point to what has been placed there; the order of distribution is conditioned by local topological circumstances that *never act separately or on their own*. In this way, everything is connected to a multiplicity of other things through a continuum. If matter, life, and mind coexist, they do so as different forms of integration or disintegration. They coexist because they are distinguished from one another by stages of integration and disintegration that are organized according to a philosophy of form.[15]

The chapters in part one, "Interiority," are committed to an exploration of the idea of continuity that magnifies the role of interiority or inner life in the face of the material and even social demands of the world. These chapters examine Merleau-Ponty's use of nonspatial language to describe the workings of inner life and its connections to the world, his notion of transcendence emerging out of immanence, and Merleau-Ponty's development of a notion of the unconscious that maintains a relation to the world. Part two, "Gestalt Connections and Disconnections," focuses on the gestalt as the connector between interiority and exteriority, whether in the form of the body-image or broken up into nothing but connections. The chapters in the third part of this volume, "Exteriority, Life in the World," demonstrate that life in the social and material world is infused with interiority. As the final chapter in this volume explains it, following Merleau-Ponty, we can no longer maintain an idea of nature according to which various processes are known in isolation, though this is not to go so far as to say that everything is literally dependent upon everything else. What we can say is that physical laws, like the law of falling bodies, are possible only within a de facto structure, a reality supported and maintained at each instant by the ensemble of relations of the physical universe (in this case that of the stability of the speed of the earth's rotation).[16] Merleau-Ponty insists that not only are physical laws operating within a structure but that structure can be located in those physical laws, since the ensemble of relations of the physical universe can itself be integrated into a continuous tissue of relations with the rest of the universe. Given that physics makes use of mathematics to characterize the objects of its knowledge, it must be the case that numbers remain numbers and when even physicists want to speak about the physical phenomena they are measuring, they can do so only by expressing them as "laws of certain concrete wholes . . . . Thus form is not a physical reality, but an object of perception," a perceived whole.[17] With this, we are turned to the world of perception, where, as these chapters argue, the truth of Merleau-Ponty's continuum of interiority and exteriority will have to prove itself in terms of phenomena ranging from the unconscious, to the body-image, to the organization of the state, and even the order of the cosmos.

In a powerful and moving chapter on the interiority of thought, heart, dream, and memory, titled, "Inside and Outside: Ontological Considerations," Galen Johnson asks pointedly if there is still a place in philosophy for inner life or if it has not been overwhelmed by the determinative power of the exterior world. He notes that philosophers as diverse as Levinas, Foucault, and Deleuze seem to agree that thought is exteriority and that the exterior has philosophical privilege. Perhaps, Johnson ventures, even Merleau-Ponty can be attributed with such a philosophy. When Merleau-Ponty moved from the prevailing Husserlian thetic intentionality to an incarnate and operative intentionality, was this not to loosen our intentional grasp upon the world? Johnson concludes, however, that even this move has to be seen as an inadequate basis for understanding our relation with the outside. There are at least three prevailing reasons why this is so. First, intentionality marks an inside aiming at an outside and so at least implies dualism; second, while reflection invokes the world, it certainly does not coincide with it; and third, thought and speech as systems overtake any intentional act.

Johnson argues that in spite of Merleau-Ponty's move toward a philosophy of Being, that is, a philosophy of the fold, there is no denying that Merleau-Ponty's thought is a thought of the inside. Yet there is a question, posed, oddly enough, by Gilles Deleuze, whose own thought may not be as fixed on the outside as Johnson suggests it is. That is, is Merleau-Ponty's thought of the inside a stranglehold? Johnson suggests that it is a matter of thinking the inside carefully, of paying close attention to the spatial metaphors that we make use of in explicating this notion. Specifically, he points out that *l'être au monde* is not *l'être dans le monde*, and that if we are to make use of spatialized metaphors to clarify the work of Merleau-Ponty, it might be preferable to avoid saying that the inner life is "inside" us. In a move that connects this chapter with the editors' introduction, Johnson argues that perhaps we can do better if we spatialize inner life in a way that connects it to the exterior, to all the places in which we dwell, to the light above us and the earth beneath. What Johnson proposes, is a rethinking of Merleau-Ponty's notion of "flesh" so that it does not merely juxtapose interior and exterior but rather reflects the sense in which they are bonded together. As Johnson so aptly points out, in choosing the notion of "flesh," *la chair*, Merleau-Ponty gives us a flesh-and-blood feel and smell for what our time is, for our origin and our end; and it is by engaging thoughtfully with this sense of the connection between inner life and the exterior that we can avoid the collapse into the interiority of thought.

While a chapter titled "Transcendence in Merleau-Ponty," might not appear to be concerned with interiority, in this instance, paradoxically, it is, in that as Michael B. Smith argues, exteriority always remains tied to inner life. He notes that while the Husserlian move was to bracket the question of the existence of transcendent being so as to preserve its essence as meaning within immanence, Merleau-Ponty takes up the immanence/transcendence distinction in earnest in order to work out the parameters of transcendence available to human existence. Smith too endorses the focus of this volume when he argues that the "/" symbol in Merleau-Ponty stands less for dichotomy and opposition than for "mediation," and that this crucial difference distinguishes Merleau-Ponty's sense of transcendence from that of Husserl, Sartre, and especially, Levinas.

Smith articulate three sorts of transcendence in the work of Merleau-Ponty, types that are themselves defined in terms of the mediating slash: phenomenological/epistemological, existential/ontological, and quite rarely, metaphysical/theological. On the phenomenological/epistemological level, Merleau-Ponty's concept of "flesh" operates so as to break through the opposition Meno's paradox establishes between knowledge and ignorance, by positing flesh as seer and seen, immanence and transcendence. Smith also argues that existential/ontological transcendence brings Merleau-Ponty closest to Heidegger whose concept of thrownness into the world makes transcendence into a feature of existence that opens up freedom, choice, virtuality, and consciousness. For, when *Dasein* transcends entities by projecting itself toward the world taken as the totality of entities, then a human being in this movement becomes a transcendence, a being-at-the-world. Finally, Smith contends that Merleau-Ponty's mediation of metaphysical/ontological transcendence can best be explained by contrast to that of Levinas. Merleau-Ponty sees the relation between immanence and transcendence as an "inner" one, in which transcendence arises out of immanence. He considers such an emergence to be more rationally satisfying and more politically subversive than transcendence as pure exteriority, such as is found in Emmanuel Levinas.

Smith concurs that Merleau-Ponty seeks to expand being and knowledge so as to accommodate all being and experience within a coherent manifold, thereby containing transcendence within a unified field of being. Merleau-Ponty accomplishes this, principally, through epistemological means: Reason, reflection, and knowledge draw transcendence toward immanence. Yet, Smith warns, if philosophy merely constitutes transcendence, it simultaneously relativizes it, thereby compromising its alterity. Thus, the importance of phenomenological description in this process becomes apparent. Merleau-Ponty avoids relativizing alterity by giving priority to description over constitution and by broadening the meaning of reason to include fleshly mediation. Ultimately, Smith claims, what makes Merleau-Ponty's philosophy so valuable to us is that rather than constituting transcendence and the exterior, it seeks, with its evocative language, to describe the inception of subjectivity within the sphere of interiority and immanence, and from there, to trace the birth of ideality; neither immanent, nor transcendent, but mediatory.

Edward Casey is also interested in matters reflecting upon interiority and its relation to the continuum of life by means of the relation to Freud's theory of the unconscious. His chapter, "The Unconscious Mind and the Prereflective Body," addresses the question of the difference between Freud's notion of the unconscious mind and Merleau-Ponty's conception of the prereflective body. What, he asks, motivates each to locate the nonconscious or preconscious aspect of life in the mind and the body respectively? Freud, Casey argues, was re-acting to nineteenth-century philosophies such as Schelling's, which located the unconscious in the natural world. By midcentury, the unconscious was clearly identified with the physiological body, "an obdurate and self-unknow-ing mass" of nature that is nothing more than the absence of consciousness. Yet alongside this conception of the unconscious as obdurate body, subsisted a no-tion of the unconscious as a dynamic agency outside of consciousness and ev-idenced in artistic and other creative acts.

While Freud reacts against the nineteenth-century notion of the uncon-scious, he does so by elaborating the second notion, that of dynamic agency. The unconscious is capable of its own acts of representation and brings forth effects—symptoms and dreams—that do not correspond to the products of consciousness. Yet, while recognizing the physiological instinctual basis of the unconscious, Freud stubbornly maintains that the unconscious is representa-tional, that it is the ideational representation of those instincts. But this im-plies, according to Casey, that mental means more than mind in Freud. Freud's psyche is soulful, and psychic life is often obscure to itself insofar as conscious life is invaded by the products of the unconscious.

Given this same data, Merleau-Ponty attributes the obscurity or ambi-guity of the unconscious to the body and the world because everything we live and think is pervaded by ambiguity in the sense of multiple meanings. But specifically and additionally, Merleau-Ponty links the prereflective with the body insofar as he is reacting to the French rationalist tradition established by Descartes according to which objects (bodies included) are nothing but opaque matter and minds simply mirror the world. Casey argues that both Freud and Merleau-Ponty are correct because body or flesh and mind or psy-che are involved in a relationship of reciprocal expression, what we have been calling the continuum of life, with its structures and forms. Each thinker de-veloped new terms to rethink and recharacterize the tradition each inherited. For Freud, "psyche" overtook and multiplied the meaning and role of "mind," while for Merleau-Ponty, "flesh" exhibits a dynamism not found in the Carte-sian notion of body. Together, Freud's and Merleau-Ponty's thinking about the unconscious constitutes a "chiasm," that is, each crosses over into the realm abandoned by the other, intersecting at the point of signification, such that nowhere in prereflective or psychic life do we discover a pure mind in isolation from a pure body.

David Pettigrew's chapter, "Merleau-Ponty and the Unconscious: A Po-etic Vision," also juxtaposes Merleau-Ponty's vision of unconscious interiority with Freud's. Pettigrew argues that the continuum of life gives the unconscious a different character. For Merleau-Ponty, he maintains, a subject's dreams, memory, and sexuality are not hidden, but are coextensive with life, so that attributing them to an unconscious constitutes an illusion. However, rather than simply ignoring or denying the phenomenon of the unconscious, Pettigrew concludes that Merleau-Ponty blurs the distinction between consciousness and the unconscious and accepts the term *unconscious*, but only in a highly qualified manner. That is, rather than reinvest the unconscious with the causal authority given to it in Freud's account, Pettigrew argues that Merleau-Ponty enlists the language of poetry in order to come to terms with the ambiguous nature of the unconscious.

Already this is more complicated than it appears since, as we have already seen, for Merleau-Ponty, if the unconscious and consciousness are indiscernible, then so are the body and the world, inside and outside. In fact, the body is the medium of the poetic disclosure of the world, and thus is comparable to a work of art, for both works of art and the body are beings in which the expression is indistinguishable from what is expressed. This is why the world openly acts upon the body as well, for although every use of the human body is a primordial expression that retrieves and remakes it, the world acts upon the body first, and thereby opens it to an infinite number of possibilities. Pettigrew also invokes Aristotle's *Poetics* to indicate that psychoanalysis should be considered in terms of drama and poetry and so (as Aristotle does with the latter) be placed in the context of the world and science.

In the final section of Pettigrew's intricate argument, he maintains that insofar as, for Merleau-Ponty, the unconscious is interwoven with the world of our experience and manifest in an authorless poetic disclosure, Heidegger's *Ereignis* is evoked: poetic expression disrupts temporal coherence and efficient causality. If this is the case, then the primary task of the therapist would be to coexist with the patient and to engage with the patient's narrative as with a poetic vision, neither true nor false, but still graspable by reason even while it both precedes and exceeds it.

A final approach to the interiority of the unconscious is presented in the final chapter of part one, a chapter that takes us from the interiority of the unconscious to the middle realm of the gestalt, which is the starting point of part two of this volume. In "From the Unseen to the Invisible: Merleau-Ponty's Sorbonne Lectures as Preparation for His Later Thought," James Phillips examines Merleau-Ponty's Sorbonne lectures from the point of view of the later writings. Phillips argues that those lectures contain an implicit understanding of psychoanalysis as well as the first flashes of insight into how psychoanalysis contributes to Merleau-Ponty's later ontology of the flesh. With this, Phillips brings us back full circle to the question of ontology in relation to the continuum between interiority and exteriority.

Phillips argues that in connecting the Sorbonne lectures to the later ontology, the chief problem centers on how to describe the relationship between
sexuality and life. For, if sexuality reflects the general trend of one's life, does
it lose its specificity and become lost in existence? Or, if all existence has sexuality as a substructure, is the general structure of life merely an effect of sexuality? Phillips concedes that for Merleau-Ponty, neither position is acceptable.
Even though it is a mistake to recognize only the manifest content of existence
presented in distinct representations as the philosophies of consciousness prescribe, it is also a mistake to redouble manifest content with latent, unconscious representations in the manner of psychologies of the unconscious.

To resolve the problem of the relationship of sexuality and existence,
Phillips argues, Merleau-Ponty brings it into the larger discussion of sensation
and perception, particularly the gestalt. In gestalt theory, even the smallest
sense-datum is presented as patterned and related to the brain as a whole. With
a brain injury, the visual or auditory side of the datum will predominate depending on the affected area of the brain. Likewise, while sexuality carries the
general intentionality of the subject's existence, in the case of neurotic illness,
sexuality bears a special relationship to that neurosis. For while not all human
conflicts take place on a sexual plane, such conflicts find their most intense expression in sexual relations. In conflicts of power and possession, Phillips concludes, sexuality appears to play a dominant role insofar as it acts out the larger
conflicts with more intensity than other aspects of our existence. Thus, Phillips
argues, for Merleau-Ponty, sexuality is the arena in which basic human struggles of power, autonomy, and dependence are most dramatically acted out in
the world among others. This gives us new insights into the lectures where
Merleau-Ponty states that we tend to forget the ground of perceptual gestalten
even though it gives the figure its meaning. We forget because we are ourselves
that ground, that is, we always caught up in circumstances; we are part of
the continuum and we cannot see beyond its circumstances whether they are
defined by operative intention, existential trend, or sexual conflict.

The chapters in part two turn to the middle ground in the continuum
between interiority and exteriority. In particular, they focus on the development of the gestalt notion of structure or form to make sense of the relation
between matter, life, and mind in Merleau-Ponty's philosophy. I have argued
that according to the notion of the gestalt that Merleau-Ponty adapts, every organism has an overall organization that continually determines the position
and function of its parts. Lawrence Hass takes this use of the perceptual gestalt

as central to Merleau-Ponty's understanding of perception and ultimately of the otherness of exteriority. In "Sense and Alterity: Rereading Merleau-Ponty's Reversibility Thesis," Hass argues against critics of the reversibility thesis who complain that it is obscure, that it presupposes the other that it should account for, and that it ultimately eliminates any consideration of difference between self and others by reducing the other to the same. These criticisms, Hass believes, arise from a failure to take into account the extent to which reversibility and sensibility are intertwined in Merleau-Ponty's account of perception.

To this end, Hass also proposes a rethinking of the perceptual gestalt. Rather than conceiving of the gestalt as an immobile figure-ground relationship, Hass proposes to make sense of it on the basis of the human form or structure, that is, on the basis of meaningful embodiment. Hass's essay supports the point of this volume, that embodied being in the world is a behavioral gestalt such that human projects are internally related to specific perceptual figurations. Behavioral and perceptual gestalten together embody multiple meanings and senses, effecting not only one's own corporeality, but that one that constitutes "alterity" as well, that is, the sense of other and exterior perceptual comportments with their accompanying meaning(s). Additionally Hass argues that because the gestalt perception includes a third element, the separation between figure and ground, the gestalt in fact prevents the self and the other from simply merging or collapsing into one another. With this, Hass clarifies the gestalt structure, demonstrates its perceptual, thus lived quality, and guarantees that the other retains its separateness.

The alterity or "ambiguity" of gestalt perception is central to the chapter by Nobuo Kazashi, who, in "Bodily Logos: James, Merleau-Ponty, and Nishida," explores the realm bordering interiority and exteriority by studying the relation between Merleau-Ponty's phenomenology of ambiguity in experience, William James's radical empiricism, and the experience of Buddhist illumination in the work of Kitaro Nishida. For Merleau-Ponty, writes Kazashi, the philosophy of ambiguity (the name conferred by Alphonse de Waelhens) refers to the indeterminacy or vagueness that permeates our existence in the world and derives from our embodied existence, which itself is irreducible to either the transparency of self-consciousness or the inertia of matter. For Kazashi, the ambiguity of experience remains a key element of Merleau-Ponty's thought, thus Kazashi insists that "ambiguity" was given the name "flesh" in Merleau-Ponty's later philosophy.

Kazashi also argues that the notion of ambiguity can be regarded as one of the key notions in William James's *Essays in Radical Empiricism*. James, however, calls it "pure experience," by which he means the instant field of the present that is only virtually object or subject, an unqualified field which we act upon or which is an act. For Kazashi, James's definition of pure experience is an attempt to bring to light the ontologically primordial layer of experience that makes overcoming the dualism between interiority and exteriority thinkable. The similarities between Merleau-Ponty and James arise from their shared anti-Cartesian perspective on the body, that is, their refusal of the split between inner life and the world of objects, as well as attention to what he identifies as the phenomenological enterprise to return to the stream of life, a phrase that evokes the continuum. As such, both philosophers' critiques of mind-body dualism were directly correlated with their critiques of subject-object dualism. Pure experience and flesh are respectively the names James and Merleau-Ponty gave to the ontological milieu of the immediately given. Unfortunately, Kazashi argues, James's concept of pure experience fails because it is overloaded and supposed to be capable of functioning as perception, perceiver, or perceived, depending on the context. Nevertheless, it is precisely this failure that brought Nishida, who had struggled with the psychologistic character of James's notion, so close to Merleau-Ponty.

Thus, Kazashi maintains, in spite of the radically different terms each philosopher employs, they share the ontological notion of the bodily, expressive self as obtaining in and through the chiasmic (Merleau-Ponty) or self-contradictory (Nishida), that is, the relationship between the bodily self and the world. For both, Kazashi maintains, the ambiguous body is essential to considering our existence in the world because the body plays the pivotal or mediating role in the self-reflexive structuring of the bodily field of experience. While Nishida's awkward terminology may seem to enforce the kinds of dualism Merleau-Ponty struggled so much to undermine, Kazashi concludes that a careful reading reveals a philosopher who, like Merleau-Ponty, sought to express the fragile nature of the integration between the self and world prior to subjectivity and objectivity.

Gail Weiss also revisits Merleau-Ponty's notion of gestalten by arguing that the conception of the body image developed by Merleau-Ponty situates the body image within a continuum organized by physiological, libidinous, and socially structured phenomenon. Furthermore, she claims, this continuum overcomes some of the most serious feminist and minority objections to Merleau-Ponty's position. To prove her point, Weiss makes extensive use of the ideas of the psychologist Paul Schilder, whose monumental work, *The Image and Appearance of the Human Body*, was the first full-length study of the body image ever to be published. In her chapter, "Body Image Intercourse: A Corporeal Dialogue between Merleau-Ponty and Schilder," Weiss argues that by developing and extending the implications of Merleau-Ponty's and Schilder's accounts of the body image, a richer understanding of how racial, gender,

class, age, ethnic, and cultural differences are corporeally registered and reproduced can be achieved. Her compelling use of the work of Frantz Fanon
makes the point that unless philosophers recognize the role of the body image
in reflecting and sustaining individual, social, and political inequalities, there
is a danger that positive social and political changes will not address the individual's own corporeal existence in the intimate manner necessary to move
successfully toward the eradication of sexism, racism, classism, ageism, and
ethnocentrism.

This means that, for Weiss much more than for some of the other
thinkers who have contributed to this volume, the social construction of the
body image must be emphasized. Weiss argues that both Schilder and Merleau-Ponty recognize the importance of others and the exterior or social world
in the ongoing development of the body image. She argues on the basis of the
connections between interior and exterior that, like Merleau-Ponty, Schilder
stresses that "the body-image is a social phenomenon," that "there exists a deep
community between one's own body-image and the body-image of others,"
and that the "body-images of human beings communicate with each other either in parts or as wholes." This makes it possible for Schilder to claim that the
body itself may be a kind of phantom, a possibility that can materialize itself
in any number of shapes or forms. Weiss is careful to reiterate the point made
by feminist theorist Elizabeth Grosz, that this does not mean that "anything
goes." Rather, she concludes, this implies that it is possible to construct a new
morphological imaginary, nonetheless, feminist and other minority critics
must continue their task of articulating the social and bodily forces that con-
strain and enable the development of the body image.

Elizabeth Grosz investigates a later and broader version of Merleau-
Ponty's conception of the body image in her chapter, "Merleau-Ponty and Irigaray in the Flesh." As we have seen, Merleau-Ponty's philosophy is subtle and
shifting, thus it is not easy to say whether or not his conception of "flesh" is
useful to feminist conceptions of subjectivity or hostile to them. While Grosz
acknowledges that Merleau-Ponty's work may well be misogynist either
through a neutralization of sexual categories or through intent, she is focused,
in this chapter, on articulating points of alignment and intersection between
Merleau-Ponty and feminist theories, particularly that of Luce Irigaray.

Grosz's argument, that Merleau-Ponty anticipates Derrida by refusing to
make use of dualisms and, instead, reclaims the space between binaries, reflects
the general theme of this volume, that rather than positing perception in terms
of interiority and exteriority as binaries, Merleau-Ponty developed a continuous connection between them. In feminist theory, Merleau-Ponty's conception
of "flesh" as the reversibility of interior and exterior in a structure that encom-

passes both is of great importance for undermining binaries and producing a new conception of the continuity of relations between mind-body and interior-exterior. To this same end, Merleau-Ponty's insistence on the notion of lived experience as phenomenologically given to the embodied subject is indicative of his method, for the embodied subject is flesh incarnated in the body as the relation between interior and exterior. While Grosz warns against naive views of experience, she nonetheless takes experience to be the starting point for the establishment of new theoretical systems, sociopolitical and aesthetic constructs, and moral values.

A central concern of Grosz's chapter is the relation Luce Irigaray establishes between her own work and that of Merleau-Ponty. Although, according to Grosz, Irigaray embraces Merleau-Ponty's call to return to prediscursive experience as well as his conception of it as the basis of later more highly integrated and complex experience, she disagrees with Merleau-Ponty's description of that experience. Grosz argues that for Irigaray, the earliest mother-child relations take place in the womb prior to a coordinated and fully constituted vision. The womb is in darkness yet it is fully and positively tactile. Thus, intrauterine existence is a positivity, the tactile precondition of vision as of all embodied experience. What this means, however, is that the visible does not precede or overrun the tactile, as Merleau-Ponty appears to argue, but that the tactile, fluid world serves as the precondition of all sensations, in a system of (as Merleau-Ponty would have it) increasingly integrated organization. Thus, the tactile cannot be subordinated to the visual, since as the intrauterine precondition of all sensation, the tangible is the fluid medium of the visible and is neither in a reciprocal relation with it nor merely dependent upon it.

Having said this, Grosz concludes by noting that from Irigaray's point of view, Merleau-Ponty at least makes use of conceptions such as that of "flesh" and "embodied subject" that open the way to the sexualization of ontology and the recognition of the importance of sexual difference as an ontological issue. While this does not erase the phallocentric if not misogynist point of view he so often espouses, it nonetheless puts Merleau-Ponty among those few philosophers whose conceptualizations evoke feminist theoretical concerns.

In making sense of the relation between matter, life, and mind in Merleau-Ponty's early work, we have seen the importance of the gestalt notion of structure or form, that is, every organism has an overall organization determined by its milieu that continually orders the position and function of its parts. According to this notion, perception is a figure against a ground, and thus, the body does only one thing at a time insofar as it perceives only one thing at a time and operates in only one milieu at a time. Any single movement of hand, face, or leg is taken to express that whole. Against this view of the human being's fully integrated and engaged faculties operating in an ordered continuum extending from self to world, Alphonso Lingis posits an alternative view of the interior-exterior relation in his chapter, "Segmented Organisms." Turning explicitly to Marx, and implicitly to Michel Foucault, Gilles Deleuze, and Félix Guattari, he points to the recent generalized recognition that talk relating to the person as such is a confused extension of juridic discourse. On the one hand, he points out, people are insisting you have to relate to the cabby, the desk clerk, the bartender as a man—or more often that you have to relate to the waitress, the hotel manager, the massage girl as a woman, that is, as an integrated and fully engaged human being.

Against this, Lingis argues that to envision someone as a man or as a woman rather than as a cabby, a desk clerk, a waitron, is to envision them as abstract wholes, wholes that can somehow be wholes even though the times when anyone is there as a whole with fully integrated and engaged faculties are very rare. Yet, the problem remains that society demands of us that we be present as wholes, and that we act as if others are too. Language contributes to this illusion, Lingis argues, because in society there is the expectation that the integrated being will answer for what she said, live up to what she promised, be responsible for everything she sees, says, and does. Not to do so, not to account for what she has seen or done is considered irresponsible, amoral, or immoral. Paradoxically, the same social field that demands engaged and integrated beings also dismembers all who enter its structures. For capitalists, human beings are nothing but hands, strong backs, calculative minds, and ambitions, each with a corresponding job in the labor force. For marketers, humans are hair, teeth, feet, and stomachs, each with a corresponding set of products to consume. Capitalism has stripped away all connections between men except naked self-interest even while demanding that to exist as a self one must maintain all of one's properties and attributes.

Lingis concludes that because we live in a society that makes us sell off our body parts in order to survive, the self that is left is not engaged and integrated but organized wholly in terms of the other, whether that means prostitution, the corporation, or God. To recognize this, claims Lingis, takes an act of courage. Thus, rather than the futile attempt to relate to the whole person or to present ourselves as whole and our world as an extension of ourselves, what takes courage in contemporary society, is to connect to people concretely, as segmented organisms. Unlike gestalten, segmented organisms contain all their functions in each segment, but their moves are small and do not express a whole compressed into each small gesture. Each small conjunction of body parts, like the thumbs-up of the Cariocas cabby that terminates each and every cab ride and payment, concretely makes sense of the social field and conveys a sense of rightness, which, Lingis concludes, Merleau-Ponty's integral human being, with its demand for universal ethics and distributive justice, fails to account for and fails to see as both right and intelligible.

The chapters in part three expand the movement of Merleau-Ponty's thought of the interior in the direction of the exterior world. Specifically, they explore the themes of intersubjectivity and the role of the other in developing the self, the impossibility of separating interior and exterior life, and the mind's integration with matter. The first of these chapters, "Envisioning the Other: Lacan and Merleau-Ponty on Intersubjectivity," by Helen Fielding, takes up the Lacanian critique of Merleau-Ponty's conception of how the subject's relation to intersubjective worldly life is mediated by the body. Fielding seeks to redefine the areas of compatibility and incompatibility between the two thinkers, beginning with Lacan's claim that Merleau-Ponty's notion of phenomenological vision does not distinguish between the eye and the gaze. For Lacan, this distinction is necessary to disrupt the unity of a subject who would be a Cartesian eye, seeing according to laws of physics and light, registering flat optics, and transmitting messages back to the subject.

Against Lacan's attack, Fielding unfolds the disunity of the phenomenological subject in her bodily manifestation rather than as an intrapsychic phenomena. She argues that, for Merleau-Ponty, otherness arises with latency and is not experienced at the level of consciousness, since, as embodied, humans experience relations of simultaneity between what they see and what they feel or smell or taste. That is, activities, moods, and passions intertwine and flow into one another. Thus, Fielding argues, vision is not just visual signification, but also bodily experience intrinsically tied to touch and motility, and the body mediates between inner life and the world. Lacan's theory of intersubjectivity, Fielding argues, does not include a developed theory of the body that could resolve the split between the intrapsychic and the intersubjective, the inner self and the world. Because Lacan focuses principally upon the body as mediated by drives, he fails to account for the lived body of daily experience as well as for our lived experience of others, our contact with the world.

This said, Fielding is not interested in merely defending Merleau-Ponty against Lacan's critique. She digs deeper to argue that Lacan adapts one of Merleau-Ponty's central themes, a theme that would bring Lacan to embrace Merleau-Ponty's notion of the mediation between interior and exterior life. In Merleau-Ponty's notion of reversibility, Fielding uncovers the core of Lacan's notion of the doubling up or split that comprises the subject. Since, for Merleau-Ponty, by means of reversibility the subject is a subject for herself as well as for the other. This, she claims, is the Lacanian inside-out structure of the gaze. When Merleau-Ponty describes the point where the two sides of a glove meet as a nothingness that one can turn over to see things, Fielding concludes that this point of negativity configures Lacanian subjectivity. Such a subject sees but cannot see herself and so can only imagine herself there through the reflection in the gaze of the other. Thus, the other and the world remain essential to the constitution of a self. Ultimately, what interests Fielding here is how the two thinkers work out this schema of interiority and exteriority, that is, the same insight is taken up by one as the opening to the outside world and by the other as the opening to the self. Indeed, it may well be both.

As these chapters reveal, the continuum of life from interiority to exteriority operates in all spheres for Merleau-Ponty and is definitive of how life is constituted both with regard to the self and with regard to the world. Wilhelm Wurzer takes this connectedness to its furthest point in his account of Merleau-Ponty's notion of inner life in relation to Marx and the concept of capital. In a chapter that seeks less to analyze the texts of these thinkers than to operate within the freedom they grant, Wurzer risks thinking entirely *without* the immanence-transcendence distinction, that is, without a separation but with a continuum between interiority and exteriority. Calling upon Heidegger and Derrida, as well as Merleau-Ponty, Wurzer argues that when Merleau-Ponty and Derrida turn to Heidegger, even while evading Heidegger's transcending textuality and project, they do so precisely in order to generate a continuity. In rejecting Heidegger's *ekstasis*, Wurzer follows Merleau-Ponty's claim that the philosopher does not have the right to shut herself up in an inner life, but must think the world of everyone. This world combines the seamlessness of the electronic web with increasing ethnic rivalry, violence, and civil unrest: it is wild being, flesh, operating chiasmatically, neither immanent nor transcendent, but continuous in a particular manner.

Wurzer claims that Merleau-Ponty's phenomenology is valuable for our world now insofar as it moves us from the Heideggerian rhetoric of ecstatic temporalizing to the borders of Derrida's spectralizing temporality. In this move, temporalizing brings us to recognize Merleau-Ponty's claim that philosophy cannot express by traditional means what the world, what "we" are living through now, that is, even though we live in the world and in Being, neither can be fully explained by whatever current framework we may utilize; there is always a certain "wildness." This wildness, on Wurzer's account, is Merleau-Ponty's redefinition of Heideggerian Being, but one defined now out of a concern for difference. As such, it gives rise to the movement of a time that resists how things are, so as to return as what is different, the becoming-of-world.

Although Merleau-Ponty's reflections on Marx in *The Visible and the Invisible* are brief, yet, Wurzer maintains, Merleau-Ponty does propose the historical question of *how* philosophy opens up the world rather than *what* philosophy thinks. In rethinking "capital," Wurzer argues that a hypertextual reading, interpreting, and rewriting is necessary. To this end he claims that capital is not just a monetary sign, but as always ahead of the game, capital is the historical question of evading the distinction between immanence and transcendence. Thus, time and capital, interior and exterior, come together as *Zeitkapital*, a capital that resists our time by always running ahead of it. This would mean that, for Merleau-Ponty, there are perceptions that evade structure and so meaning. While this is not Marxist orthodoxy (nor perhaps Merleau-Pontean orthoxodoxy either), it is, concludes Wurzer, what Derrida has called "a certain spirit of Marxism" for on this account, capital is neither simply "out there" (exterior and transcendent) nor limited to philosophical textuality (interior and immanent).

The final chapter in this volume, "Chaos Theory and Merleau-Ponty's Ontology: Beyond the Dead Father's Paralysis toward a Dynamic and Fragile Materiality," is a complex interweaving of themes. In it, Glen Mazis argues that Merleau-Ponty's ontology and the diverse developments in recent science called "chaos theory," can be used to bring about a rapprochement between philosophical thinking about human life and scientific thinking regarding matter. Traditionally, he argues, science has operated with a logic of change according to which the material world was taken to be predictably, incrementally, and mechanically ordered. Given this paradigm (the same one, we have argued, that Merleau-Ponty seeks to alter) human unpredictability has been explained by recourse to concepts that inevitably set the human in opposition to the material world.

To understand how science can now comprehend sudden, disproportionate change and unpredictable transformation, Mazis argues that it is important to grasp how the notion of feedback has displaced linear causality insofar as science has begun to look at the world in terms of "open systems." In contrast to mechanism, feedback consists of nonlinear plots that show breaks, loops, recursions, and various forms of turbulence. The power of iteration—the feedback that involves the continual reabsorption or enfolding of what has come before—mathematically represented, also creates a sensitivity to initial conditions that seem to get lost in the process of unfolding but can suddenly reappear. Even in a mathematical representation, self-amplifying open systems demonstrate alternation, a tension of order and chaos.

It is this tension that Mazis focuses on when he claims that when Merleau-Ponty wrote "man is but a network of relationships," Merleau-Ponty was attending, not only to the effulgence of new sense from our intertwining with the world, but also to the "dark side" of human being in a chiasm with the world. Mazis insists that we must not overlook the fragility of being a seer caught up in the seen (an interiority caught up in the exterior) but, like Wurzer, he argues that this will only happen insofar as we are attuned to the temporal unfolding of the intertwining. He argues that the writer Virginia Woolf expresses temporal unfolding when she "writes of the whisperings of the wind, night, material shiftings of the world, the rhythms of the season," for she does so only by recognizing that in time's passing, "illumination and darkness are inseparable moments of a fragile process." Thus, he maintains, Merleau-Ponty's subject is not discrete and identifiable but a reversibility of the shared power of the human world, as well as darkness, disintegration, and recalcitrance. Likewise, Mazis argues, for Merleau-Ponty, this insight comes about through the recognition that time is the subject and the subject is time.

Maziz concludes his moving chapter, dedicated to the memory and life of the feminist philosopher Linda Singer, by insisting that both chaos theory and Merleau-Ponty's theory of perception are "open system[s] . . . keeping alive the reiterating factors that were part of its unfolding." More darkly, he sees in classical rationalistic philosophy and science—the "dead father" of the title—a refusal of the shadowy and material side of reversibility, a side that was simultaneously identified with women. Mazis argues that even while suffering under the oppression of this identification, women have, nonetheless, gained valuable insights from it, insights that classical science has been largely indifferent to. And chief among these insights is, Mazis point out, that we cannot screen out the uncontrollable, so that unpredictable change and death itself belong to the articulation of human identity. This realization of ongoing cycles of creation and dissipation is, Mazis concludes, something Merleau-Ponty fully realized and sought throughout his work to conceptualize.

Mazis's conclusions are, in many respects, central to this volume's goal, which has been to argue that from his earliest work Merleau-Ponty searched for ways to break through the subject-object, immanence-transcendence distinction and that he did so by conceiving of interiority and exteriority as connected. Each of these chapters explores that connection; each articulates it differently, some arguing that perhaps Merleau-Ponty did not think radically enough about the nature of this connectedness, others arguing that no one has yet thought it more radically than Merleau-Ponty. The relevance of Merleau-Ponty's work in the continuity of interiority and exteriority is, I think, also made clear throughout these chapters. The importance of this move for ontology, ethics, psychoanalysis, artistic creation, feminism, intersubjectivity, politics, and science, as well as its relation to the ideas of a world of philosophical theorists, is the point of drawing these particular chapters together. This volume is proof of the power and creative energy of this aspect of Merleau-Ponty's thought. And perhaps it is not going too far to say that future developments of Merleau-Ponty's work will depend upon the degree to which this aspect of his thought endures and continues to be the source of new philosophical insights and theories.

## NOTES

1. Maurice Merleau-Ponty, *The Visible and the Invisible*, trans. Alphonso Lingis (Evanston:Northwestern University Press, 1968), p. 267.

2. Maurice Merleau-Ponty, *The Structure of Behavior*, trans. Alden L. Fisher (Boston: Beacon Press, 1967), p. 3.

3. Maurice Merleau-Ponty, *The Structure of Behavior*, p. 4.

4. Maurice Merleau-Ponty, "Phenomenology and Psychoanalysis: Preface to Hesnard's 'L'Oeuvre de Freud,'" trans. Alden Fisher, in *The Essential Writings of Merleau-Ponty*, ed. Alden Fisher (New York: Harcourt, Brace and World, 1969), p. 69.

5. Maurice Merleau-Ponty, *The Structure of Behavior*, pp. 103, 88.

6. Maurice Merleau-Ponty, *The Structure of Behavior*, p. 114. See W. Koehler, *The Mentality of Apes*, trans. E. Winters (London: Routledge and Keegan Paul, 1925).

7. Maurice Merleau-Ponty, *The Structure of Behavior*, p. 115.

8. Maurice Merleau-Ponty, *The Structure of Behavior*, p. 118.

9. Maurice Merleau-Ponty, *The Structure of Behavior*, p. 125.

10. Maurice Merleau-Ponty, *The Structure of Behavior*, p. 125.

11. Maurice Merleau-Ponty, *The Structure of Behavior*, pp. 125–26.

12. Maurice Merleau-Ponty, *The Structure of Behavior*, p. 129. K. Koffka, *Principles of Gestalt Psychology* (New York: Harcourt, Brace, 1939), p. 28.

13. Maurice Merleau-Ponty, *The Structure of Behavior*, p. 133.

14. Maurice Merleau-Ponty, *The Structure of Behavior*, pp. 133, 131. Merleau-Ponty cites Koffka who, in *Principles of Gestalt Psychology*, remains willing to give way to physical causality in matters of ultimate explanations (pp. 49, 48).

15. Maurice Merleau-Ponty, *The Structure of Behavior*, pp. 134, 135.

16. Maurice Merleau-Ponty, *The Structure of Behavior*, pp. 140, 141.

17. Maurice Merleau-Ponty, *The Structure of Behavior*, p. 143. It is of interest that Merleau-Ponty attributes this view to Edmund Husserl, *Ideas I*.

# PART ONE

# Interiority

CHAPTER 1

# Inside and Outside

## ONTOLOGICAL CONSIDERATIONS

## GALEN A. JOHNSON

The idea is this level, this dimension. It is therefore not a *de facto* invisible, like an object hidden behind another, and not an absolute invisible, which would have nothing to do with the visible. Rather it is the invisible *of* this world, that which inhabits this world, sustains it, and renders it visible, its own and interior possibility, the Being of this being

—Merleau-Ponty, *The Visible and the Invisible*[1]

In the field of power as a problem, thinking involves the transmission of particular features: it is a dice-throw. What the dice-throw represents is that thinking always comes from the outside. . .

—Gilles Deleuze, *Foucault*[2]

There is an inner life. It is the life of thought, the life of the heart, the life of dream and memory. These are interiors that encounter lines of exterior force that shape, fold, or break them. Exteriority is an outer bound where thought and words unravel in the enigmas of desire, the sublime, forgetting, silence, solitude, suffering, night, death, and nothingness. It is philosophically difficult to speak of interiority in light of the weight of the outside. Image dominates word, information replaces thought, and either interiors are erased or they are so reduced in significance as to command only marginal philosophical attention. What used to be the most important subject for philosophical attention, consciousness, thought, or reflection, becomes one of the least important.

Not only in modern philosophy, but in our best social scientists, philosophers of social science, and philosophers of history, the inside has inevitably been set in opposition to the outside, consciousness to thing, for-itself to in-itself, knowledge to power, creating the syllabus of philosophic difficulties that flow from dualism. Kant described time as the "inner" form of intuition, Marx found the human species-being in free, "self-conscious" activity, Collingwood referred to thought as the "inside" of historical events, and Max Weber contrasted the "outside" of cultural phenomena with a "within" that bestows "significance" (*Sinn*). Merleau-Ponty's phenomenology of our "being-in-the-world" and ontology of visible and in-the-visible no less demand from us an account of the meaning, force, and variations of the "inside."

The problem of this chapter was referenced in the subtitle of Levinas's *Totality and Infinity: An Essay on Exteriority*, published in the same year as work on *The Visible and the Invisible* was brought to a close (1961). It was taken up by Foucault's reflections on the fiction of Maurice Blanchot entitled "Thought from the Outside" (1966), and once again in Deleuze's critical commentary on Foucault in chapters entitled "The Thought of the Outside (Power)" and "Foldings, or the Inside of Thought" (1986).[3] In his chapter entitled "The Experience of the Outside," Foucault traced the genealogy of the thought from the outside, the first renderings of which he referred to Sade and Holderlin.[4] Sade gave voice to the nakedness of desire that outrages religious and moral law, while the poetry of Holderlin manifested the shimmering absence of gods and the obligation to wait for the healing of "God's failing." Both authors worked against the grain of the Enlightenment,[5] in the era of Kant, Hegel, and Marx that demanded the total interiorization of experience, the end of all alienation, the humanization of nature, and the creation of the treasures of heaven on earth. From Sade and Holderlin, the lineage of exteriority extends through Nietzsche's attack on Western metaphysics as tied to grammar and to those who hold the power over how and to whom we shall speak, to Bataille's discourse of ruptured subjectivity, eros, and transgression, and to Blanchot.[6]

The thesis of the authors of exteriority may be summarized more or less strongly. In *Totality and Infinity*, Levinas contended that Being *is* exteriority, and "no thought could better obey Being than by allowing itself to be dominated by this exteriority."[7] This is a thesis of the *philosophical privilege* of the outside. For Levinas, not even language can bind self to the other, for no concept can lay hold of the alterity of the face to face. No idea is capable of absorbing the face of the other in the contemplative soul. Genuine language is produced only in the face-to-face relation as teaching, a way for truth to be created such that it is not the work of my consciousness and could not be derived from my own interiority. Language, therefore, confirms the abyss of separation of inside and outside, and affirms the philosophical primacy of the outside.

Levinas's thesis of the philosophical privilege of exteriority (the other, the face, God) is milder than what we find in the middle to late texts by Foucault on the history of discipline and punishment and of sexuality. There the notion is probably best expressed as a *constructionist* one, that thought, knowledge, and self are historical effects that arise from the invisible power structures that discipline docile bodies. The culturally constructed "soul" becomes the prison of the body[8] as the invisible lines of exterior force double themselves in interior self-reflection. In his book on *Foucault*, Deleuze articulated Foucault's position by using the image of the dice-throw in which the faces of the dice that come up are the result of the exterior forces at play in their tumble. "There is a liberation of forces which come from the outside and exist only in a mixed-up state of agitation, modification and mutation. In truth, they are dice-throws, for thinking involves throwing the dice."[9]

The constructionist thesis on the power of exteriority over interiority escalates into an explicit criticism of the ontology of Merleau-Ponty, which Foucault had already hinted at in the foreword to the English edition of *The Order of Things* when he took the trouble to single out phenomenology as a philosophy of subjectivity and as the one philosophical approach he explicitly rejected.[10] If thinking is a dice-throw in the play of forces, then consciousness cannot be exhaustively understood in terms of intentionality. Intentionality is the notion that the world comes to us as meaningful and our grasp binds us to the world-as-meant in acts that coherently cement inside and outside. The dice-throw means that you get what comes up, good luck and bad, order and disorder, continuity and discontinuity, coherence and incoherence of meaning and intention. Certainly the Husserlian account of intentionality as the relation ego-noesis-noema portrays our relation to the world as the conscious and self-conscious idea or mental representation of things. Merleau-Ponty's own movement from Husserlian thetic intentionality to an incarnate and operative intentionality in the *Phenomenology* had already loosened our intentional grasp on the world, but Merleau-Ponty came to understand that the intentionality of consciousness, whether thetic or operative, is an incomplete basis for understanding our relation with the outside. In the first place, in order to posit the relation of intentionality, we already posit the difference between the inside and the outside. We thereby implicitly reinstate the old dead ends of dualism, or psychologism vs. naturalism. Second, consciousness has its blind spot when

we reflect on our experience or on ourselves, and this is a blindness in principle. Reflection can only evoke our contact with the world and not coincide
with it. Third, there are those overpowering experiences of transcendence and
trans-descendence or vertical time, in which it is no longer we who have
thoughts or speech but there is a Thought and a Speech that has us. For all
these reasons, surface intentionalities conceived in terms of a two-dimensional
Euclidean space must be deepened by a topological account of the heights and
depths of the world beneath and above experience at its horizons. This does
not mean that Merleau-Ponty abandoned intentionality as an account of the
nature of consciousness and self-consciousness. He simply came to believe that
intentionality, whether thetic or embodied and operative, could not provide a
complete or exhaustive account of consciousness and self-consciousness.

To this point, there is little to separate Levinas, Foucault, Deleuze, and
Merleau-Ponty, all of whom, in varying ways, turned philosophy toward the
tasks of intellectual archeology. In *Totality and Infinity*, Levinas had written:
"One of the principal theses of this work is that the noesis-noema structure is
not the primordial structure of intentionality."[11] Nevertheless, in a fashion
similar to Heidegger, Merleau-Ponty sought to go beyond a philosophy of our
being-in-the-world to a philosophy of Being. Deleuze, on behalf of Foucault,
argues that this movement to Being is too rapid, it rushes things, for it still assumes that we are able to find a voice, a language in which Being will speak
and disclose itself, once again interlacing knowledge and Being, articulating
the chiasm of thing and word. This model of the interlacing of visible and ar-
ticulable (invisible), does little more than reestablish the Platonic model of
Being = Knowing as a replacement for the model of subjective intentionality.
"But this interlacing is in fact a stranglehold,"[12] and Merleau-Ponty remains a
philosopher of interiority and immanence seeking the adequation of Knowledge and Being.

In beginning to reflect on this reading of Merleau-Ponty, it would be
tempting, although ultimately disingenuous, to make an argument for including Merleau-Ponty among the philosophers of exteriority in light of Merleau-Ponty's phenomenology of our incarnation and his own path away from
intellectualism and the philosophy of consciousness. The preface to the *Phenomenology of Perception* proclaimed: "Truth does not 'inhabit' only 'the inner
man,' or more accurately, there is no inner man, man is in the world, and only
in the world does he know himself."[13] This was written against Husserl's reap-
propriation at the end of *Cartesian Meditations* of Augustine's thesis that "truth
dwells in the inner man." The denial of an "inner man" is a forceful rejection
of all philosophies of reflection, Augustinian, Cartesian, and Husserlian. The
reflection of Husserlian intuition does not give us the things themselves, for

both thought and the world are an ongoing genesis, and thought always exists in language as a more and less faithful articulation of the world and itself. Reflection must be replaced with a hyperreflection, an interrogative articulation that is as originary, creative, and promiscuous as the visible and as subtle, dimensional, and horizonal as the invisible.

Nevertheless, Merleau-Ponty's objections to Husserlian reflection cannot be taken as a declaration for exteriority. There is no inner man as pure, reduced *ego cogito*, yet there remains an inner life and an approach to the interior heart of Being. The *Phenomenology* says that "we present our thought to ourselves through internal or external speech."[14] *The Visible and the Invisible* sought to develop an "endo-ontology," an "intra-ontology," which is articulation of an "ontology from within."[15] Jean-Francois Lyotard has said that though Merleau-Ponty was "one of the least arrogant of philosophers" it remains the case that "the arrogance of philosophers is metaphysics."[16] Though *The Visible and the Invisible* is exceedingly hesitant to make proclamations, nevertheless, Merleau-Ponty's lateral ontology concludes that Being is depth, Being is dimensionality, Being is horizon, Being is invisibility.[17] In contrast to both versions of the thesis of exteriority, Merleau-Ponty described human being as being-in-the-world, and Being as invisibility. There can be no denying that this is a philosophy and a thought of the inside. The question to be asked is whether this "inside" is a "stranglehold."

There has been a pervasive fault in the philosophical use of the term *in* to construe the inside in a spatializing sense. Thereby we are led to think of consciousness, thought, word, and significance as located in a space or container, as "wine is in the jar." This is why it is always worth being reminded that in saying we are being-in the-world we mean that we are "l'être *au* monde." We are not "l'être *dans* le monde," which might tempt us to search for our being in the room that contains us. This is not to deny that a geographic space or landscape can become for us a place of habitation with which we dwell. Quite the opposite. It is to say that we must beware of spatializing mind and Being, and that to say we are in the world is to say that it is our inseparable habitation. In accord with Aristotle's analysis in the *Physics*, this is the sense in which we use the word *in*, to designate encompassment or inclusion as the part/whole relationship, for example, when we say that "she is in the family," "health is in the body," "science is in her soul," or "metaphysics is in his blood."[18] Merleau-Ponty wrote: "I must no longer think myself *in the world* in the sense of ob-jective spatiality, which amounts to autopositing myself and installing myself in *Ego uninteressiert* (disinterested Ego)."[19] We dwell in the world, it is our inhabitation. This is why spatial metaphors are an exceeding danger for understanding our interiority as inhabitation and inclusion. If we must be spatial, it is better to say not that our inner and spiritual life is inside us, but in front of us in the places with which we dwell and the relationships we treasure, or that it is above us in the sky that lightens and the stars that warm, or that it is beneath us in the shadows of the dusk, the earth and water that sustain, and the memories of graves and dead loves. Metaphors such as "dice-throw" or the "fold" at the intersection of "lines of exterior force" inevitably mislead as to the nature of the inner life.

Though he was aware of the dangers, Merleau-Ponty's own account of Being is not altogether free of spatializing metaphors. The "fold" of subjectivation or thinking, so much highlighted by Deleuze, is a term introduced by Merleau-Ponty.[20] Our inhabitation is itself both held and holding within Being, that is, the ongoing genesis of inclusion and exclusion, encompassing and marginalizing, identity and difference, self and alterity. This crossing over from inside to outside easily leads us to spatial metaphors of folding over, the hollow of Being, two laps, two leaves, two sides of an abyss, a glove turned inside-out. Even the term "element" in the Greek sense, to which Merleau-Ponty analogized the term *Flesh*, is subject to the same danger. Moreover, *so is the term* Flesh *itself.* Flesh is *la chair*, meat. These spatializing metaphors tempt us to begin making two-dimensional line drawings of Being,[21] and to make of Flesh an impossiblity, for space without time is a static ontological region in which exclusion and laws of either/or dominate. In a static moment, to be in two different spaces is a geometer's fiction. We must rid ourselves of spatializing being-in-the-world and Being as a "total philosophical error." From this point of view, Being as Flesh is imbued with the same philosophical dangers of monism as Spinoza's doctrine of Substance, and one would prefer Heidegger's account of Being as Time.

The genius of Merleau-Ponty's name for Being, Flesh, is that it gives us a flesh-and-blood feel and smell for what Time is. Merleau-Ponty did not want an abstract concept—Substance, Time—to carry the heaviest philosophical weight of our encompassment, our origin and our end. Truly, neither was he content with the elemental terms of the Greek alchemy. The Milesian elements were the presuppositions in which things have their origin and life, and to which they return in death. The Greek elements, were, therefore, eternal. Merleau-Ponty gave us a rich and long list of temporal metaphors for Flesh as a genesis: emergence, transcendence, coming of itself to itself, coiling up, reversal, doubling back, divergence from inside to outside. These are the more helpful metaphors that avoid spatializing inside and outside when thinking of Being as "in-the-visible." The Flesh is flesh and blood Time. It is the explosion of seed pods, united and separated, it is the dehiscence of the colors of fire, it is the labor of pregnancy, the joy and pain of new life and separation, it is the shock of death and the work of mourning and grieving. "I call the world flesh," Merleau-Ponty wrote, "in order to say that it is a *pregnancy* of possibles."[22] Flesh is the name for the ontological hinge on which the outside passes over to the inside and inside passes over to outside. Flesh is not a totalizing stranglehold of Being-Knowing, for the Flesh that is flesh-and-blood time is as inscrutable, strange, foreign, and other as it is colorful, creative, and promiscuous. This is why Merleau-Ponty's ontology is not an idealism nor purely a Thought from the Inside. Though the relation of our being to the world is inhabitation or part/whole, and though the relation of our being-in-the-world to Flesh is also that of encompassing or part/whole, this ontology does not collapse all relations into internal relations. The whole of which all things are part is itself porous and polymorphous. We should not be unhappy with characterizing this as a double-aspect ontology, as Merleau-Ponty himself has given his assent to doing,[23] as long as we speak of Flesh as Time and not as Substance. In discussing Sartre's dualist ontology of being and nothingness, Merleau-Ponty commented: "For me it is structure or transcendence that explains, and being and nothingness [in-itself and for-itself] are its two abstract properties."[24] Regardless of vocabulary and philosophic taxonomy, nothing is to be gained from opposing the authors of exteriority who speak to us so profoundly against a supposed Thought from the Inside, for Interiority and Exteriority share a bond by birth as nonidentical twins, they are flesh and blood time that at any moment unravel and turn the one into the other. This hinge and this turning has been poignantly captured in a few lines from a poem by Antonin Artaud: "There is a mind in the flesh, but a mind as quick as lightning. And yet the agitation of the flesh partakes of the mind's higher matter."[25]

If it is important not to divest the inside of its outside, it is also important not to fall prey to identifying the inside with the right side and the outside with the world's wrong side. It is undeniable that inside and outside bear moral as well as ontological weight and meaning, and the lineage of the authors of exteriority, Sade to Foucault, is also the lineage of outsiders. There is a well-known story, entitled not "Inside and Outside" but "The Right Side and the Wrong Side" ("L'Envers et l'endroit"). It is a brief and poignant account of a woman encumbered by an inheritance too small to change her way of life yet too large to ignore or consume idly. Nearing death, she wanted a shelter for her old bones, and used her legacy to purchase her cemetery plot. On it was erected a large, black marble tomb with her name engraved in gold letters. This woman became seized by love for her tomb, and paid herself a visit every Sunday afternoon. She would go into the vault, carefully close the door behind her, and alone with herself, kneel on the prayer bench. One All Saints Day some passers-by honored her memory with violets, and she came to realize that in the eyes of the world she had already passed over and was dead. Nevertheless, in this way, she regularly travelled from outside to inside and back again, and slowly made her peace with the wrong side of the world. The author of this tale reflected on these events in the following way: "One man contemplates and another digs her grave: how can we separate them? I do not want to choose between the right and wrong sides of the world, and I do not want a choice to be made."[26]

Merleau-Ponty has given us the beginnings of a postmodern metaphysics in which we do not have to make this untenable choice. The Flesh of flesh-and-blood Time is polymorphous, porous, and promiscuous, interior and exterior, where the life of thought, the heart, dream, and memory constantly cross over and unravel in the enigmas of desire, the sublime, forgetting, silence, solitude, suffering, night, death, and nothingness. "I am not resigned to the shutting away of loving hearts in the hard ground."[27]

## NOTES

This chapter is dedicated to my friend, neighbor, and colleague, R. Ken Forcé (1946–1994).

1. Maurice Merleau-Ponty, *The Visible and the Invisible*, translated by Alphonso Lingis (Evanston: Northwestern University Press, 1968), p. 151.

2. Gilles Deleuze, *Foucault*, edited and translated by Sean Hand (Minneapolis: University Press, 1986), p. 117.

3. This paper is also indebted to Françoise Dastur for her essay entitled "Merleau-Ponty and Thinking from Within," which she read at the meetings of the International Merleau-Ponty Conference in November 1991 at the University of Louvain, Belgium, and which was subsequently published in *Merleau-Ponty in Contemporary Perspective*, ed. P. Burke and J. Van der Veken (The Hague: Kluwer Academic Publishers, 1993), pp. 25–35.

4. Foucault comments that it may seem that the thought from the outside was born of the mystical thinking prowling on the borders of Christianity since Pseudo-Dionysus. However, on Foucault's acount, the mystical experience of going "outside of oneself" is done ultimately in order to find oneself as united with the most dazzling interiority of a Being who is Logos, Thought, and Speech.

5. For a Deleuzian reading of the significance of Sade, which moves much more toward an analysis of Sade as typifying Enlightenment rationality and systematicity, see the essay by Dorothea Olkowski entitled "Monstrous Reflection: Sade and Masoch—Rewriting the History of Reason," in *Crises in Continental Philosophy*, ed. Arlene B. Dallery and Charles E. Scott (Albany: SUNY Press, 1990), pp. 189–99.

6. See Michel Foucault, *Maurice Blanchot, The Thought from the Outside*, trans. Brian Massumi (New York: Zone Books, 1987), pp. 16–19.

7. Emmanuel Levinas, *Totality and Infinity: An Essay on Exteriority*, trans. Alphonso Lingis (Pittsburgh: Duquesne University Press, 1969), p. 290.

8. This is Foucault's remarkable turn of phrase and inversion of Plato's *Phaedo* in *Discipline and Punish*: "The soul is the instrument and effect of a political anatomy; the soul is the prison of the body." See Michel Foucault, *Discipline and Punish: The Birth of the Prison*, trans. Alan Sheridan (New York: Vintage Books, 1977), p. 30.

9. Deleuze, *Foucault*, p. 87.

10. Michel Foucault, *The Order of Things: An Archeology of the Human Sciences*, English translation of *Les mots et les choses*. (New York: Vintage Books, 1970), p. xiv.

11. Levinas, *Totality and Infinity*, p. 294.

12. Deleuze, *Foucault*, p. 112.

13. Maurice Merleau-Ponty, *Phenomenology of Perception*, trans. Colin Smith (London: Routledge and Kegan Paul, 1964), p. xi.

14. Merleau-Ponty, *Phenomenology of Perception*, p. 177.

15. Merleau-Ponty, *The Visible and the Invisible*, pp. 226, 225, 237.

16. Jean-Francois Lyotard, "Philosophy and Painting in the Age of Their Experimentation: Contribution to an Idea of Postmodernity," in *The Merleau-Ponty Aesthetics Reader: Philosophy and Painting*, ed. Galen A. Johnson (Evanston: Northwestern University Press, 1993), p. 331. This essay first appeared in *Camera Obscura*, no. 12 (1984): 110–25.

17. Merleau-Ponty, *The Visible and the Invisible*, pp. 227, 237.

18. Here, I am relying upon Aristotle's analysis of the eight senses of the word *in* that is found in the *Physics*, Book IV, 3. The analysis occurs in the context of Aristotle's discussion of the category of place. The Oxford English Dictionary lists forty definitions of "in" as a preposition and twenty-one definitions of "in" as an adverb of motion or direction, e.g., "he went in."

19. Merleau-Ponty, *The Visible and the Invisible*, p. 227.

20. Merleau-Ponty, *The Visible and the Invisible*, p. 227.

21. See Deleuze's line drawing of the line of the outside and the fold of subjectivation or thinking, in *Foucault*, p. 120, which appears to be a diagram of the stratified and highly organized field of present, past, and future. We should be mindful that Deleuze also sometimes diagrams the deterritorialized and destratified assemblages that express the simultaneity of past, present, and future.

22. Merleau-Ponty, *The Visible and the Invisible*, p. 250.

23. Merleau-Ponty, *The Visible and the Invisible*, p. 237.

24. Merleau-Ponty, *The Visible and the Invisible*, p. 237.

25. Artaud's poem is entitled "The Situation of the Flesh," and also contains these remarkable lines on interiority and exteriority: "It seems to me one must above all reckon with man's incomprehensible magnetism and with what, for want of a more telling phrase, I am forced to call his life-force. My reason will certainly one day have to receive these unformulated forces exteriorly shaped like a cry which are besieging me, and they may then supplant higher thought. There are intellectual cries, cries which stem from the marrow's delicacy. This is what I personally call the Flesh." Antonin Artaud, *Collected Works*, Volume One, trans. Victor Corti (London: John Calder, 1978), pp. 164–65.

26. Albert Camus, "The Right Side and the Wrong Side," in *Lyrical and Critical Essays*, ed. Philip Thody, trans. Ellen Conroy Kennedy (New York: Vintage Books, 1968), p. 61. Camus's own reflections on this story also include the remark: "It's odd all the same to live among people who are in such a hurry" (p. 61).

27. Edna St. Vincent Millay, "Dirge Without Music," from the collection *The Buck in Snow* (1928), reprinted in *Selected Poems of Edna St. Vincent Millay: the Centenary Edition*, Colin Falck (New York: Harper, 1991), p. 79.

CHAPTER 2

# Transcendence in Merleau-Ponty

### MICHAEL B. SMITH

It is quite impossible to have a firm grasp of what is at stake in the philosophy of phenomenological existentialism without beginning with Husserl and his radical solution to the epistemological riddle of transcendence versus immanence. The pair of terms, transcendent/immanent, had been central to the epistemological problem at least since Descartes. At ground level, they designate what is within me (immanent) as opposed to what is without (transcendent). But this appears to be a naive view, since (anatomically) what is within me may be considered part and parcel of the "outer world," and no amount of peeling will get us to the inside of an apple without transforming it to a new "outside" in the process. True immanence is not a point of arrival, but where we set out from the moment we say "I." Descartes founded all philosophical certainty on the proposition involving this articultion of selfhood. "I think, therefore I exist." Now Husserl carefully trims back Descartes's findings, to "I think thoughts, therefore thoughts exist." This restricts us to the realm of immanence quite unequivocally, since concluding the existence of a thinker might lead to the unfounded assertion that the real, three-dimensional philosopher's status as a *transcendent* entity had somehow been established. Husserl's most portentous decision was to solve the epistemological problem that seems inherent in the transcendence/immanence problematic by "bracketing" the question of the existence of transcendent being, while preserving its essence in the form of meaning *within immanence*, i.e., within the *cogitationes*. Immanence henceforth contains transcendence qua idea.

In the following pages I shall distinguish three sorts of transcendence: phenomenological (or epistemological), existential (or ontological), and metaphysical (or theological). In Merleau-Ponty's work, the meaning of the term is sometimes phenomenological, more often existential, and only rarely metaphysical. Transcendence is a word so full of historical resonances that it can hardly be used in any new, personal way within a fresh philosophical configuration. It never becomes one of Merleau-Ponty's key words. It is mediation, not transcendence, that is the focus of his philosophy. There is something too "magical" about transcendence, too discontinuous to play a key role in his own thought. Perhaps that is why, where Husserl was led to speak of a "transcendence-in-immanence," Merleau-Ponty speaks of a *"dépassement sur place,"* translated as a "surpassing that does not leave its field of origin," a noteworthy expression to which I shall return. Nevertheless, as I shall attempt to show, transcendence does play an important role in one aspect of Merleau-Ponty's philosophy: it designates the passage, not to the superhuman (as it has often done in its metaphysical sense) but to the fully human. It is in the movement toward meaning (the cultural manifestations of which movement are but its most obvious and broadly recognized phenomena) that transcendence has its place in Merleau-Ponty. Other existential phenomenologists assign transcendence related but not indistinguishable roles. By establishing a clearly, almost pedagogically defined backdrop of "transcendences," we hope to gain insight into this perhaps essentially elusive movement. (Is not the "term" *transcendence* a term in both senses? Both name and end point? A Bergsonian doubt arises as to whether the noun's status must not stop the movement, destroying its phenomenological evidence.) Let us proceed by distinguishing the three above-mentioned varieties of transcendence.

## EPISTEMOLOGICAL TRANSCENDENCE

The first and most philosophically well-established sense of transcendence in Merleau-Ponty I shall dub, following Heidegger's distinction, epistemological transcendence.[1] It is the transcendence evoked by Martin Dillon in the second chapter of his illuminating study, *Merleau-Ponty's Ontology*.[2] There the transcendence/immanence dichotomy is seen as the "matrix" of the dualisms Merleau-Ponty's philosophy is intended to overcome. The Meno paradox, an epistemological roadblock, stems from the wrongful application to knowledge of the principle of excluded middle: either we know something or we do not. How then could we ever find something the nature of which is unknown to us? It is the mediation of this dualism in Merleau-Ponty that allows us to understand our possibility of partial and progressive understanding. His aesthetic ontology of flesh—a development of his study of the lived body, which is both seer and seen, a blend of immanence and transcendence—provides us with the element necessary for a mediation between knowledge and ignorance, but also between knower and known, activity and passivity, etc. Dillon takes up the two terms Merleau-Ponty uses to designate the philosophies of transcendence and of immanence—empiricism and intellectualism—respectively. He shows that neither of these philosophies can offer adequate epistemological fields because intellectualism is not subject to error (being closed to all extramental correction) and empiricism, always open to skepticism, can never supply certainty.[3]

Intellectualism generates its own world. Like the Greek gods, who by virtue of their divinity have the innate gift of recognizing any of the other (Greek) gods, so the mind of intellectualism need not fear stumbling upon an entirely unknown entity. How can intellectualism's consciousness (which is immanence) discover a world, with all the haecceity and surprise associated with our everyday notion of "world," if it has itself (if it is of the Husserlian variety) constituted it? Let us note in passing that Michel Henry makes the sensible suggestion that it can do so only if the act of constitution is unconscious. Henry attributes this very doctrine to Schelling and Merleau-Ponty,[4] and associates the domain of immanence with Night. The role of the *punctum caecum*, the famous blind spot of consciousness, would seem to be that of the darkened theater out of which subjectivity, the spectator, can observe.[5]

But Merleau-Ponty passes from this epistemological to what we shall term an ontological interpretation of transcendence when he suggests that there is in the nature of perception itself a tendency to set up a world of immanence in which its own transcendence is repressed. I quote from the "Working Notes" appended to *The Visible and the Invisible.*

> With life, natural perception (with the savage mind) is perpetually given to us the wherewithal to set up the universe of immanence—
> And yet, this universe tends of itself to become autonomous, realizes of itself a repression of transcendence—.[6]

And what is this transcendence? Clearly not that of the external object, separate from the self. On the contrary, the external world of material objects has become "the universe of immanence," which has the perverse tendency to "become autonomous" by realizing "a repression of transcendence." As the continuation of this same working note makes clear, this transcendence is a "latent intentionality, *being at*—." The last, Heideggerian expression makes it apparent that we are dealing with the self as transcendence, i.e., with the existential or ontological sense of transcendence.[7]

## ONTOLOGICAL TRANSCENDENCE

Ontological (or existential) transcendence is the result of existentialism's rejection of Husserl's reduction of "real" transcendence to the status of a meaning, a transcendence in immanence.[8] Transcendence is thus well on its way to becoming (specifically in Sartre) a feature of existence, i.e., of the human mode of being, or of "for-itself" being. It is the negation that opens up freedom, choice, virtuality, and consciousness. Consciousness finds itself henceforth obliged to be "of" something and at the same time be aware of itself—for otherwise it would be pure "ex-stasis," losing itself in its object. Heidegger rejects Descartes's and Husserl's transparent presence of self to self or the sphere of epistemological immanence. What *Dasein* transcends is not immanence, or even less subjectivity, but entities, and projects itself toward the world as horizonal totality of entities, though itself no entity.[9] Sartre's and Merleau-Ponty's transcendence is no longer the name of a movement but of that which moves in the movement: *a* transcendence, a human being, a subjectivity, which is described as a temporalizing upsurge of being directed largely toward virtuality, a modality of nonbeing.

We have been speaking of "the existentialist" notion of transcendence, and although it is possible to do so to some extent, there are important differences between the transcendence of Heidegger, Sartre, and Merleau-Ponty. Merleau-Ponty's existential use of transcendence is less extreme than that of Sartre, since the latter's ontology posits consciousness as nothingness, so that transcendence tends to be an all-or-nothing affair, precisely: consciousness as nothingness versus the in-itself as being. Whereas, for Merleau-Ponty, "the for-itself is a *hollow and not a void,* not absolute non-being."[10] When Merleau-Ponty defines transcendence as an act that "takes up, for its own purposes, and transforms . . . a situation,"[11] he is using the term in a specifically existentialist sense, a sense that, once more, is close to but not identical with that of Sartre, for whom transcendence is oriented toward freedom, consciousness or for-itself, and the future. Merleau-Ponty's transcendence would have us "assume" a situation, and define, though not in total freedom, the way in which a set of circumstances are to be lived—as, e.g., El Greco assumes and lives his astigmatism, or as human beings assume their sexuality and collaborate in its eventual meaning.

Here, Merleau-Ponty's notion is closer to that of Heidegger's *Geworfenheit* "thrownness" than to Sartre's radical freedom. The precise close reasoning that leads Merleau-Ponty to reject the "summary rationalism" that would make our freedom either total or nonexistent is contained in the last chapter of *Phenomenology of Perception,* titled "Freedom," in which Merleau-Ponty's own position, still bearing the linguistic trace of its Husserlian chrysalis, is clearly stated. "There is an autochthonous significance of the world which is constituted in the dealings which our incarnate existence has with it, and which provides the ground of every deliberate *Sinngebung*."[12]

We shall have more to say about this notion of transcendence in Merleau-Ponty when we discuss the role it plays in Merleau-Ponty's attempt to trace the genesis of meaning; let us simply mention that it is developed in connection with both the analysis of meaningful bodily gestures and the structuring of the Gestalt in perception.

## METAPHYSICAL TRANSCENDENCE

This conception of transcendence is perhaps more theological than philosophical, but can the distinction be maintained? In his radio interview with Georges Charbonnier, Merleau-Ponty shows how the "quasi-theological" problem of transcendence versus immanence reappears in the midst of a group "as little religious as the revolutionary society of Russia in 1917."[13] In one sense, for Marx, the revolution is immanent to history and the fruit of the development of capitalism. But on the other hand no one knows exactly, on the practical plane, what decision is or is not "revolutionary," or precisely where the line of the future will cut through concrete life. In the religious sphere proper, and in French Catholicism specifically, Merleau-Ponty says he sees a theology of irreconcilable opposites in the notion of a transcendent God, for whom the world is "surplus," and on the other hand a God who did "positive work" in creating man capable of sin "as if God alone were less than the totality God and the world." And after a brief discussion of the Vatican's decision to end the worker-priest initiative, Merleau-Ponty adds with some irony:

> Well, you know the reactions of the hierarchy. The hierarchy usu-
> ally doesn't go overboard in the direction of immanence—the idea
> of an organic relation, a constant communication between the su-
> pernatural and the natural, between the visible history of the
> Church and its invisible meaning. Those are not typically admin-
> istrative ideas, and we have here an administration.... No admin-
> istration, as far as I know, is immanentist. Administrations and
> spontaneity . . . don't go together. (Charbonnier 1959, 97)

To summarize, Merleau-Ponty sees the relation between immanence and transcendence as an "inner" one, in which transcendence (as subjectivity and "spontaneity") arises out of immanence. He considers such an emergence to be more rationally satisfying and more politically subversive than transcendence as pure exteriority, such as we find in Emmanuel Levinas's essay on exteriority,

*Totality and Infinity.*[14] But does Merleau-Ponty's philosophy of the *Ineinander*[15] do justice to the exteriority of transcendence?

## TRANSCENDENCE AND EXTERIORITY

Exteriority is an important conceptual component of transcendence. In the epistemological transcendence of Descartes, what is exterior to me is doubtful, and in Kant, the "transcendent" is unknowable. Husserl, as we have seen, abstracts from the question of the existence of the transcendent world: it is knowable, but is it anything more than knowledge? Husserl rejects the terms *outer* and *inner* in place of *transcendent* and *immanent*, as being those of a mere "neophyte."[16] For Merleau-Ponty, however, the terms *inner* and *outer* are recruitable terms for philosophical reemployment because they form part of our everyday understanding of perception and are not laden with technical meaning. In speaking of the image and of painting, Merleau-Ponty rejects the notion that they are a copy of the external aspect of things. "They are the inside of the outside and the outside of the inside,"[17] he writes, clearly in consonance with his theory of reversibility. The "carnal obverse" exposed to view for the first time—that is what painting really is. In calling the painting the outside of the inside, he is referring to the way painting gives external manifestation to the invisible inner structure of things; in saying it is the inside of the outside, he is referring to that same invisible structure of the "outer world." Merleau-Ponty's aesthetic ontology is really a complex and implex topology. It is an "endo-ontology," in which "transcendence [is a] synonym of incarnation."[18] This would suggest that, in addition to Cartesian or Euclidean space, which is but one of polymorhism's possibilities, in which the *ens realissimum* obtains *partes extra partes*, there is (and no doubt flesh is its "emblem") a way for Being to be *partes intra partes*. While traditional transcendence was a movement from self to what is outside of self, Merleau-Ponty's transcendence of perception does not stop at the exteriority of the outer world, but loops back: that movement is but one strand of a "*chiasme,*" an "*Ineinander*" or crossing, a Husserlian "*Überschreitung*" that moves from self to world and from world to self, via the mediating elemental flesh. This circular schema, according to Merleau-Ponty, "does not present the difficulties that the relation between 'layers' or linear orders presents (nor the immanence-transcendent alternative)."[19]

Hence, Merleau-Ponty's "existentialist" use of the term *transcendence* includes the feature of exteriority, that is, an exteriority enmeshed in a Husserlian "*Ineinander*" and one that will be caught up in the reversibility of the visible and the invisible. But exteriority, from a less topological and more psychological perspective, has another name, which may capture the subjective source of exteriority more adequately: alterity. The movement of transcendence beyond the self encounters otherness. How does Merleau-Ponty's transcendence stand in this respect?

## TRANSCENDENCE AND ALTERITY

If we consider transcendence and immanence in the traditional or epistemological sense, it seems legitimate to identify immanence with sameness and transcendence with otherness (or alterity). The Cartesian self is identity itself, and its sphere, that of subjectivity, is totally transparent to itself. Hence what characterizes its pendant term, transcendence, is opacity.

In order to clarify Merleau-Ponty's understanding of alterity it may prove useful to contrast it with that of Emmanuel Levinas. For the latter, the alterity of the physical object is but a first step on the ladder of alterity. The non-me, everything I can encounter or know in the world, is other, but only in a very relative sense. The absolute other cannot even share a common border separating it from myself. In very approximate terms, this absolute, metaphysical alterity is the other person, and God.[20] Merleau-Ponty's understanding of the otherness of transcendence follows much more closely the problematic of Edmund Husserl's *"Fremderfahrung Analyse"* (analysis of the experience of otherness) in chapter 49 of his *Cartesian Meditations*.[21]

The paradox facing Husserl is: How can I, as meaning giver, generate a heterogenous meaning, a meaning that would be that of another? The marvelous discoveries of Husserl's phenomenological analyses in his fifth Cartesian Meditations notwithstanding (the derivation of objectivity from intersubjectivity being perhaps the most outstanding of them), it is a foregone conclusion that all Husserl can find is the *meaning* "truly existing others." But could we reasonably expect anything better than a meaning? Is Husserl after all doing anything other than adding the prefix "meaning" to all entities, thus assuring them right of passage into a realm in which only meanings may reside?

Let us note in passing that Husserl (though he was the first philosopher to undergo Derrida's deconstruction) might well be viewed as the philosopher of deconstruction; indeed, the realm of subjective essences he describes would seem to correspond precisely to the world of the text. Deconstruction is exactly as open to the charge of being incapable of getting outside the text as is Husserl of exiting the essences belonging to the transcendental Ego.

The ultimate rejection of Husserl's world of essences by Merleau-Ponty is well known, and constitutes a significant portion of his writings.[22] His philosophy is centered on restating the terms of the insoluble problem of the immanence/transcendence dichotomy. His works contain three solutions to the problem of the relationship between inner and outer (and I am assimilating, for the moment, inner to immanent and outer to transcendent). In his early works he critiques the abstract nature of subject and object, in terms very close to those of Husserl. The relation is more real than the terms. The relation itself is the mediation. Later, it is the ontologically "simple" element, flesh, that resolves the irreconcilables, essence and existence. Finally, inner and outer are "reversible." They are identical.

Emmanuel Levinas does not change the terms of the problem fundamentally. He takes up Husserl's notion of the idea of otherness within the realm of the self, but problematizes it by contrasting the finitude of the idea of the other with the incommensurable infinity of otherness. In approximate terms, we could say that Levinas thematizes what in Husserl was a problem, dramatizing the self/other dialectic and transposing it to the ethical realm of persons and perhaps God—in any case, the realm of "who" more urgently than of "what."

How profound is the difference between the "who" and the "what"? Both possess individuality, specificity, but the "haecceity" of the thing is that of the egocentric particular: it emanates from the *hic et nunc* I bring with me. It is therefore a prolongation of self, of identity, of same. The uniqueness of the alterity of the "who" on the other hand emanates from the non-me, from an otherness that is related to me by a relation originating completely outside myself.

Levinas's tendency, following Martin Buber, is to introduce a transcendence neither ontological nor epistemological, but metaphysical (or theological). One is faced with the question of whether such a move can be construed philosophically in the traditional sense, as love of knowledge. Love of knowledge yields to love of the other. We have, most of us, I suspect, who have ever taught an ethics course, wondered vaguely whether a good grade corresponded to any moral amelioration. Before we scoff at such considerations, let us pause to remember that no lesser a philosopher than Aristotle spelled out the subservience of all ends to the highest good. It is not surprising, considering how closely epistemology and ontology are related, that once we withdraw primacy from knowledge, we may be launched toward a transcendence that outdistances being altogether.

Merleau-Ponty's most intimate philosophical movement seems to be exactly the opposite. He wishes to expand the notion of being and of knowledge so that all being (human and nonhuman) and all experience (mute and inarticulate or discursive, scientific) can be accommodated within one coherent manifold. Hence his version of transcendence must be containable within a unified field of being. I will, accordingly, conclude with a few brief remarks on that transcendence that does not declare itself such, and that Merleau-Ponty redescribes as a "*dépassement sur place.*"

## IDEAS WITHOUT EQUIVALENTS

The striking formulation, "*dépassement sur place*," or "surpassing that does not leave its field of origin,"[23] appears very close to the end of the last pages Merleau-Ponty wrote. Therefore we are made aware of the dramatic force of: "It is too soon now to clarify . . ." which serves to introduce it. There is a point at which Merleau-Ponty, breathlessly leading the reader into the labyrinthine depths of the intertwining of vision and flesh of the world pauses, as if suddenly fearful of having succeeded too well.

> But once having entered into this strange domain [of mixed essences and existences, etc.] . . . there is to be sure a question as to how the "ideas of the intelligence" are initiated over and beyond, how from the ideality of the horizon one passes to the "pure" ideality, and in particular by what miracle a created generality, a culture, a knowledge come to add to and recapture and rectify the natural generality of my body and of the world. (*The Visible*, 152)

His strategy will have to be to show how an architectonics of interlacing visibility and invisibility, and particularly how music and language can catch the inner dimensionalities in their mesh, transpose them, pass from Proust's "ideas without equivalents" to Plato's hypostatized ideas. We know enough about Merleau-Ponty's conception of the relation of painting to language from his "Indirect Language and the Voices of Silence" to realize that no meanings ever emerge clean and clear from the medium of their expression. Pure ideality "already streams forth along the articulations of the aesthesiological body" and "slips through ways it has not traced" (ibid., 152). There is, then, no transcendence in the sense of absolute separation in Merleau-Ponty. The animals depicted in the cave paintings at Lascaux seem to move, to inhabit a different space from that of their material support—but they never quite break free from their invisible moorings.

Transcendence tends to be drawn into the web of immanence through rationality. Reason, reflection, knowledge—such are the ties that bind transcendence, drawing it toward immanence. The philosophy that succeeds in constituting transcendence relativizes it, thereby compromising its alterity. Merleau-Ponty avoids this outcome by giving priority to description over constitution, and by broadening the meaning of reason. His philosophy seeks to surprise the inception of subjectivity within the sphere of immanence, and to trace the birth of ideality. The result is an aesthesiological ontology.

Martin Dillon's work on Merleau-Ponty's ontology[24] has performed an important task in offering a systematic analysis of that philosopher's main accomplishment. It has done so largely because it has succeeded in correctly locating the central philosophical issue to which Merleau-Ponty's work is a response: namely, the transcendence/immanence dichotomy. This rift is an ontological one, giving rise to mutually exclusive accounts of the world. But should we conclude that this dualistic matrix has given rise to a host of noxious binary oppositions from which our culture is now longing to be free? Is not Merleau-Ponty's text itself animated by such oppositions at every turn? Indeed, it would be difficult to imagine that dramatization of being (up to and even including its denouement of savage being and reversibility) without the cast of dramatis personae whose inert bodies litter the philosophical theater of operations: subject/object, essence/existence, immanence/transcendence, *parole parlante/parole parlée*, and so on.

One of the inconveniences of perfection is that it is over. Merleau-Ponty has generated his share of secondary literature, but he has become "classic" in the sense that his texts are quoted more than they are synthesized: as if the wording itself contained the mysterious formula of their efficacy. He may be looked upon, like Proust whom he admired so deeply, as the culmination of a tradition, despite his originality. And is not expression usually a kind of ontological promotion from existence to essence?

To read Merleau-Ponty as the philosopher who overcomes the dualisms of mind and body, form and matter, etc., is to read him as he should be read, but is it not also to be seduced by the power of a prose that is itself constantly nourished by all the rich array of oppositions that have for so long sustained European philosophy? These philosophemes—subject/object, transcendence/immanence, and the rest—are at the root of all the most impressive personal productions of Husserl, Heidegger, Sartre, Levinas, and Michel Henry, as well as Merleau-Ponty. Perhaps what has made these particular concept pairs so fecund is their aptness to be modified and redescribed, reinvested with personal experience. Whence the unmistakable blend of extreme personalism and ontological generality that characterizes so much of phenomenological existentialism.

## NOTES

1. See Frederick Olafson's *Heidegger and the Philosophy of Mind* (New Haven and London: Yale University Press, 1987), p. 67.

2. M. C. Dillon, *Merleau-Ponty's Ontology* (Bloomington: Indiana University Press, 1988), pp. 35–50.

3. It should be noted, of course, that these two ways of philosophizing, designated as empiricism and intellectualism, and correlated with transcendence and immanence, respectively, represent philosophical idealizations both in Merleau-Ponty and in Dillon: all

historical empiricisms have had some sort of epistemological accounting for the possibility of knowledge.

4. See Michel Henry, *The Essence of Manifestation*, trans. G. Etzkorn (The Hague: Martinus Nijhoff, 1973), pp. 395, 396, esp. note 40.

5. See Merleau-Ponty, *The Visible and the Invisible*, trans. A. Lingis (Evanston: Northwestern University Press, 1968), p. 248; *Phenomenology of Perception*, trans. Colin Smith (London: Routledge and Kegan Paul, 1962), p. 100–101; *The Structure of Behavior*, trans. A. L. Fisher (Boston: Beacon Press, 1963), p. 217.

6. Merleau-Ponty, *The Visible and the Invisible*, p. 213.

7. Perhaps it is because Merleau-Ponty had become aware of the possible misunderstandings to which his use of the terms *immanence* and *transcendence* might give rise that he uses them abundantly in his working notes but seldom if at all in the portion of *The Visible and the Invisible* intended for eventual publication. Clear enough for his own notes, in which he is differentiating his position from that of Husserl, Piaget, Sartre, etc. (and therefore more inclined to employ stock terminology), he becomes increasingly creative and poetically scrupulous in the main text.

8. See Edmund Husserl, *Ideas Pertaining to a Pure Phenomenology and to a Phenomenological Philosophy*, First Book, trans. F. Kersten (Dordrecht: Kluwer Academic, 1982), p. 133 (Husserl's chapter 57).

9. Frederick A. Olafson, *Heidegger and the Philosophy of Mind* (New Haven and London: Yale University Press, 1987), p. 68.

10. *The Visible and the Invisible*, p. 233.

11. *Phenomenology de la Perception*, p. 169.

12. *Phenomenology de la Perception*, p. 441.

13. Georges Charbonnier, "Douze entretiens avec Maurice Merleau-Ponty," (Recorded for the Radio-Télévision Française between May 22 and August 8, 1958. Transcript, 149 pages. Property of the Institute National de l'Audiovisuel, Paris; my translation.) p. 93.

14. Emmanuel Levinas, *Totality and Infinity: An Essay on Exeriority*, trans. A. Lingis (Pittsburgh: Duquesne University Press, [1969]): see esp. pp. 33–52 (Section I, A., "Metaphysics and Transcendence").

15. Husserl's term for what Merleau-Ponty naturalized into French and his own philosophy as "chiasme" and "entrelacs." See *The Visible and the Invisible*, pp. 130, 268; and *Le visible et l'invisible* (Paris: Gallimard, 1964), pp. 172, 322.

16. See Edmund Husserl, *The Idea of Phenomenology*, trans. W. P. Alston and G. Nakhnikian (The Hague: Martinus Nijhoff, 1973), p. 3.

17. Maurice Merleau-Ponty, *Eye and Mind*, in *The Merleau-Ponty Aesthetics Reader*, ed. G. Johnson (Evanston: Northwestern University Press, 1993), p. 126. The expression *carnal obverse* occurs on the same page.

18. Merleau-Ponty, *The Visible and the Invisible*, pp. 226, 229 (from the "Working Notes").

19. Merleau-Ponty, *The Visible and the Invisible*, p. 268.

20. This view is developed in the first section of the first part of Levinas's *Totality and Infinity*, pp. 33–52.

21. Edmund Husserl, *Cartesian Meditations,* trans. Dorion Cairns (The Hague: Martinus Nijhoff, 1973), pp. 106–108.

22. See in particular *The Visible and the Invisible,* chapter 3 (pp. 105–29.) Here, Merleau-Ponty does not reject all aspects of Husserl's philosophy, but submits the notion of essence to a searching critique.

23. Merleau-Ponty, *The Visible and the Invisible,* p. 153; *Le Visible et l'invisible* (Paris: Gallimard, 1964), p. 200.

24. See note 2 above.

CHAPTER 3

# The Unconscious Mind and the Prereflective Body

EDWARD S. CASEY

For the most part, we are the [mere] plaything of obscure representations.

—Kant, *Anthropology from a Pragmatic Point of View*, Part I, Book I, sect. 5

"Unconscious mind," "prereflective body": it is not often that we pause to ponder how strange these particular pairs of terms are. Unconscious *mind*—not body? Prereflective *body*—not mind? Which mind? Whose body? In the wake of Freud and Merleau-Ponty, the respective progenitors of the pairs under scrutiny in this brief chapter, we do not usually ask such questions. We tend to take both the terms and their pairing for granted, not wondering why these particular affiliations have become so prominent, so widely presumed to be true, in late modern times. It is a postmodern preoccupation to begin to feel how bizarre such combinations can be—how much of a pastiche, or simply how contingent or limited, they can be upon examination. It is time, I think, to look into the *mysterium coniunctionis* which these binary pairs of terms present. I will do so by asking two leading questions whose answers will fall into two unequal parts. These questions are: why, for what good reason, does Freud tie the unconscious domain so stringently to the mind? Why, for what good reason, does Merleau-Ponty link the prereflective realm so closely to the body?

## TWO SENSES OF THE UNCONSCIOUS

Strange, to begin with, that Freud should tie the unconscious so fully to the mind when there was already an entire tradition in the nineteenth century that linked unconsciousness exclusively to the body and, more generally, to nature. Schelling, the first systematic thinker of the unconscious, located the unconscious squarely in the natural world. In his *System of Transcendental Idealism* (1800), he proclaims:

> The sum of all that is purely objective in our knowledge we may call Nature; whereas the sum of everything subjective may be termed the *Ego*, or Intelligence. These two concepts are mutually opposed. Intelligence is origin[ari]lly conceived as that which solely represents, and nature as that which is merely capable of representation; the former as the conscious—the latter as the unconscious. But in all knowledge there is necessary a mutual agreement of the two—the conscious and the unconscious *per se*. The problem is to explain this agreement.[1]

Freud would demur on all counts: not only is the unconscious not to be identified with nature (or "natural phenomena" as Schelling sometimes puts it),[2] but it is capable of representational activity of its own (and is not something merely represent*ed*). Moreover, precisely in its representational power, the unconscious brings forth things that do *not* agree with the products of consciousness: symptoms, dreams, parapraxes, and the like. Only at the most general hermeneutical level do Freud and Schelling converge. Just as Freud claims that the major task of psychoanalytic interpretation is to render the unconscious conscious, so Schelling holds that "the complete theory of Nature would be that by virtue of which the whole of Nature should be resolved into an intelligence,"[3] which is to say, a conscious intelligence.

Half a century after Schelling's *System of Transcendental Idealism*, the unconscious was identified not with Nature as a totality but with the human body or, more exactly, the physiological body. This was the step taken by the British physician Maudsley in the middle decades of the nineteenth century. Freud was aware of Maudsley's work via Brentano, his erstwhile mentor in philosophy. Indeed, his own training in medicine, along with his even earlier inclination to a dogmatic materialism, might have inclined him to accept this quasi-plausible view, whereby the body—itself a chunk of Nature—is regarded as an obdurate and self-unknowing mass of matter. But he did not. Why not?

Here, we must distinguish between two senses of the unconscious. The first, in effect espoused by both Schelling and Maudsley, holds that the unconscious is merely the absence of consciousness—and thus of knowledge (and, a fortiori, of self-knowledge). As Schelling put it quite explicitly, "the meeting of the two (of the conscious and the unconscious) gives *without* consciousness the real, *with* consciousness the aesthetic world."[4] The real—the real of nature and thus of the body—is what lacks consciousness, yielding the unconscious as nonconscious. A second sense of unconsciousness is importantly different: the unconscious as a dynamic agency, operating outside the sphere of consciousness. (This latter qualification is crucial, since Schelling admits that consciousness itself can harbor unconscious aspects, e.g., when the artist creates something consciously and volitionally and yet does not know how or why he or she has done so, resulting in an "unconscious knowing,"[5] an unconscious under-edge of knowing itself.) For Freud, of course, the unconscious is a realm of its own, having its own operations (i.e., "primary processes"), laws (e.g., the primacy of the signifier), products (e.g., dreams), effects (e.g., ranging from normal to psychopathological phenomena), and dynamics (i.e., primary and secondary repression).

But now the question becomes: granting that the unconscious may be such an energetic and independent domain, why does Freud insist that it is mental? Especially when its sources and resources are said to be "instinctual," that is to say, biologically driven? Notice, first of all, that it is precisely because the unconscious is representational that the instinctual, physiological basis is transformed into a mental unconscious—i. e., by the production of unconscious representations taken as ideational representatives of instincts. Instinct may well exist as a source (*Quelle*) of psychological life, but its biological format is insufficient to explain the vagaries and vicissitudes of that life: a life that is resolutely representational and that takes the form of fantasies, wishes, memories, etc. Second, by "mental" (*seelische*) Freud means something more than what the English word connotes. As Bettelheim has pointed out, *Seele* implies not just the limpid lucidity of "mind" in the tradition of Descartes, Berkeley, Hume, and even Kant. It also means "soul" or "psyche," where these latter terms bring with them a sense of dense historicity, the deep and slow internalization of a lifetime (or perhaps even several lifetimes) of experience. Mind qua soul is not a matter of that transparency which finds its appropriate model in mirrors or, more generally, in reflections. It cannot therefore be judged according to the Cartesian criteria of clarity and distinctness, which reinforce each other by their common demand for determinate presence. As Merleau-Ponty says, mind for Descartes is "a being wholly present to itself without distance."[6] Here is the metaphysics of presence in its modern guise and with a vengeance! In any case, such presence is precisely what *Seele* cannot deliver in Freud's view, for *Seele* is something that is continually complicating itself, thickening itself, yet also deceiving itself, alienating itself, holding itself at a distance, etc. The point is not that "psyche" is entirely opaque to itself: if it were this, there would be no possibility of psychoanalysis as an interpretive procedure yielding insight. The point, rather, is that psychic life is very often obscure to itself, self-obscuring in fact: "for the most part," says Kant, "we are the [mere] plaything of obscure representations"—our *own* psychic representations. Merleau-Ponty remarks that when one begins with the body, "obscurity spreads to the perceived world in its entirety."[7] Freud would say the same of the unconscious mind: here, too, obscurity prevails, an ambiguity such that concerted procedures of disambiguation must be constantly employed. The guile of the unconscious, as Ricoeur has put it, "will be met with double guile."[8]

In fact, Freud situates the unconscious mind midway between blatant matter and mirrorlike conscious mind, those Cartesian extremes that ultimately rejoin each other in an oddly comparable transparency: "the transparency of an object with no secret recesses" is only the counterpart of "the transparency of a subject which is nothing but what it thinks it is."[9] Just as the Schellingian natural object (i.e., matter) is "productive without consciousness" and not merely "dead and unconscious,"[10] so the Freudian subject is *not what it thinks it is.* As Lacan says memorably, "I think where I am not, therefore I am where I do not think. . . . I am not wherever I am the plaything of my thought; I think of what I am where I do not think to think."[11] The conscious subject is continually invaded by the products of the unconscious: products that ambiguate and complicate its life immeasurably. Concerning this subject, we can say with Merleau-Ponty that "ambiguity is of the essence of human existence, and everything we live or think has always several meanings."[12]

Merleau-Ponty makes this last statement in the context of discussing the role of the human body in sexuality. Affirming Freud's recognition of this body's "original intentionality,"[13] he finds that it is systematically polysemous. For the French thinker, the paradigmatic *Vieldeutigkeit* lies in the body, while for the Austrian analyst it is found in the mind. True, both attempt to steer a course between the Charybdis of obstinate materialism and the Scylla of crisp mentalism, and both discover that the middle realm between these dangerous extremes consists almost entirely of indeterminacies, of actions and thoughts that are essentially multimorphic. Yet they draw together only, finally, to fall apart: the realm in between is designated as "corporeal" in one case and "psychical" in the other. As if to reinforce the falling apart, Merleau-Ponty contrasts the ambiguity of the bodily middle world with the unconscious. Characterizing the body as "that ever slumbering part of ourselves which we feel to be anterior to our representations," he remarks that "there are here blurred outlines, distinctive relationships which are in no way 'unconscious' and which, we are well aware, are ambiguous."[14] On *this* point, Merleau-Ponty and Freud are in at least minimal agreement: the unconscious is not to be located in the body. But the question remains: is the ambiguity of human existence to be found paradigmatically in the mental or in the bodily realm?

At issue here is not just the debate as to whether Freud espouses a poly-semantic model of meaning—Ricoeur affirms the model, Derrida and Lacan deny it—but whether ambiguity spreads to the world of the human subject "in its entirety," or whether it stays situated in a privileged part of this subject: to wit, its body or its mind?

Merleau-Ponty, in his own characteristically ambivalent way, both suggests a straightforward answer to this question and yet puts the question itself into question. The answer is that ambiguity does indeed spread to the whole subject, since the two dimensions here at stake themselves exist in an intimate relation of reciprocity with each other. Thus, what is true of one must be true of the other as well: "the life of the body, or the flesh, and the life of the psy-che are involved in a relationship of reciprocal expression."[15] It follows that if one life is inherently ambiguous, then the other is so as well.

Yet Merleau-Ponty also raises a disturbing question: might it not be the case that what we call "body" and "mind" are themselves contrived conceptions peculiar to modernity? Then the very issue of whether ambiguity inheres in one or both is itself at issue. This line of thought emerges from a statement such as this one in the *Phenomenology of Perception*:

> [the body] expresses total existence, not because it is an external accompaniment to that existence, but because existence comes into its own in the body. This incarnate meaning is the central phenomenon of which body and mind, sign and sense are abstract moments.[16]

What, then, if "body" and "mind" are creatures of modern philosophical (and psychological) abstraction? If this is true—and I think in some large mea-sure it is true—then Freud and Merleau-Ponty rejoin each other on three counts: first, each tries to replace at least one of these two quintessential mod-ernistic terms ( the one that is most important to him) with a more adequate ex-pression. Thus Freud opts for *Seele* or "psyche" instead of *Geist* ("spirit"), while Merleau-Ponty chooses "flesh"(*la chair*) rather than "body" (*le corps*).[17] Second, both move to "meaning" as something more basic than "mind" or "body." This is what Merleau-Ponty explicitly suggests by saying that "incarnate meaning" (*sens incarné*) precedes the mind/body distinction and makes it possible. Freud, for his part, continually insists on the inherent meaningfulness of somatic symptoms: in the Dora case, for example, he says expressly that meaning is "welded on to" hysterical symptoms in such a way as to become inseparable from them.[18] He would not hesitate to concur with Merleau-Ponty that "the bodily event always has a psychic meaning."[19] Third, both authors propose that, if there is to be a contrasting dichotomy, the proper binary pair is not mind/body but something else. Merleau-Ponty continually juxtaposes "body" not with "mind"—or even "psyche"—but with "existence": body and existence "presuppose each other, and [this is so] because the body is solidified or generalized existence, and existence a perpetual incarnation."[20] Freud makes a different but closely parallel step: psychic life is most usefully paired not with the life of the body (for him a properly medical matter and outside the domain of psychoanalysis) but with human existence overall, i.e., with its history and especially its suffering, thus with the life of the person in its full scope and sweep.

## MIND AND/OR BODY?

A converse line of questioning opens just here: just as we have wondered why Freud should tie the unconscious so exclusively to the mind, why should Merleau-Ponty link the prereflective mainly with the body? (I say "mainly" since Merleau-Ponty does invoke the "prereflective *cogito*" at one crucial juncture in the *Phenomenology*.)[21] Is there not an equal but opposite error here? We have just seen the unconscious to be more than mental and, indeed, *other than* mental in a strictly Cartesian sense. On Freud's expansive view, the unconscious is truly psychical, a matter of *Seele*, and perhaps also fleshly, thus more than sheerly bodily. Maudsley's physiological unconscious, in which the unconscious is reduced to its corporeal components, needs to be supplemented or, perhaps, sublimated in an unconscious that is *charnelle* and not just *corporelle*. Such an unconscious is found, for example, in Drew Leder's notion of the "absent body" as exemplified in the viscera. The visceral unconscious is not merely nonconscious; in its convoluted workings, it possesses all the dynamism of primary process: it is itself a kind of primary process in the flesh and of the flesh.

We have seen that Freud's embedding of the unconscious in the mind was partly a reaction to earlier nineteenth-century efforts to submerge it in nature and body and partly a result of Freud's conviction that the unconscious is the very scene of conversion from instinctual states to ideational representations, the place in which psyche emerges from soma. Merleau-Ponty, on the other hand, maintains that prereflective mind arises from the lived body and is inseparable from it. Freud, wishing to put his physiological and neurological past behind him, displaces psychoanalysis onto the psyche; Merleau-Ponty, attempting to distance himself from his own Cartesian origins, plunges phenomenology into the flesh. A chiasmatic moment in short, as each crosses over into the domain abandoned by the other. Do they not, however, meet at the crossing of the chiasm, at the very point where psyche and flesh conjoin? Thus Merleau-Ponty can call for "a psychoanalysis of Nature,"[22] while Freud provides a phenomenology of the psyche in distress.

One might wonder whether it makes sense to think of a prereflective mind or psyche that exists in parallel (or some other relation) with a prereflective body or flesh. Let us dismiss one obvious candidate for such a mediatory psyche: the "preconscious mind." Although this latter term is an official part of Freudian metapsychology from *The Interpretation of Dreams* to *The Ego and the Id*, it is a threshold concept. At the most, it is the site of the ego's agency of censorship; at the least, it is merely a place of passage between consciousness and the unconscious. In neither respect does it possess the rich resources inherent in the prereflective realm on Merleau-Ponty's thick—or, indeed, even on Sartre's inaugural—description. We need to look elsewhere for better models of a psychical mediatrix. Three of these come promptly to mind: Polanyi's "tacit dimension," Heidegger's "fore-structure" of understanding, and de Saussure's "virtual memory." (a) On Michael Polanyi's model, the mind (prototypically the mind of the scientist) grasps in advance, albeit implicitly, the structures to be explored in experimentation and formulation. (b) The Heideggerian *Vorstruktur*, "forestructure," applies still more generally to any and all situations, scientific or not, in which we are called upon to understand something new. (c) Ferdinand de Saussure's virtual memory serves to put an entire language at the disposal of a collective speaking mass. "Tacit," "fore," "virtual": these are three ways in which the "pre-" of "prereflective" realizes resourceful depths not otherwise available. All are mental or on the very verge of mind, whether by way of the abductive projection of hypotheses in scientific theory formation, or by that empathic *Verstehen*, "understanding," in which *Dasein* grasps the sense of its being-in-the-world, or by a grasping of the syntactic and semantic structures of a given natural language. Finally, each of these three modes of prereflective mind bears on the understanding of *meaning*, whether the meaning be that of a puzzling natural phenomenon, spoken or written words, or being-in-the-world as a caring creature. In every case, the pertinent meaning is more felt than articulated, more inflected than reflected. By coming to meaning, moreover, we come back to a basic dimension of the unconscious, which is itself meaning-oriented and meaning-saturated at every step (e.g., in the interpretation of somatically specified symptoms). Indeed, the common crux of the chiasmatic structure to which I have pointed is found in incarnate meaning itself.

I do not mean to imply, of course, that in the three areas of prereflective mind I have just singled out there is an absence of corporeal or fleshly activity. On the contrary! It is just because there is such a rich immersion of prereflective mentation—or "psychation" as we might call it—in particular bodily practices that thinking can take off on its own: can take the imaginative and insightful leaps it does in science, language, and everyday life. These practices include various experimental procedures, forms of speech in which gesticulation is important, and those basic bodily habitudes described so tellingly by Merleau-Ponty in the chapter on "The Spatiality of One's Own Body and Motility" in the *Phenomenology of Perception*. The point is not to deny prereflective corporeal comportment but to see how it is continuous with—and actively supports—prereflective moves of mind and psyche. The first prereflectivity makes possible the second, while the latter takes up and carries forward what has already been accomplished (and is still being currently accomplished) by the body.

We have said much the same of the unconscious: here, too, what happens in *en tē psychē* gets extended to bodily engagements in a continuous (and continually compounding) series of interinvolvements. Nowhere, neither in unconscious life nor in prereflective endeavors, is there pure mind in splendid isolation from sheer body, much less vice versa. Everywhere, in all cases, there is commixture of body and mind, flesh and psyche, sexuality and existence, all within the circumambience of incarnate meaning. Ultimately, the unconscious and the prereflective themselves, each meaningful in bodily and mental modes alike, intersect at the still point of signification to which they both belong and to which they both contribute so profusely and profoundly—yet still so perplexingly.

## NOTES

1. Schelling, *System of Transcendental Idealism*, trans. B. Rand in his *Modern Classical Philosophers* (Boston: Houghton Mifflin, 1908); reprinted in B. Wilshire, ed., *Romanticism and Evolution: The Nineteenth Century* (New York: Putnam's, 1968), p. 130.

2. Schelling, *System of Transcendental Idealism*, p. 131. I am thinking of Freud's statement in *The Ego and the Id*: "all our knowledge is invariably bound up with consciousness. We can come to know even the *Ucs.* only by making it conscious" (*The Ego and the Id*, trans. J. Strachy [New York: Norton, 1962], p. 62).

3. Schelling, *System of Transcendental Idealism*, p. 131. By "intelligence" Schelling means reflection or reason in which nature has become "self-objective," i.e., known to itself. See also Schelling's claim that "the nature of the transcendental mode of thought must consist, therefore, in general in this: that, in it, that which in all other thinking, knowing, or acting escapes the consciousness, and is absolutely non-obejctive, is brought into consciousness, and becomes objective" (p. 135).

4. Schelling, *System of Transcendental Idealism*, p. 138; his italics. Ironically, Freud considered the unconscious to be the *psychically* real: see *The Interpretation of Dreams*, ch. 7.

5. "Activity [i.e., productive activity as epitomized for Schelling in art], at once conscious and unconscious, can be shown in the subjective, that is, *in consciousness itself*"(*op.cit.*, p. 138; my italics). With respect to art, Schelling maintains that "long ago it was recognized that in art not everything is performed with consciousness; that with the conscious activity an unconscious activity must combine; and that the loftiest in art is born of the perfect unity and interpenetration of the two"(*The Relation of Plastic Art to Nature* [1807], tr. B. Wilshire in *op.cit.*, p. 129). On unconscious knowing, consider the following statement: "[Art] works that lack the seal of unconscious knowing are detectable by the clear absence of a life that is self-sufficient and independent of the producer"(*ibid.*, pp. 129–30). Even so, the unconsciousness that can become part of conscious projects stems ultimately from nature: "when the unconscious acts, art imparts to its work, along with the greatest clarity to the understanding, that unfathomable reality in which it resembles a work of nature"(*ibid.*, p. 130).

6. Maurice Merleau-Ponty, *Phenomenology of Perception*, trans. C. Smith (New York: Humanities, 1962), p. 198. Ironically, Descartes uses the term "soul" (*âme, anima*) for what has come to be meant standardly by "mind" in English.

7. Maurice Merleau-Ponty, p. 199: "*l'obscurité gagne le monde perçu tout entier.*"

8. Paul Ricoeur, *Freud and Philosophy,* trans. D. Savage (New Haven: Yale University Press, 1970), p. 34; in italics in the text.

9. Maurice Merleau-Ponty, *Phenomenology of Perception*, p. 198. Merleau-Ponty adds: "the reflective attitude [evident in Descartes] simultaneously purifies the common notions of body and soul by defining the body as the sum of its parts with no interior, and the soul as a being wholly present to itself without distance. These definitions make matters perfectly clear both within and outside ourselves. . . . The object is an object through and through, and consciousness a consciousness through and through"(*ibid.*).

10. Schelling, *System of Transcendental Idealism, op.cit.*, p. 137 and p. 131 respectively. Modifying Schelling slightly, we might say that an unproductive, unreflective nature is "dead *as* unconscious."

11. Jacques Lacan, "The Agency of the Letter in the Unconscious, or Reason Since Freud" in *Écrits*, trans. A. Sheridan (New York: Norton, 1977), p. 166.

12. Maurice Merleau-Ponty, *Phenomenology of Perception*, p. 169. On the same page, Merleau-Ponty writes that "there is in human existence a principle of indeterminacy."

13. Maurice Merleau-Ponty, *Phenomenology of Perception*, p. 157: bodily sexuality possess "an intentionality which follows the general flow of existence and yields to its movements . . . sexual life is one more form of original intentionality."

14. Both citations are from Maurice Merleau-Ponty, *Phenomenology of Perception,* p. 168.

15. Maurice Merleau-Ponty, *Phenomenology of Perception*, p. 160. The word *expression* is italicized. On "reciprocal expression," see also *ibid.*, p. 157 and esp. p. 166, where Merleau-Ponty writes that "the relation of expression to thing expressed, or of sign to meaning, is not a one-way relationship like that between original text and translation. Neither body nor existence can be regarded as the original of the human being, since they presuppose each other . . ." ("nor existence" is italicized).

16. Maurice Merleau-Ponty, *Phenomenology of Perception*, p. 166.

17. This move is already evident in a sentence cited just above in the *Phenomenology of Perception*: "the life of the body *or the flesh* [*la vie corporelle ou charnelle*] and the life of the psyche [*psychisme*] are involved . . ." (p. 160; my italics). Notice that here Merleau-Ponty opts for "*psychisme*" rather than "*esprit.*"

18. Sigmund Freud, *Dora: An Analysis of a Case of Hysteria*, trans. J. Strachey (New York: Macmillan, 1963), p. 57.

19. Maurice Merleau-Ponty, *Phenomenology of Perception*, p. 160.

20. Maurice Merleau-Ponty, *Phenomenology of Perception*, p. 166; On the body/existence pair, see also p. 169: "there is interfusion between sexuality and existence."

21. "There is a world for me because I am not unaware of myself; and I am not concealed from myself because I have a world. This pre-conscious possession of the world remains to be analyzed in the pre-reflective *cogito*" (*Phenomenology of Perception*, p. 298).

22. "Do a psychoanalysis of Nature: it is the flesh, the mother" (working note of November 1960; *The Visible and the Invisible*, trans. A. Lingis [Evanston: Northwestern University Press, 1968], p. 267).

CHAPTER 4

# Merleau-Ponty and
# the Unconscious

## A POETIC VISION

DAVID E. PETTIGREW

### THE INDEX OF AN ENIGMA

Freud asserted that the unconscious was the "true psychical reality,"[1] yet for Merleau-Ponty the psyche lay in a reciprocal relationship with the body; in a "relationship of reciprocal *expression*."[2] This reciprocity, it seems, eclipses the primary causal status of the psyche. Indeed, Merleau-Ponty asserts that pathologies are in no way "unconscious" (Merleau-Ponty 1962, 168), and that there is no inner self (Merleau-Ponty 1962, xi).[3] The subject's dreams, its memory, and its sexuality, which "spread forth like an odor or sound," are not hidden or unconscious; they are coextensive with life and fundamentally ambiguous and indeterminate.[4] For Merleau-Ponty the notion of an unconscious is an illusion. There is no interior monologue but an openness played out on rays of the world.[5] The unconscious, he writes,

> is to be sought not at the bottom of ourselves, behind the back of our "consciousness," but in front of us, as articulations of our field. It is "unconscious" by the fact that it is not an *object*, but it is that through which objects are possible, it is the constellation wherein our future is read. . . . It is the *Urgemeinshaftung* of our

57

intentional life, the *Ineinander* of the others in us and of us in them. (Merleau-Ponty 1968, 180)

Merleau-Ponty blurs the distinction, then, between the strictly unconscious, on the one hand, and the strictly conscious, on the other, which amounts to a "de-entification" of the unconscious as such. The disappearance of the unconscious as an object, or as an entity, evokes a motif that lies at the heart of Merleau-Ponty's project. He writes, "We cannot remain in the dilemma of having to fail to understand either the subject or the object. We must discover the origin of the object at the very center of our experience; we must describe the emergence of being" (Merleau-Ponty 1962, 71). With this motif, Merleau-Ponty thematizes as well the collapse of the distinction between the body and its world. He writes:

> The body unites us directly with the things through its own ontogenesis, by welding to one another the two outlines of which it is made, its two laps: the sensible mass it is and the mass of the sensible wherein it is born by segregation and upon which . . . it remains open. (Merleau-Ponty 1968, 136)

For Merleau-Ponty there are no longer clearly differentiated discrete objects, subject and object, conscious and unconscious, or body and world, but, more profoundly, the "inspiration and expiration of Being, action and passion so slightly discernible that it becomes impossible to distinguish between what sees and what is seen, what paints and what is painted."[6] His ontology proposes an intertwining of the visible and the invisible such that: "Every visible something, as individual as it is . . . gives itself as the result of a dehiscence of Being. What this ultimately means is that the proper [*le propre*] essence of the visible is to have a layer [*doublure*] of invisibility in the strict sense, which makes it present as a certain absence" (Merleau-Ponty 1964a, 187).[7]

The unconscious then fades in a phenomenology, a phenomenology that, as Merleau-Ponty says, is a return to the cogito in search of a more fundamental *Logos* (Merleau-Ponty 1962, 365). In his essay entitled "*Logos*," Heidegger writes that "the unconcealing of the concealed into unconcealment is the very presencing of what is present. We call this the Being of beings."[8] As in the case of Merleau-Ponty's notion of the visible and invisible, for Heidegger:

> *Logos*, is in itself and at the same time a revealing and a concealing. . . . Unconcealment needs concealment . . . as a reservoir upon which disclosure can, as it were, draw. *Logos* remains infinitely different from what we tend to represent as a connecting or binding together. The unifying that rests in *Legein* is neither a mere comprehensive collecting nor a coupling of opposites. (Heidegger 1984, p. 71)

Merleau-Ponty's *Logos*, the site of unconcealment and concealment, is no less than the name for the Being of beings. Merleau-Ponty asserts, indeed, that "It is the invisible of this world, that which inhabits this world, sustains it, and renders it visible, its own and interior possibility, the Being of this being" (Merleau-Ponty 1964a, 151).

Thus, to speak of a particular unconscious as opposed to a consciousness or to speculate as to the location of the unconscious seems to be an egregious impropriety. In a project that collapses the simple bifurcation of subject and object maintained by traditional metaphysical categories, one cannot find the unconscious in a new location, such as the in body or in the flesh. Such an effort would invest those phenomena with a discrete causal or psychical status, which would seem inappropriate. Challenging the notion of an efficient causality of the psyche, Merleau-Ponty writes that the existentials of the world are between our acts and not behind them (Merleau-Ponty 1968, 232). A childhood memory, for example, is not the cause of a dream or behavior, rather, the subject lives as a child, not unconsciously, but ambivalently.[9] Merleau-Ponty writes:

> Without calling into question the role which Freud assigns to the erotic infrastructure and to social regulations, what we would like to ask is whether the . . . psychological mechanisms which he has described really require the system of causal notions. . . . For it is easy to see that causal thinking is not indispensable here and that one can use *another language*. (Merleau Ponty 1963, 177, my emphasis)[10]

Merleau-Ponty's notion of the unconscious cannot be placed or located, it seems to be its nature to be spreading, splayed out indeterminately: *Unheimlich*.

Even as the unconscious slides from its psychoanalytic pedestal, however, the term *unconscious* remains in Merleau-Ponty's discourse. Merleau-Ponty, one must note, does accept the term *unconscious*, if only in a highly qualified manner:

> Since our philosophy has given us no better way to express that *intemporal*, that *indestructible* element in us which, says Freud, is the unconscious itself, perhaps we should continue calling it the unconscious—so long as we do not forget that the word is the index of an enigma—because the term retains, like the algae or the stone that one drags up, something of the sea from which it was taken.[11]

The unconscious, it seems, is both eliminated as a discrete entity and maintained as an enigma that plays a part in the unfolding synthesis of the body and the world: not hidden but enigmatic, invisible but present. The unconscious is neither in full possession of itself nor entirely estranged from itself. We may consider, analogously to Merleau-Ponty's notion that "No one is saved and no one is totally lost," that nothing, not even Freud's unconscious, is ever completely lost (Merleau-Ponty 1962, 171). Such ambiguity is not an accident, but is rather a necessary, central theme in Merleau-Ponty's discourse. Any approach to the status of "the unconscious" in Merleau-Ponty's work must concern itself with this ambiguity. Merleau-Ponty writes:

> Ambiguity is of the essence of human existence, and everything we live or think has always several meanings. . . . Existence is indeterminate in itself, by reason of its fundamental structure . . . whereby the hitherto meaningless becomes meaningful. (Merleau-Ponty 1962, 169)

## AN EPISTEMOLOGICAL REORIENTATION

This necessity of ambiguity in Merleau-Ponty's work, particularly with respect to the unconscious, reminds us of Husserl's caveat that we must reject the model of the so-called exact sciences, and meet the psyche on its own terms. As Husserl wrote:

> It has already become clear to us that an "exact" psychology, as an analogue to physics (i.e., the dualistic parallelism of realities, of methods, and of sciences), an absurdity. Accordingly, there can no longer be a descriptive psychology which is the analogue of a descriptive natural science. In no way, not even in the schema of description vs. explanation, can a science of souls be modeled on natural science or seek methodical counsel from it. It can only model itself on its own subject matter, as soon as it has achieved clarity on this subject matter's own essence.[12]

Merleau-Ponty, indeed, attempts such an epistemological reorientation with respect to the unconscious, interweaving body, consciousness, and world, as well as challenging the traditional notion of causality, particularly efficient causality. He seeks to come to terms with the ambiguous essence of the unconscious, the "subject matter's own essence," in "another language."

The "other language" which Merleau-Ponty's discourse suggests, and which incorporates the body's acts, its ambiguity, and its spontaneous mystery; a language by which we may approach the ambiguity of the unconscious, is the language of *poetry*. Poetry has, he writes, an "existential modulation" by which it makes itself "eternal"(Merleau-Ponty 1962, 151). Philosophy, he writes, is not the reflection of a preexisting truth, but, "like art, the act of bringing truth into being." It is a disclosure of the world (Merleau-Ponty 1962, xx). For Merleau-Ponty the medium for that poetic disclosure is the body:

> A novel, poem, picture, or musical work are individuals, that is, beings in which the expression is indistinguishable from the thing expressed, their meaning accessible only through direct contact, being radiated with no change of their temporal or spatial situation. It is in this sense that our body is comparable to a work of art. (Merleau-Ponty 1962, 151)

Indeed, for Merleau-Ponty the body—as comparable to a work of art—is a fabric into which all things are woven (Merleau-Ponty 1962, 235). The aesthetic quality of the body's poetic disclosure of the world is underlined in Merleau-Ponty's essay, "Eye and Mind," where he writes that "The body of the painter is site of a 'secret and feverish genesis of things'" (Merleau-Ponty 1964a, 167). Moreover, the body's expression, the site of disclosure, is like an artistic performance (Merleau-Ponty 1962, 151). He writes:

> The movement of the artist tracing his arabesque in infinite matter amplifies but also prolongs the miracle of oriented motion or grasping movements. The body not only flows over into a world whose schema it bears in itself but possesses this world. . . . The gesture of expression . . . retrieves the world and remakes it. . . . All perception, and all action which presupposes it, in short, every human use of the body, is already *primordial expression*.[13]

For Merleau-Ponty the chiastic performative play of body and world is an active nexus in which the two merge. "Your act is you," Merleau-Ponty asserts, yet this activity is not a one-way subject-object pole: the world also acts upon, or holds us (Merleau-Ponty 1962, 456). First "we are acted upon," he writes, then "we are open to an infinite number of possibilities."[14] The flux of the world is one in which he writes, a being is in pursuit of itself outside (Merleau-Ponty 1962, 451).

This consideration of the unconscious in terms of poetry has its antecedents. For it was Freud who posited the poetic status of the psyche. In his 1908 article entitled, "Creative Writers and Day Dreaming," he suggested that our creative abilities have a relation to, and indeed spring from, our childhood phantasies.[15] Our childhood phantasies are an attempt to rearrange the world in a way that is more agreeable to us. Freud gives special emphasis to the play, the *Spiel* of these phantasies as contained in the terms *Lustspiel* or *Trauerspiel*, terms that, for him, preserve the relationship between child's play and poetic creation (Freud 1986, IX, 144). Freud proposes, significantly, that the creative writer's poetic production touches a desire that we share and offers us a "yield of pleasure" that is only possible through the *ars poetica* (Freud 1986, IX, 153). Thus, the act of creative writing springs from the unconscious, and its poetic creation activates the unconscious desire that we share, in a Freudian version of a "collective unconscious." These fundamental poetic truths provide a unique access to the unconscious: another royal road, as it were. In this regard, we could refer to Freud's own references to "Hamlet," from as early as his October 15, 1897, Letter to Fliess (Freud 1986, I, 265–66). Freud emphasizes the collective *well* that drama draws from when he writes, in the same letter to Fliess, that the Greek legend Oedipus, that "drama of destiny," "seizes on a compulsion which everyone recognizes because they feel its existence within themselves" (Freud 1986, I, 265). In a paper entitled, "Psychopathic Characters on the Stage," Freud invoked Aristotle's classical formulation reflecting on the way drama, particularly through its cathartic effects, opens areas of our emotional life that are otherwise inaccessible (Freud 1986, VII, 305). Freud's reference to Aristotle indicates that psychoanalysis, his "new science," should be considered in terms of drama or poetry, that is, placed in the context of a more comprehensive view of the world and of science. Further, it raises the question of the epistemological status of psychoanalysis and challenges the narrow conception of the exact sciences.

Indeed, for Aristotle, the principles of each science are relative to their respective subject-matter domains. His view of science was not as limited as our contemporary understanding, that is, physics and mathematics, but rather was broad enough to include ethics and poetics. Poetry involves "the variable" rather than "the precise." Poetry responds to those instances in which the variable or imprecise is advantageous, even a preferred mode of discourse. Moreover, Aristotle found poetry to be philosophically superior to and of graver import than history as the narration of facts.[16]

Poetry, in Aristotle's well-known formulation, consists in the authorship or staging of a scene in which human acts are portrayed, performed, or acted out. The action takes the form of comedy or tragedy, good acts or bad. In the case of tragedy, the portrayal produces a catharsis of pity and fear (Aristotle 1947, *Poetics* 6, 1449b 20–30). The actions portrayed are not particular historical events but rather interpretations of what might have been or what ought to have been (Aristotle 1947, *Poetics*, 9, 1451b). Poetry projects a possible past and a more desirable future. While poetry has its origin in the human propensity to imitate nature and the delight we take in that imitation, it is also the case that in the process of dramatizing poetry, the dramatic characters and the audience are brought to make discoveries about the concrete universals of human nature: not theoretical or precise truths, according to Aristotle's terms, but poetic truths (Aristotle 1947, *Poetics*, 4, 1448b 15). The movement toward discovery and the nature of the universals are an essential part of what, for Aristotle, gives form to poetry as a science.

Certain aspects of Freudian psychoanalysis can be considered in the light of Aristotle's treatment of poetry. The psychoanalytic scene is like a staging in which forms of actions are under consideration. The staging narrates possible worlds. The analysand's speech, neurotic symptoms, hysterical acting out, projections, identifications, and transferences are all parts of the drama. The drama does not portray an actual history but the symptoms and metaphors of a more fluid and hidden temporal drama. The transferences and catharses provoke a series of discoveries: discoveries by the analysand, the analyst, and the community. The discoveries may lead to certain truths, not those that pertain to the mathematical sciences, but are, so to speak, "poetical truths."

By virtue of this analogy between psychoanalysis and tragic drama, and through this recourse to Aristotle, one may gain an alternative epistemological perspective from which to read Merleau-Ponty's epistemological reorientation with respect to the unconscious. Merleau-Ponty's emphasis on action, the artistic performance of the body, and the provocative imprecision of the ambiguity of existence—along with its indeterminate causality—seems well suited to the Aristotelian model. For Merleau-Ponty the psychoanalytic scene provides the patient and the analyst with the opportunity to relive acts. "Psychoanalytical treatment," he writes,

> does not bring about its cure by producing direct awareness of the past, but in the first place by binding the patient to his doctor through new existential relationships. It is not a matter of giving scientific assent to the psychoanalytical interpretation, and discovering a notational significance for the past; it is a matter of reliving this or that as significant, and this the patient succeeds in doing only by seeing his past in the perspective of his co-existence with the doctor. (Merleau-Ponty 1962, 455)

Merleau-Ponty asserts, moreover, that even in its most canonical and respectable forms psychoanalysis reaches the truth about a life only through "the rapport it establishes between two lives in the solemn atmosphere of transference."[17]

## AN EVENT OF POETIC DISCLOSURE

The poetic scene, for Aristotle, is one of discovery; a discovery of concrete universals of human existence. For Freud, the poetic nature of the analytic session led to discovery as well, in his case, to the discovery of the unconscious. What does Merleau-Ponty's discourse reveal with respect to the status of the unconscious in his work? Aristotle asserted that "All art is concerned with coming into being, contriving and considering how something may come into being . . . ," and that "the origin is in the maker."[18] Can it be said that, for

Merleau-Ponty (for whom art was as well an act bringing truth into being and disclosing a world) there is an author—a maker, unconscious or otherwise—of the subject's actions and its poetry? Merleau-Ponty's collapse of the subject-object distinction, his characterization of the estatico-horizonal nature of our existence, and perhaps most fundamentally, his critique of causality, inveigh against such a conclusion. His consistent cautions against the causal status of the unconscious appropriate even Freud's discourse:

> [W]hat Freud wants to indicate are not chains of causality; it is the fixation of a "character" by investment of the *openness to Being in an Entity*—which henceforth takes place through this entity.[19]

Rather than a particular author or cause, the "index of an enigma" of which Merleau-Ponty writes could be considered in terms of Heidegger's rethinking of and challenge to Aristotle's theory of causality. Arguing that our contemporary view of *causa efficiens* is a misreading of Aristotle's intention, Heidegger suggests that the four causes are rather a unity that "bring something into appearance."[20] The "causes," or four modes of occasioning, "occasion," or "induce to go forward" to appearance (Heidegger 1977, 292). For Heidegger, this unified occasioning, this "bringing-forth," is rather a "*poiesis*" (Heidegger 1977, 293). Similarly, Merleau-Ponty's phenomenology does not concern the particular location or causal agency of the unconscious but rather its spreading or splaying in the horizon of human experience. As we have noted above, the unconscious is not at the bottom of our acts, it is out in front, interwoven with the world of our experience, manifest in what is essentially an authorless poetic disclosure.

   This poetic dispersion of the unconscious evokes Heidegger's notion of *Ereignis:* the event of appropriation or, simply, the event of being. Significantly, Heidegger's theme of "the event," or *Ereignis*, disrupts the coherence of time either as a succession of discrete nows, as in the case of Aristotle's formulation, or as a "mere duration" linking past present and future, as in the case of Augustine's treatment.[21] Such an event is an ineffable unconcealment, an openness. Heidegger's more radical interrogation of time rejects the mechanical scientific thinking linked to efficient causality. In the face of such a fundamental disruption, no logic, no syntax, and no scientific system, can be adequate.[22] Hence, Heidegger's recourse to poetry and meditative thinking. In the *Phenomenology of Perception*, Merleau-Ponty echoes Heidegger's treatment of time as an ecstatic event as he similarly refers to the subject's experience of time as a "thrust."[23] Merleau-Ponty asserts that this "upsurge of time," is an "outrunning" or negation of ourselves (Merleau-Ponty 1962, 423 and 426). For the Merleau-Ponty of *The Visible and the Invisible*, the phenomenal world is just such a disruptive event; the result of "one sole explosion of Being which is forever" (Merleau-Ponty 1968, 265). This "intemporal" unconscious—in the sense that it is neither a now-point nor mere duration—even as it has been maintained in Merleau-Ponty's discourse, would have to be said to have been pulverized by the explosion into a glittering fabric of metaphors. Such is the poetic quality of Merleau-Ponty's discourse in search of a more fundamental *Logos*.

In an interesting and revealing sense, Merleau-Ponty's ontological allegory of the "inspiration and expiration of Being," to which we referred earlier, could be said to reinscribe the psyche as breath-soul within the question of being. The return to the breath-soul of Homer recalls, as well, Heraclitus's account of a soul as an exhalation with no boundaries.[24] Insofar as there is a soul in Heraclitean discourse it is undulating, and interwoven with the world: a fiery ether that is constitutive of nature (Barnes 1987, 121). The treatment of the unconscious in Merleau-Ponty's work points, perhaps, to the *Logos* of Heraclitus. *Logos*, with its multiplicity of translations and the poetic visibility and invisibility of the Heraclitean lightning flash, offers yet another alternative paradigm to efficient causality. The unconscious, in Merleau-Ponty's text, would not be hidden, but rather unapparent, in a Heraclitean sense that is fully constitutive of what is apparent; a sense that is also evocative of Husserl's notion of an inner structure of meaning.[25] Symptomatic occurrences of this unconscious would be the unexpected flashes that ignite the soul in the process of its expurgation; its *Logos*.

## A THRESHOLD OF DISCOVERY

Finally, this approach to Merleau-Ponty's treatment of the unconscious clearly does not begin to offer a prescription for therapeutic practice but is rather a philosophical interrogation of the ontological character of that which therapy attempts to treat. Yet if we were to be guided by Merleau-Ponty in our speculation, the primary task of the therapist would be to enter into a relationship—a "co-existence"—with the patient in a new experience of being. The patient's narrative would not be subjected to a reductive causality. The conclusion, findings, or interpretations would be neither theoretical nor practical but only poetical in a way that would remain to be discovered in its fullest dimensions. The challenge for therapeutic practice would be to recognize this poetical dimension—indeed, to gain a new poetic vision—and understand that which by its very nature resists conceptualization.

Annie Dillard, in her *Pilgrim at Tinker Creek*,[26] perhaps offers guidance toward such a new poetic vision; insight into this "index of an enigma." She refers to Marius von Senden's *Space and Sight*,[27] a text reflecting on the effect of the early cataract operations of individuals who had been blinded since birth. The sudden birth of vision left the seers without adequate concepts of space and place. The patients could only see, initially, "'an extensive field of light, in which everything appeared dull, confused and in motion. They could not distinguish objects." Another patient saw, "nothing but a confusion of forms and colours." These "newly" sighted see the world in a dazzle of color patches. Dillard subsequently reports on her own re-visioning of the world, on a sunny evening at Tinker Creek:

> Again and again, one fish, then another, turned for a split second across the current and flash! the sun shot out from its silver side. I couldn't watch for it. It was always just happening somewhere else, and it drew my vision just as it disappeared: flash, like a sudden dazzle of the thinnest blade, a sparkling over a dun and olive ground at chance intervals from every direction. I blurred my eyes and . . . saw a new world. I saw the pale white circles roll up, roll up, like the world's turning, mute and perfect, and I saw the linear flashes, gleaming silver, like stars being born. . . . Something broke and something opened. I filled up like a new wineskin. I breathed an air like light; I saw a light like water. I was the lip of a fountain the creek filled forever; I was ether, the leaf in the zephyr; I was fleshflake, feather, bone. When I see this way I see truly. (Dillard 1985, 31–32)

The question of the unconscious in Merleau-Ponty's work suggests the possibility and calls for the necessity of such a poetic vision. Through Merleau-Ponty's phenomenology the body is unveiled and opened to the world. The body is opened to a world of experience without cause, without precision, and without Cartesian position or origin; thereby poised on the threshold of discovery, the discovery intrinsic to Aristotle's and Merleau-Ponty's treatment of the poetic. The "unconscious" would be considered in the context of Merleau-Ponty's assertion that psychoanalysis is neither true nor false but rather is a myth (Merleau-Ponty 1964b, 122). For Aristotle, myth was fundamentally important for discovery. Aristotle wrote in the *Metaphysics* that "even the lover of myth is, in a sense, a lover of wisdom, for the myth is composed of wonder." Wonder is central to our thinking of Merleau-Ponty's treatment of the unconscious. For he held that our task is to broaden our reasoning to make it capable of grasping what, in ourselves and in others precedes and exceeds reason (Merleau-Ponty 1964b, 122). This excess is, with Merleau-Ponty, where we must always already agree to begin again. That excess is not simply a postmodern critique of reason, but is rather the foundation of the existentialist theme of freedom.

# NOTES

1. Sigmund Freud, *The Interpretation of Dreams*, trans. James Strachey (New York: Avon Books, 1965), p. 651.

2. Maurice Merleau-Ponty, *Phenomenology of Perception*, trans. Colin Smith (Atlantic Highlands: The Humanities Press, 1962), p. 160.

3. "I am never a thing and never bare consciousness" (Merleau-Ponty 1962, 453).

4. For Merleau-Ponty, memory is not discrete unconscious phenomena that require discovery but rather a "direct possession of the past with no interposed contents" (Merleau-Ponty 1962, 265).

5. Merleau-Ponty, *The Visible and the Invisible*, trans. Alphonso Lingis (Evanston: Northwestern University Press, 1968), p. 240.

6. Merleau-Ponty, *The Primacy of Perception*, trans. James Edie (Evanston: Northwestern University Press, 1964), p. 167.

7. "It is the invisible of this world," he writes, "that which inhabits this world, sustains it, and renders it visible, its own and interior possibility, the Being of this being"(Merleau-Ponty 1964a, 151).

8. Martin Heidegger, "Logos," in *Early Greek Thinking*, trans. David Farrell Krell and Frank Capuzzi (San Francisco: Harper & Row, 1984), p. 64.

9. Merleau-Ponty, *The Structure of Behavior*, trans. Alden L. Fisher (Boston: Beacon Press, 1963), p. 179.

10. One hears echoes, for example, of Bergson's critique of a mechanistic conception of mind on pages 146–147 of *Time and Free Will*, trans. F. L. Pogson (New York: The Macmillan Company, 1959).

11. Merleau-Ponty, "Phenomenology and Psychoanalysis: Preface to Hesnard's *L'Oeuvre de Freud*," trans. Alden Fisher, in *Merleau-Ponty and Psychology. Review of Existential Psychology and Psychiatry* XVIII, nos. 1, 2, & 3 (1982–1983): p. 71.

12. Edmund Husserl, *The Crisis of European Sciences and Transcendental Phenomenology*, trans. David Carr (Evanston: Northwestern University Press, 1970), p. 223.

13. Merleau-Ponty, *The Prose of the World*, trans. John O'Neill (Evanston: Northwestern University Press, 1973), p. 78.

14. "There is, therefore, never determinism and never absolute choice . . . " (Merleau-Ponty 1962, 453).

15. Sigmund Freud, "Creative Writers and Day Dreaming," in *The Standard Edition of the Complete Psychological Works of Sigmund Freud*, trans. James Strachey (London: Hogarth Press, 1986.), IX., p. 143.

16. Richard McKeon, ed., *Poetics* in *The Basic Works of Aristotle*, trans. Ingram Bywater (New York: Random House, 1947), 9, 1451b 5–10.

17. Merleau-Ponty, "From Mauss to Claude Lévi-Strauss," in *Signs*, trans. Richard C. McCleary (Northwestern University Press, 1964b), p.122.

18. Richard McKeon, ed., *Ethics*, trans. W. D. Ross, in *The Basic Works of Aristotle*. (New York: Random House, 1947), VI 4 1140a.

19. Merleau-Ponty, "From Mauss to Claude Levi-Strauss," p.122, my emphasis.

20. Martin Heidegger, "The Question Concerning Technology," in *Basic Writings* (New York: Harper and Row Publishers, 1977), p. 292. "They set it free to that place and so start it on its way, namely into complete arrival. This principal characteristic of being responsible is this starting something on its way to arrival. It is in this sense of such a starting something on its way into arrival that being responsible is an occasioning or an inducing to go forward [Ver-an-lassen]" (Heidegger 1977, 292).

21. Martin Heidegger, *On Time and Being*, trans. Joan Stambaugh (New York: Harper & Row, 1972), pp. 11–12.

22. "We are not dealing with statements that are always fixed in the sentence structure of the subject-predicate relation . . . we must give up the declaratory sentence that is anticipated by the question we have raised" (Heidegger 1972, 19–20).

23. "We must understand time as the subject and the subject as time" (Merleau-Ponty 1962, 422).

24. Jonathan Barnes, *Early Greek Philosophy* (New York: Penguin Books 1987), p. 116.

25. Edmund Husserl, *The Origin of Geometry*, in *The Crisis of European Sciences and Transcendental Phenomenology*, trans. David Carr (Evanston: Northwestern University Press, 1970), p. 371.

26. Annie Dillard, *Pilgrim at Tinker Creek* (New York: Harper and Row Publishers, 1985), p. 25.

27. Marius von Senden, *Space and Sight. The Perception of Space and Shape in the Congenitally Blind Before and After Operation*, trans. Peter Heath (Glencoe, Ill.: The Free Press, 1960), pp. 130–132.

CHAPTER 5

# From the Unseen to the Invisible

MERLEAU-PONTY'S SORBONNE LECTURES
AS PREPARATION FOR HIS LATER THOUGHT

JAMES PHILLIPS

On the occasion of assuming the chair in child psychology at the Sorbonne in 1949, Merleau-Ponty undertook an intense reading of the field of child development. The reading covered the areas of anthropology, child psychology, and psychoanalysis. For the most part the readings and the lectures based on them provided a confirmation and a deepening of the analyses carried out in *The Structure of Behavior* and the *Phenomenology of Perception*. In this regard they offer a striking confrontation of Merleau-Ponty's phenomenology with current findings in child development. The lectures, however, may be viewed in another manner—that in which they advance beyond the earlier thought and anticipate Merleau-Ponty's later ontology. To the extent that this is the case we may question whether the Sorbonne investigations played a formative role in the development of the later thought.

In this chapter I will focus on Merleau-Ponty's reading of the psychoanalytic literature in the Sorbonne lectures; for if there is any area of the Sorbonne researches that clearly advanced his thought, it is that of psychoanalysis.[1] We know that he was interested in Freud and psychoanalysis throughout his life. The two are dealt with in both of the early books, and references to psychoanalysis abound in the posthumous *The Visible and the Invisible*. He speaks of the convergence of phenomenology and psychoanalysis in the well-known "Preface,"[2] published in 1960; and in an interview near the end of his life he reiterated his position regarding the reciprocal need of philosophy and psychoanalysis for one another.

> Does psychoanalysis render the human individual transparent? Does it allow us to dispense with philosophy? On the contrary, the questions that psychoanalysis now asks, even more energetically than ever before, are questions that one cannot begin to answer without philosophy: How can the human being be at once wholly spiritual and wholly corporeal? The psychoanalyst's techniques contribute in conjunction with many other investigations in resolving this question, and philosophy is again at their crossroads.[3]

As suggested above about the Sorbonne lectures in their entirety, the investigation into psychoanalysis may be viewed in two ways. On the one hand the dialogue between phenomenology and psychoanalysis initiated in the early books is pursued, and in this regard we have the opportunity to witness a phenomenological reading of psychoanalysis, as well as an enrichment of phenomenology through the reading of psychoanalysis. On the other hand, certain aspects of the Sorbonne reading make most sense only when viewed from the vantage point of the later thought. They both adumbrate the later thought and may indeed have stimulated it. It is this relationship of the psychoanalytic readings to the later thought that will be pursued in this chapter.

## SORBONNE LECTURES: RECAPITULATION OF EARLY THOUGHT

Let us begin, however, with the backward glance of the lectures. To do this I will focus first on Merleau-Ponty's treatment there of the unconscious, which remains essentially that of the *Phenomenology*. The unconscious is a concept that has always troubled phenomenologists and that preoccupied Merleau-Ponty for most of his philosophic career. For that reason it offers a vantage point both on his changing understanding of psychoanalysis as well as on the viscissitudes of the latter's influence on his thought. Indeed, this chapter will be framed around his changing understanding of this concept, beginning now with the Sorbonne discussion that points back as it does to the *Phenomenology*, and concluding with the transformation the concept has undergone by the end of his life.

As just indicated, the Sorbonne definition of the unconscious repeats Merleau-Ponty's treatment of the concept in his early work. In the lectures the unconscious is understood in terms of the figure-ground phenomenon of

Gestalt psychology. The unconscious is the *unseen ground*. One of the clearest expressions of this understanding is found in the lecture entitled "Methodology in the Psychology of the Infant." As Merleau-Ponty explains it, when something is called unconscious, this refers to a failure to distinguish figure from ground—that is, to recognize the ground that defines the figure and gives it meaning. The unconscious is thus the unseen ground. As he says:

> In order to know [ourselves] we need a certain distance that we are not able to take by ourselves. It is not a matter of an unconscious that would play tricks on us; the problem of mystification [of a deceptive consciousness] stems from the fact that all consciousness is the privileged consciousness of a "figure" and tends to forget the "ground" without which it has no meaning (cf. Gestalt theory). We do not know the ground although it is lived by us. We are for ourselves our own ground. For knowledge to progress, for there to be scientific knowledge of that "other" [the ground], it is necessary for what was ground to become figure. (BP 113/474)

To appreciate the continuity of this statement with Merleau-Ponty's treatment of the unconscious in the *Phenomenology*, we must briefly review the latter.[4] In the *Phenomenology* the unconscious is, in fact, not often explicitly evoked, for the reason that it is *equivalent* to perceptual consciousness. Merleau-Ponty shows in the *Phenomenology* how the phenomena uncovered by psychoanalysis and described by it under the rubric of the unconscious may indeed be accounted for, in language more philosophically acceptable, in terms of perceptual consciousness. He replaces the conscious/unconscious distinction with a consciousness that is opaque and ambiguous. As ambiguous perceptual consciousness, man is never in complete possession of himself: "[T]he lived is never entirely comprehensible, what I understand never quite tallies with my living experience, in short, I am never quite at one with myself" (PP 347).

Psychoanalysis is taken up explicitly in the *Phenomenology* in the discussion of sexuality—the latter introduced, it may be recalled, to demonstrate in the clearest manner the bond of embodied subject and world. Sexuality and the affective life represent, as Merleau-Ponty puts it later, "a consciousness that is not so much knowledge or representation as investment" (Pref 68). In his discussion of sexuality Merleau-Ponty takes great effort to articulate the ambiguous relation of sexuality and the whole of one's existence. He insists that sexuality is not an autonomous behavior but rather that it "has internal links with the whole active and cognitive being, these three sectors of behavior displaying one typical structure, and standing in a relationship to each other of reciprocal expression" (PP 157). Sexuality reflects one's existence, and one's existence is experienced in one's sexuality. He sees Freud's contribution, whatever his theoretical statements, as that of connecting sexuality with the rest of one's life. Psychoanalytic research "led to an explanation of man, not in terms of his sexual substructure, but to a discovery in sexuality of relations and attitudes which had previously been held to reside in consciousness . The significance of psychoanalysis is less to make psychology biological than to discover a dialectical process in functions thought of as 'purely bodily,' and to reintegrate sexuality into the human being" (PP 158).

It is in attempting to account for the Freudian notion of an unconscious sexual conflict with his analysis of sexuality that Merleau-Ponty evokes the figure-ground terminology of Gestalt psychology. As a dimension of human existence that is never fully transcended albeit routinely unnoticed, sexuality is present like an atmosphere. "Taken in this way, as an ambiguous atmosphere, sexuality is co-extensive with life. In other words, ambiguity is of the essence of human existence, and everything we live or think has always several meanings" (PP 169). A consequence of this ambiguity is that we can never determine absolutely the proportion of sexual to nonsexual motivation in any human act. For the sexual to be distinguished at all, it must be set off against the nonsexual. The peculiarity of the dream is that this demarcation of the sexual as figure against the nonsexual as ground is completely absent. As Merleau-Ponty writes, "The 'latent content' and the 'sexual significance' of the dream are undoubtedly present to the dreamer since it is he who dreams his dream. But precisely because sexuality is the general atmosphere of the dream, these elements are not thematized as sexual, for want of any non-sexual background against which they may stand out" (PP 381). In the dream, sexuality is everywhere and nowhere. It does not make sense to call the sexual themes of the dream either "conscious" or "unconscious," because those categories apply to an ability to separate figure and ground, theme and horizon, that is completely lost in the dream.

## SORBONNE LECTURES:
## FURTHER TREATMENT OF PSYCHOANALYSES

Let us now look further at Merleau-Ponty's treatment of psychoanalysis in the Sorbonne lectures themselves. His exploration of psychoanalysis is extensive and proceeds from Freud's own texts to those of his successors, culminating finally with the application of psychoanalysis to anthropology and sociology.[5] I will focus on what in all of this material seems most relevant for the present discussion.[6]

It should be noted that the bulk of the psychoanalytic reading occurs in the lecture course entitled "The Child's Relations with Others."[7] The course has been translated into English, but the published translation contains only the first part of the course, which treats the cognitive dimension of the child's relations with others. The most relevant part of that section for this paper is Merleau-Ponty's discussion of "syncretic sociability" and "transitivism," whose relation to the later notion of reversibility has been examined by Dillon.[8] Merleau-Ponty relates this material to the psychoanalytic discussion that follows it. He makes the connection explicit in comparing transitivism and imitation with the psychoanalytic mechanisms respectively of projection and introjection.

In his general discussion of Freud's early thought Merleau-Ponty first focuses in on the "Three Essays on the Theory of Sexuality" and the notions of sexuality and libidinal development elaborated in that early work. He finds an ambiguity in Freud's presentation concerning the libido and sexuality: on the one hand a description in realistic language of the libido as a physiologic process; on the other a treatment in which the notion of sexuality is found to be far more complex than simple physiology. This latter reading of Freud on infant sexuality certainly follows the thematic of sexuality in the *Phenomenology of Perception*. In the lecture under discussion, for instance, Merleau-Ponty says of Freud's thought: "The idea is at bottom that of an *incarnation*: man is situated in a body without being reduced to it" (BP 309/335).

But the analysis in the Sorbonne lecture is developed beyond the general idea of incarnation. After reviewing the phases of libidinal development in Freud's "Three Essays," Merleau-Ponty questions why Freud insists on calling the pregenital phases—the oral and anal phases—sexual. Does he intend that "the same libido that will later support genital life is already present in the pregenital phases and applied to the anal and oral apparatuses" (BP 307/332). Such a notion does not concur with Freud's further description of genital activity as an elaborate product of the individual's history. Further, the original libido cannot have anything to do with what is ordinarily called the "sexual instinct," since "the work of Freud consists in large measure in showing that there does not exist any instinct *already complete*" (BP 308/332). Why then, Merleau-Ponty asks again, does Freud call pregenital activity sexual? "He means that there is a behavior relating to the differences of the sexes of the father and mother, inasmuch as they are different, without any knowledge of how they are different, or of the genital mechanism. There is sexuality in the sense of an anticipation, of a discrimination of the sexes prior to the total functioning of the genital apparatus, of a premature sexuality" (BP 308/333). Challenging again Freud's contrary notion of a more concretized libido, Merleau-Ponty repeats, "Several suggestions permit us to correct the realist conception of the libido. When he declares that the activity of the infant is sexual from the beginning of life, Freud means only that the infant distinguishes between the sexes of his parents" (BP 308/333). Merleau-Ponty summarizes this sense of an indeterminate, ambiguous libido by invoking Freud's own description of the infant's sexuality as polymorphous, perverse.

Merleau-Ponty develops this discussion of infant sexuality further with a discussion of the Oedipus complex. The infant has "the remarkable power to transport itself into the relations of adult life without being able truly either to represent it or participate in it" (BP 308/333). He locates in Freud's discussion an idea that helps to explain the precocious sexuality of the infant. Freud reports that in the oedipal development there is an identification with the parent of the same sex that is prior to the attraction to the opposite-sex parent. Thus, if the young boy has an experience of his mother as a sexual being, this is because he has identified himself with his father. "'Sexuality' is less the search for the other sex than the infant's recognition of his own sex" (BP 308/333). The infant then, without being able to understand the situation, is completely caught up in the affective relationships of the adult world. His or her relationship with each parent is conditioned by the relation of that parent with the other. This condition is further complicated by Freud's later finding of the negative Oedipus complex, also a part of normal development and connected to the inherent bisexuality of everyone. In the negative Oedipus complex the infant forms an identification with the opposite-sex parent and then models that parent's attraction to the same-sex parent. Thus, in the case of the boy, he not only follows the primary oedipal path in identifying with his father and being attracted to his mother, but at the same time follows an opposite path in identifying with his mother and being attracted to his father. This discussion recalls—because it is their origin—Merleau-Ponty's words in the "Preface" at the end of his life: "The oedipus complex is spoken of as a cause, while actually it only imposes on the child certain poles, a system of references and dimensions, the child's position (or his successive positions) in this context being a matter of individual history" (Pref 68).

In his further reading of the Freudian corpus Merleau-Ponty continues to elaborate these themes found in the early works: an infantile sexuality that is ambiguous, diffuse, premature, and anticipatory of adult sexuality; and associated with this premature sexuality a personal life that is also anticipatory and that is fashioned out of complex identifications with the significant adults. Freud's later writings demonstrate an increasing preference for psychological over physiological explanations. The notion of a series of clearly delimited libidinal phases is replaced by a recognition of a great overlapping of phases in which the earlier phase is rarely fully abandoned.

Finally, Freud's description of the three psychic agencies—ego, id, and superego—represents the final elaboration of the individual's complex relations with others. "There exists a bond between one's relations with others and one's relations with oneself. . . . The relation with the other passes through the relation with oneself" (BP 309/336). A narcissistic wound to the self may be compensated by aggression toward others. The mechanism of projection allows self-protection through projection into the other of what is unacceptable in the self. Merleau-Ponty concludes this section by contrasting the true object relation from the more common pseudo-object relation. Describing the latter he says,

> [W]hen we identify ourselves with the other, the presence of the other does not make us get out of ourselves, for there is in fact a failure of the true relation. . . . The infant is every minute oriented toward a life for which he does not have the technique, and it is then inevitable that he wishes "to be" those whom he cannot "have." Identification threatens all our relations with others. . . . It is possible that certain individuals never achieve a true object relation. The relations with the other appear like an inevitable tension between one term of the relation and the other. The subject wishes to remain in his immanence that it is difficult to surpass. The otherness of the other can only be reached in the true object relation. (BP 311/339)

Following his discussion of Freud, Merleau-Ponty undertakes detailed discussions of his successors. The one on whom I will focus, and who seemed to have the greatest impact on Merleau-Ponty, is Melanie Klein. The themes Merleau-Ponty takes from Melanie Klein extend the Freudian analyses presented above. He emphasizes Klein's focus on the infant's body and on the manner in which the infant's relations with the world are carried out through the body. For Merleau-Ponty the phenomenal or lived body is given a dramatic illustration and development in Klein's treatment of infantile experience. Three aspects of Merleau-Ponty's treatment of Klein need to be emphasized. First, with regard to the psychological mechanisms of introjection and projection, Klein points out that with the infant these are initially physical and that they function at a level that is prior to the differentiation of the physical and the mental. Merleau-Ponty writes: "The psychological mechanisms of introjection and projection, instead of appearing as mental operations, should be understood as the very modalities of the activity of the body. The phenomenal body is the vehicle of the infant's relations with the outside" (BP 319/359). At each libidinal stage there is an exchange between the inside and the outside. The respective organs—mouth, anus, genitals—serve as vehicles of incorporation and expulsion. For the infant the division of the interior and exterior world is understood in terms of what is inside and outside the body.

Second, Klein's emphasis on introjection and projection leads to a revised and extended conception of the superego. The superego is no longer simply the

result of the completion of the Oedipus complex, as with Freud. Rather, it begins to develop as early as the first relations with others. For the infant all perception is also introjection. This begins with the introjection of the bodily parts
(part-objects) of the mother and then extends to the rest of the perceptual
world. "The superego is understood as containing not only the body of the parents but also all objects: every perception, every relation is 'digested' by us. It is
a world, an entire universe" (BP 320/361).

   Finally, these notions just developed imply a revised understanding of
symbolism in the infant. The infant's experience must be appreciated as it is
and not understood through the imposition of adult categories. What is involved is mainly a state of undifferentiation in the infant. As Merleau-Ponty
writes: "Between an image, a fantasy, the meaning of an experience, an introjection, an internalized object, the superego, there is no longer any great difference. The totality of the infant's activity appears simplified, and owing to
that Melanie Klein makes of it an activity that is corporeal as much as psychical" (BP 323/368). He then summarizes: "These extracts show that the
Freudian notions receive an extreme simplification [in Klein]. Every perceived
object is also taken in as an 'internal object.' The distinction between the fan-
tasied and the real is less sharp. Between corporeal activity (sucking, swallow-
ing) and introjection there are no longer well established boundaries. The
superego ceases to be an identification with one person but is encountered in
a diffuse state in every relation with the exterior" (BP 323/368)[9]

## COLLÈGE DE FRANCE LECTURES

   From the point of view being developed in this chapter Merleau-Ponty's
lectures at the Collège de France represent a transition between the Sorbonne
lectures and the final ontology. In his discussion of the human body he takes up
a number of the themes that I have drawn from the Sorbonne lectures, both restating them and developing them somewhat in their implications for an ontology of the flesh. He reaffirms the general point made in the *Phenomenology
of Perception* that the affective relationship is a striking case of the bond between
subject and world. "The body which possesses senses is also a body which has
desires and thus esthesiology expands into a theory of the libidinal body" (TFL
129). Specific reference is then made to Melanie Klein's contribution: "The theoretical concepts of Freudianism are corrected and affirmed once they are understood, as suggested in the work of Melanie Klein, in terms of corporeality
taken as itself the search for the outside in the inside and of the inside in the
outside, that is, as a global and universal power of incorporation" (TFL
129–130).[10] What Merleau-Ponty is here calling a global and universal power

of incorporation involves familiar themes from the Sorbonne lectures—the phenomenon of transitivism, the identity formation of the infant as a series of identifications, and the infant's primitive logic or symbolism in which inside and outside are not yet differentiated. However, what is new in the current development of these themes is precisely that the power of incorporation is global and universal, that is, that it does not only refer to the experience of the young infant. The primitive symbolism of undifferentiation, in which inside and outside are—to use the later vocabulary—reversible, is now a dimension of adult experience. Merleau-Ponty considers this Freud's "most interesting insight" (TFL 49). In speaking of dreaming he rejects any rigid distinction between the real and the oneiric and says that "[o]ur waking relations with objects and others especially have an oneiric character as a matter of principle: others are present to us in the way that dreams are, the way myths are, and this is enough to question the cleavage between the real and the imaginary" (TFL 48).

Finally, this train of thought leads Merleau-Ponty to a different notion of the unconscious. Repeating his old rejection of the unconscious as a second subject or second "I think"—the interpretation of the unconscious in terms of unconscious representations—he now connects the unconscious with what he calls "the idea of a 'non-conventional thought' (Politzer) enclosed in a 'world for us,' which is the source of dreams and more generally of the elaboration of our life" (TFL 49). Merleau-Ponty is of course close to Freud's notion of the unconscious as primary process thought. However, he has developed Freud's notion in a number of ways, and it is highly instructive to take note of the differences. First, Merleau-Ponty's conception of so-called unconscious thought is connected with what he calls "the idea of the body as a natural symbolism" (TFL 131). The logic of the unconscious does not, as with Freud, merely prescribe different rules of thought, such as a rejection of the law of contradiction, but is directly tied to a particular experience of the body. Second—and related to the first—the unconscious for Merleau-Ponty refers to a state of undifferentiation between self and other—what he calls "a permissive being, the initial yes, the undividedness of sensing" (TFL 131).[11] Finally, as suggested in the quotation concerning dreaming, the unconscious does not refer to another reality beneath appearance but is rather a dimension of waking experience.

## FINAL THOUGHT

Merleau-Ponty's last writings, published posthumously as *The Visible and the Invisible*, point to the way in which the insights from psychoanalysis first developed in the Sorbonne lectures, then elaborated in the Collège de France lectures, have contributed to his final thought. As is well known, the

latter involves an abandonment of a philosophy of consciousness for an ontology of the flesh. The problems of the *Phenomenology of Perception*, he writes in
a note, are "due to the fact that he retained the philosophy of 'consciousness'"
(VI 183). The results of the *Phenomenology of Perception* need to be brought to
"ontological explication" (VI 183). They will then be "deepened and rectified"
(VI 168). How may the psychoanalytic contribution to this ontology be characterized?

To get an initial glimpse of the psychoanalytic contribution we may
focus on the way in which psychoanalytic terminology has infiltrated philosophic description in the late writings.[12] "Polymorphism" and "promiscuity"
are heard frequently, no longer, as in the Sorbonne lectures, as attributes of infantile sexuality, rather as attributes of being or flesh. We hear of "the vertical
or carnal universe and its polymorphous matrix" (VI 221), of "the fact that the
world, Being, are polymorphism, mystery and nowise a layer of flat entities or
of the in itself" (VI 252), and that "the in itself-for itself integration takes place
not in the absolute consciousness, but in the Being in promiscuity" (VI 253).
In another note Merleau-Ponty charges himself, "Do a psychoanalysis of Nature: it is the flesh, the mother" (VI 267).

What these notes suggest is that qualities that were found in the experience of the infant are now generalized, first to the adult human world, and
then beyond that to the world itself. The infant, it may be recalled, was discovered to be polymorphous and promiscuous. In its early transitivism it begins in a state of nondifferentiation from the other. Put in the language of the
late writings, the infant and the other are simply reversible. Its sexuality is
everywhere and nowhere, promiscuous in its multidirectionality—at one moment identifying with the father and desiring the mother, at the next moment
identifying with the mother and desiring the father—and polymorphous in its
expression, taking advantage of whatever bodily part or orifice is in ascencency
for expressing its desire. The writings of Melanie Klein suggested a way in
which these primitive relationships could be symbolized through a natural
symbolism of the body. Projection and introjection, as preverbal, bodily-based
symbolic structures, describe the way in which the polymorphous, promiscuous infant takes in and relates to its world. As noted above, this early state of
nondifferentiation is continued in the 'nonconventional thought' that is found
overtly in our dreams but that persists in our waking life.

Let me now try to be more specific about the movement from psychoanalysis to ontology. Psychoanalysis has reference to the intersubjective world
of self-other relations, while ontology aims at the broader reality of perception
itself.[13] What is found through psychoanalysis about the individual's relations
with others may somehow be applied to perceptual consciousness itself. This is

how I would understand Merleau-Ponty's remark in the "Preface" concerning the convergence of psychoanalysis and phenomenology, as well as his statement in the same piece that "[p]henomenology and psychoanalysis are not parallel; much better, they are both aiming toward the same *latency*" (Pref 71). However, with respect to the relationship between perception and intersubjective relations, it appears that Merleau-Ponty's final thought involves a certain reversal of priority in comparison with the *Phenomenology*. In the latter work perceptual consciousness is privileged, and intersubjective relations are modelled on perceptual consciousness. In the posthumous notes, however, there is ample suggestion that the intersubjective bond takes priority over perception and thus becomes the model for the transformation of perceptual consciousness into an ontology of the flesh. This would of course grant a singular importance to the studies carried out in the Sorbonne lectures. Let us pursue this train of thought.

As indicated above, the insights garnered from psychoanalysis in the Sorbonne lectures and developed over the next ten years concern a certain fluidity of our relationships with others. Our intentional life, Merleau-Ponty writes in a working note, involves "the *Ineinander* of the others in us and of us in them" (VI 180). He rejects the idea of self and other as two solid individuals facing one another. Rather, the relationship of self and other involves a kind of reversibility, likened to the finger of the glove that is turned inside out. "In reality there is neither me nor the other as positive, positive subjectivities. There are two caverns, two opennesses, two stages where something will take place—and which both belong to the same world, to the stage of being. . . . There is not the For Itself and the For the Other. They are each the other side of the other. This is why they incorporate one another: projection-introjection—There is that line, that frontier surface at some distance before me, where occurs the veering I-Other Other-I—" (VI 263).

In his effort to articulate the interpenetration or mutual encroachment of self and other, Merleau-Ponty turns to a revised understanding of the unconscious. He had always rejected a realistic notion of the unconscious; and, as indicated above, in the *Phenomenology of Perception* the unconscious was made equivalent to perceptual consciousness and articulated in the figure-ground terminology of Gestalt psychology. This unconscious was gradually rejected and transformed in the Collège de France lectures into an unconscious that is the imaginary, oneiric dimension of all waking consciousness, as well as the "undividedness of sensing" (TFL 131). This unconscious forms a transitional understanding in the direction of the unconscious of the working notes of *The Visible and the Invisible*. While clearly related to the final notion, the unconscious of the Collège de France lectures is further transformed in the final writings.

The unconscious is now something else: neither the reified, second consciousness of Freud, nor the ambiguous, perceptual consciousness, the unseen ground, of the *Phenomenology* and the Sorbonne lectures, nor simply the imaginary consciousness of the Collège de France lectures. The unconscious is that structure that makes relationships possible. As he writes:

> One always talks of the problem of the "other," of "intersubjectivity," etc. . . .
>
> In fact what has to be understood is, beyond the "persons," the existentials according to which we comprehend them, and which are the sedimented meaning of all our voluntary and involuntary experiences. This unconscious is to be sought not at the bottom of ourselves, behind the back of our "consciousness," but in front of us, as articulations of our field. It is "unconscious" by the fact that it is not an *object*, but it is that through which objects are possible, it is the constellation wherein our future is read—It is between them as the interval of the trees between the trees, or as their common level. (VI 180)

Thus, the unconscious is now the "existentials" that bind us and our fellow men together. They are, "like all structures, *between* our acts and our aims and not behind them" (VI 232). These existentials are the "symbolic matrices" (VI 240) spoken of in the Collège de France lectures and in the Preface[14]—now described in Husserlian language as rays or constellations of meaning, but arising not immanently from within the subject but rather transcendently from the world.[15]

Now, what is striking about Merleau-Ponty's description of the unconscious as existentials that structure relationships is that very similar language is used to describe the ontological structure of the world. The world is a visible field that is held together by a structure of invisible meaning, "an invisible inner framework, and the in-visible is the secret counterpart of the visible, it appears only within it, it is the *Nichturpräsentierbar* which is presented to me as such within the world . . ." (VI 215). As with the existentials described above, the invisible framework is also described as "nuclei of signification" (VI 239) about which self and object pivot.[16]

There is a good reason why the description of the structure of relationships is not very different from the description of the ontological structure of the world, namely, that Merleau-Ponty does not make the distinction very sharply. In this chapter I am somewhat arbitrarily separating the relationship of self and other from that of self and thing or world, arguing that each involves its own kind of reversibility, and claiming a certain priority of the former (the level of psychoanalytic understanding) over the latter (the level of perception and ontology). At times Merleau-Ponty's descriptions justify this distinction; and, as just indicated, making the distinction is helpful in point-ing out the influence of psychoanalysis on his ontology. However, more often than not Merleau-Ponty does not distinguish the two relationships or forms of reversibility. Thus, he writes:

> [P]erhaps the self and the non-self are like the obverse and the re-verse and . . . perhaps our own experience *is* this turning round that installs us far indeed from "ourselves," in the other, in the things. Like the natural man, we situate ourselves in ourselves *and* in the things, in ourselves and in the other, at the point where, by a sort of *chiasm* we become the others and we become world. (VI 160)

The way in which the intersubjective relationship and the ontological structure of self and world are linked is highlighted in Merleau-Ponty's use of two categories: visibility and flesh. With respect to the first, the category of vis-ibility, it is not only that the visible world is held together by an invisible framework, while intersubjective relationships are held together by the uncon-scious existentials. The invisible framework and the existentials are all but in-distinguishable. Both are structures of inchoate meaning. The language of re-versibility, chiasm, dimensions, levels, pivots, and hinges applies to both of them. In one note, after describing the unconscious as the existentials that structure the interpersonal world, he goes on to describe the existentials as "the armature of that 'invisible world' which, with speech, begins to impregnate all the things we see" (VI 180). In another note he writes of the "untouchable of the touch, the invisible of vision, the unconscious of consciousness (its central *punctum caecum*, that blindness that makes it consciousness i.e. an indirect and *inverted* grasp of all things) is the *other side* or the *reverse* (or the other dimen-sionality) of sensible Being" (VI 255).

In similar manner, the notion of flesh brings together self and world as well as self and other. Flesh as the sentient sensible applies to things as well as to the sensing individual. Merleau-Ponty writes that "the thickness of flesh be-tween the seer and the thing is constitutive for the thing of its visibility as for the seer of his corporeity; it is not an obstacle between them, it is their means of communication" (VI 135). The reversibility that joins the two leaves or faces of the body as sensible and sentient, and that joins subject and object in the re-versibility of flesh, also joins self and other as both inhabited by the same anonymous, flesh-laden visibility. "There is here no problem of the *alter ego* be-cause it is not *I* who sees, not *he* who sees, because an anonymous visibility in-habits both of us, a vision in general, in virtue of that primordial property that belongs to the flesh, being here and now, of radiating everywhere and forever, being an individual, of being also a dimension and a universal" (VI 142).

This category of flesh warrants particular attention since it focuses so sharply the central theme of this paper, the influence of Merleau-Ponty's psychoanalytic studies in the Sorbonne lectures on his later thought. The notion of flesh at first seems like a great revision of perceptual consciousness that will draw us back into the primacy of perception. But Merleau-Ponty does not say, as we might expect, that he will revise his notion of bodily, perceptual consciousness to that of flesh and then apply this notion to the world. Rather, he says the opposite, that "It is by the flesh of the world that in the last analysis one can understand the lived body . . ." (VI 250). In this remarkable affirmation of the transcendence of the world he thus declares that we will understand the body as flesh through our understanding of the world as flesh. Through the category of flesh, then, the philosophy of perceptual consciousness is surpassed.

With this central category of flesh, where are we with the intersubjective relationship of psychoanalysis? If we wish to emphasize the influence of psychoanalysis on his thought, we may summarize his trajectory as follows. The experience of psychoanalysis leads to a kind of reversibility in self-other relations; this may be described in terms of an unconscious that is both the undividedness of sensing as well as the unconscious structures that structure the interpersonal world. This move away from the subject-pole of the interpersonal dyad leads to that which unifies self and other (or self and thing), now called flesh. At this point one can say equally that psychoanalysis determines flesh and that flesh determines psychoanalysis. Merleau-Ponty in fact makes statements in both directions. When he writes that "A philosophy of the flesh is the condition without which psychoanalysis remains anthropology" (VI 267), and also that "the philosophy of Freud is not a philosophy of the body but of the flesh" (VI 270), he seems to be understanding psychoanalysis through the notion of world as flesh. But when he writes, "Do a psychoanalysis of Nature: it is the flesh, the mother" (VI 267), he seems to be arguing that it is by means of psychoanalyzing nature that we will discover it to be flesh. Does the intuition of the world as flesh lead him to his particular reading of the intersubjective relationship in psychoanalysis, or, as I am suggesting, did his reading of psychoanalysis lead him to his discovery of the world as flesh? The answer is of course both. The point remains that he was strongly influence by psychoanalysis, but by a psychoanalysis itself understood with the assistance of "certain categories" brought to it by phenomenology, "certain means of expression that it needs in order to be completely itself" (Pref 67). On the one hand the discoveries of psychoanalysis clearly had a significant impact on his thinking, and there is a way of understanding the reversibility of flesh as modelled on the reversibility of the intersubjective relationship. On the other hand, once the intuition of the world as flesh is accomplished, everything is subsumed under this category, and there is a return, however transformed, to the primacy of perception.[17]

## CONCLUSION

In concluding this chapter, what may now be said concerning the Gestalt, figure-ground metaphor of the unconscious, pointed to above as specifying Merleau-Ponty's early attitude toward both the unconscious and psychoanalysis? Let me first note that Merleau-Ponty continues his traditional use of the figure-ground description of perception and consciousness to the end of his life. In one of the Collège de France lectures he says: "Every perception is the perception of something solely by way of being at the same time the relative imperception of a horizon or background which it implies but does not thematize" (TFL 4). In a working note he writes: "To be conscious—to have a figure on a ground—one cannot go back any further" (VI 191). And in another note he analyzes an example of repression in his traditional manner, writing of the patient that "[s]he would not know it in the language of conventional thought, but she would know it as one knows the repressed, that is, not as a figure on a ground, but as a ground" (VI 190).

On the other hand, he critiques his retention of a philosophy of consciousness (VI 183), and he suggests an interpretation of the Gestalt that abandons the figure-ground analysis. He writes that "[e]very Psychology that places the *Gestalt* back into the framework of 'cognition' or 'consciousness' misses the meaning of the *Gestalt*" (VI 206). He makes it clear that the invisible is not an unseen ground that can be focused on and then become the seen figure. He makes it a principle "not to consider the invisible as an *other visible* 'possible', or a 'possible' visible for an other: that would be to destroy the inner framework that joins us to it. . . . The invisible is *there* without being an *object*, it is pure transcendence, without an ontic mask" (VI 229). This analysis also changes the nature of the visibles, which "in the last analysis . . . are only centered on a nucleus of absence" (VI 229), visibility itself involving a nonvisibility (VI 247).

Figure-ground has thus been transformed into visible-invisible. In other terms of Merleau-Ponty, the horizontal relationship of figure and ground has been replaced by the vertical relationship of visible and invisible. The Gestalt is no longer the object of perception that can be analyzed into figure and ground; it is now the visible with its invisible nucleus of meaning-structures. Merleau-Ponty now speaks of the "flesh of the *Gestalt*" (VI 205).[18]

It only remains to be said that at the end the unconscious is understood according to the new interpretation of the Gestalt. We can no longer say, as in the

quotation from the Sorbonne lecture: "For knowledge to progress . . . it is necessary for what was ground to become figure" (BP 113/474). Such reversibility
of figure and ground, consciousness and unconscious, is not possible. The unconscious is now the invisible that structures the visible. As invisible rather than
unseen, it is grasped and not grasped, never available to total disclosure.[19]

## NOTES

1. The influence of psychoanalysis on Merleau-Ponty's late thought is most
strongly argued by A. Green, "Du comportement à la chair: itineraire de Merleau-Ponty,"
*Critique*, no. 211 (1964), who writes: "We pose the hypothesis that psychoanalytic thought
played a determining role in Merleau-Ponty's final turn" (p 1032). In a footnote to his "The
Unconscious in Merleau-Ponty's Thought," Pontalis writes: "Clearly, we didn't know when
these pages were written (1961) about the unfinished manuscript since published (1964)
under the title *The Visible and the Invisible*. This work reveals to what an extent the thought
of Merleau-Ponty was slowly impregnated by psychoanalysis: it is not merely the occasion
for posing problems for the philosopher. It becomes a rich source for a new ontology, as one
can see in the 'working notes'." See J. B. Pontalis, "The Unconscious in Merleau-Ponty's
Thought," *Review of Existential Psychology and Psychiatry*, XVIII, nos. 1,2,&3 (1982–83):
p. 94. See also: *Bulletin de psychologie, Merleau-Ponty à la Sorbonne*, XVIII, 236 (Nov. 1964).
Cited as BP. This text has also appeared as *Merleau-Ponty à la Sorbonne: résumé de cours,
1949–1952* (Paris: Cynara, 1988). The double pagination refers first to the original text and
second to the newer publication. Also, *Phenomenology of Perception*, trans. Colin Smith
(London: Routledge & Kegan Paul, 1962). Cited as PP.

2. "Phenomenology and Psychoanalysis: Preface to Hesnard's *L'Oeuvre de Freud*,"
*Review of Existential Psychology and Psychiatry*, XVIII, nos. 1,2,&3 (1982–83): pp. 67–72.
Cited as Pref. "As a world view psychoanalysis converges with other efforts, including phenomenology. . . . Phenomenology and psychoanalysis, in mutual encounter, would lead us
toward a philosophy delivered from the interaction between substances, toward a 'human-
ism of truth' without metaphysics. . . . This phenomenology which descends into its own
substratum is converging more than ever with Freudian research. . . . The accord of phenomenology and of psychoanalysis should not be understood to consist in phenomenology's
saying clearly what psychoanalysis had said obscurely. On the contrary it is by what phenomenology implies or unveils as its limits—by its *latent content* or its *unconscious*—that it
is in consonance with psychoanalysis. Thus the cross validation between the two doctrines
is not exactly *on* the subject man; their agreement is, rather, precisely in describing man as
a work-site (*chantier*), in order to discover, beyond the truth of immanence, beyond that of
the *Ego* and its acts, beyond that of consciousness and its objects, relations which a consciousness cannot sustain: man's relations to his origins and his relations to his models.
Freud points his finger at the *Id* and the *Superego*. Husserl, in his last writings, speaks of historical life as of a *Tiefenleben*. Phenomenology and psychoanalysis are not parallel; much
better, they are both aiming toward the same latency." (Translation altered. See A. Hesnard,
*L'Oeuvre de Freud et son importance pour le monde moderne* [Paris: Payot, 1960], pp. 5–10.)

3. "Merleau-Ponty in Person (An Interview with Madeleine Chapsal, 1960)," in Maurice Merleau-Ponty, *Texts and Dialogues*, ed. H. Silverman and J. Barry, trans. M. Smith (New Jersey: Humanities Press, 1992), p. 7.

4. Discussed at length in J. Philllips, "Latency and the Unconscious in Merleau-Ponty," *Phenomenology and Psychoanalysis: The Sixth Annual Symposium of the Simon Silverman Phenomenology Center* (Pittsburgh: The Simon Silverman Phenomenogy Center, Duquesne University, 1988).

5. Writing about Merleau-Ponty's Sorbonne lectures Jean Laplanche "point[s] out how much we can learn from Merleau-Ponty's lecture notes. A philosopher who is willing to observe! A philosopher interested in clinical observation, in the very concrete experiments involving children, and in the observations of an anthropologist! He could teach a lesson to more than one psychoanalyst." J. Laplanche, *New Foundations for Psychoanalysis*, trans. David Macey (Oxford: Basil Blackwell, 1989), p. 92.

6. See *Themes from the Lectures at the Collège de France*, 1952–1960 (Evanston: Northwestern University Press, 1970). Cited as TFL. While the focus of this chapter is those aspects of Merleau-Ponty's reading of psychoanalysis that lead into his later thought, it should be kept in mind that a good deal of the discussion of psychoanalysis in the Sorbonne lectures, like the treatment of the unconscious just discussed, maintains a strong continuity with the early works. Harking back to the analysis of the unconscious and the past in *The Structure of Behavior*, he says: "The predominance of the archaic is a ground upon which we must construct our present and our future which will present difficulties to the extent that the past has not been integrated" (BP 315/350). And he summarizes the analysis of sexuality from the *Phenomenology:* "It is far from the case that Freud wished to 'explain' behavior through sex; the latter functions as the bearer of the relation with the other" (BP 315/348). The infant of psychoanalytic developmental theory is integrated into the scheme of the existential phenomenology of the *Phenomenology:* "Freud was one of the first to take the infant seriously, in showing not that it is explained by bodily functions but that its bodily functions take place in a dynamic of the psychism. The digestive tube serves not only to digest but is also a manner to enter into a relationship with the world" is also a manner to enter into a relationship with the world. . . . Freud wished to put the infant back into the current of existence of which the body is the vehicle" (BP 316/351). Like sexuality in the *Phenomenology*, the entire digestive apparatus, as examined in psychoanalysis, is understood as a dimension of the lived body and carried into the stream of ongoing life: "The body, the digestive apparatus only play an explanatory role as carriers of a typical attitude of the person. Consequently, it is not the body as a material mass that plays an important role, but as a body integrated into the human life. . . . There would be occasion to examine the relation between the psychism and the corporeal in psychoanalysis: relation of symbolization (the body is the symbol of receptivity; the anus that of conversation; the genital apparatus that of giving). These behaviors are bound by the detectable presence of a same meaning, of a same signification in human life, in existence: they are a way of existing" (BP 315/349).

7. Maurice Merleau-Ponty, "The Child's Relations with Others," trans. W. Cobb, in M. Merleau-Ponty, *The Primacy of Perception*, ed. J. Edie (Evanston: Northwestern University Press, 1964), pp. 96–158.

8. "As Merleau-Ponty shows in 'The Child's Relations with Others,' the world prior to the emergence of the other is not a world I experience as my own: it is a world in which there is an indistinction of perspectives, a world from which the mine-alien or self-

other distinction is absent. . . . [T]hus, for him, the problem is not 'how does the infant begin to recognize others as other consciousnesses?' but rather 'how does the infant learn to differentiate himself and others as separate beings within a sphere of experience that lacks this differentiation'. Again, it is not a question of how the infant transcends an aboriginal self-centeredness, it is rather a question of how he learns to distinguish his experience of himself from his experience of others, that is, how he transcends syncretism." M. C. Dillon, *Merleau-Ponty's Ontology* (Bloomington: Indiana University Press, 1988), pp. 119–121.

9. Merleau-Ponty recalls Klein's discussion of the little girl's doll. In addition to representing herself, the doll represents her father's penis, but not in the way one thing might symbolize another for an adult. The infant does not understand sex, but sees in the male organ her father's masculinity or virility. The doll is the "incarnation" of the father's virile force. "The doll has the power to refer to the impression of virility, an impression that can be translated by a quite vague image. *There is not an association between an appearance and a different latent content, but rather a non-dissociation.* The virility is like a category in which the infant develops, and the doll locates itself in that category" (BP 320/360). The infant's symbolism is thus a way to view its surrounding world. There is not, in the adult sense, a representation of the doll to which would be added a representation of the father's sex.

10. Translation altered. See M. Merleau-Ponty, *Résumés de Cours: Collège de France, 1952–1960* (Paris: Édition Gallimard, 1968), p. 178.

11. Translation altered. See ibid., p. 179.

12. "An analysis of the style would reveal that Merleau-Ponty employs the same terms when speaking of the world of the flesh as of the Freudian world. Both are for him worlds of 'mythic and oneiric' beings" (Green, 1033).

13. For Green the ultimate divide between Merleau-Ponty and Freud has to do with the fact that for Merleau-Ponty the emphasis always falls on the body as sentient, while for Freud it is the body as a center of desire. "Here, it must be acknowledged, we confront all the difference between Merleau-Ponty and Freud. While for Merleau-Ponty the body is also a libidinal body, a body that desires, for Freud the body is above all a libidinal body. . . . Merleau-Ponty speaks of the body, of the visible and the tangible, of the there is, of structure in the sense of a bound assemblage, of archeology, of the opposition between prereflective and reflective cogito, of the Being of indivision. As for Freud, he speaks of the libido, of the partial drives, of the pair Eros-Thanatos, of structure in the sense of unconscious, of the primary process, of the opposition between the systems of the conscious and the unconscious, and finally of the subject divided by the *Spaltung*" (Green, 1037–40).

14. In the Preface Merleau-Ponty describes the body as "a sort of natural or innate complex (*une sorte de complexe naturel ou inné*)" and writes further: "What we learned from all the material drawn from dreams, fantasies, and behaviors, and finally even in our own dreaming about the body, was to discern an imaginary phallus, a symbolic phallus, oneiric and poetic. It is not the useful, functional, prosaic body which explains man; on the contrary, it is the human body which rediscovers its symbolic or poetic weight. We refused, and always will, to see behind the dream, the humorous word, the failed act, so absurd a multiplication of associations. What we have now understood is that symbolic matrices, a language of self to self, systems of equivalences built up by the past, effect groupings, abbreviations, and distortions in a simple act and which analysis reconstitutes more and more closely" (Pref 67–69).

15. In applying this conception of the unconscious as existentials to clinical phenomena, Merleau-Ponty addresses the issue of character formation. He insists that a concrete entity such as feces has no significance in itself. It is silly to assert causally that someone is a sculptor because he is anal. The relation of anality to his artistic life has to do with the significance his feces took on for him. The existential at work here is a quality of formlessness and molding that invests both the feces and the clay with which he works. "The feces give rise to a character (*Abscheu*) only if the subject lives them in such a way as to find in them a dimension of being—" (VI 269). Any entity "can be accentuated as an emblem of Being" (VI 270), and that entity will have a particular relationship to the person's character.

16. Renaud Barbaras emphasizes the displacement of the unconscious away from the human subject as well as its structuring of all worldly phenomena: "The unconscious is rather on the side of the world than at the center of the psyche; between things as the pivot or structure around which their phenomenality is constituted, it is a synonym for dimension." R. Barabas, *De l'être du phénomène: Sur l'ontologie de Merleau-Ponty* (Paris: Jérôme Millon, 1991), p. 315.

17. For a discussion of whether the categories of reversibility and flesh tend to limit or reduce the otherness of the other, see Claude Lefort, "Flesh and Otherness," in G. Johnson and M. Smith, *Ontology and Alterity in Merleau-Ponty* (Evanston: Northwestern University Press, 1990), pp. 3–13.

18. "It is moreover the same radicalization to which Merleau-Ponty will submit the theory of the *Gestalt*. If in the *Phenomenology of Perception* Merleau-Ponty takes up the psychology of form in a still faithful manner, in *The Visible and the Invisible* he radicalizes its scope. Every perception, including that of ideas, is always pereption of a figure on a ground. I always perceive more than I perceive; it is the more that permits me to perceive something, and to perceive it as I perceive it. It is the divergence (*l'écart*) between figure and ground that renders the figure visible, but this divergence, and this figure, must be conceived in a manner that is not positive. The meaning is *twisted* (*distordu*) between figure and ground. The figure does not represent a full coincidence of the signification with itself; the latter changes in accordance with the ground 'upon' which it appears. It is because the *Gestalt* opens itself in the most intimate way toward the presence-absence of a 'milieu,' of a tonality, of the total meaning, it is because it is this non-positive, these dimensions which one can not enclose, that one can perceive it precisely such a form, that is, in one sense only, encircle it. The ground is in one sense nothing other than the distortion of the figure in relation to itself, or its transcendence with respect to itself" (Anne-Marie Roviello, "Les écarts du sens," in Marc Richir and Etienne Tassin, *Merleau-Ponty, phénoménologie et expériences* [Paris: Jérôme Millon, 1992], pp. 161–84).

19. This notion of the invisible, along with the revised understanding of the Gestalt, make Pontalis's well-known characterization of Merleau-Ponty's unconscious as the Husserlian "other side," as opposed to Freud's unconscious as the "other scene," seem inadequate. (See Pontalis, 94.) While that characterization was made in an article written before the publication of *The Visible and the Invisible*, Pontalis repeats it in a later article. "And latency, for Merleau-Ponty, does not designate an elsewhere which would be, by its nature or very structure, beyond the field of the sensible. Let us repeat it: the *other side* (Husserl) is not the *other scene* (Freud). Where: the 'horizons,' the profundity of the preconscious, recoverable by a self, are not the alterity of the unconscious." See J. B. Pontalis, "Presence, entre les signes, absence," *L'Arc*, no. 46 (1971), p. 62. In keeping with his wish to maintain Merleau-

Ponty's unconscious on the side of Freud's preconscious, Pontalis insists—in apparent opposition to many of Merleau-Ponty's own statements—that the unconscious is not to be
identified with the invisible. "Let us not hasten to neutralize the feeling of strangeness, of
the familiar-unfamiliar, that the reading of *The Visible and the Invisible* induces in us; in pro-
ceeding, for example, to satisfy ourselves with analogies between unconscious (paradoxically,
now, the word reassures us!), invisible, and latent, between visible, perceived, and manifest.
Those would be not only superficial analogies but veritable contradictions to the place as
much of psychoanalysis as of the thought of Merleau-Ponty." See Pontalis, 1971, p. 62.

PART TWO

# Gestalt Connections
# and Disconnections

CHAPTER 6

# Sense and Alterity

## REREADING MERLEAU-PONTY'S REVERSIBILITY THESIS

### LAWRENCE HASS

> When I find again the actual world such as it is, under my hands, under my eyes, up against my body, I find much more than an object: [I find] a Being of which my vision is a part, a visibility older than my operations or my acts. . . . [B]etween my body looked at and my body looking . . . there is overlapping or encroachment.
>
> —Merleau-Ponty, *The Visible and the Invisible*

This passage from *The Visible and the Invisible* succinctly recapitulates Merleau-Ponty's ontology. Neither a subjectivism, which favors the constitutive function of some transcendental subject, nor an objectivism, which reduces reality to the categories of operationally "discovered" being-in-itself, Merleau-Ponty's reversibility thesis expresses reality as a reciprocal envelopment between seer and seen, touching and being touched, which defies analysis through disjunctive categories, and yet provides the very ground for them. This reversibility of "flesh," this interfolding of my corporeality in the flesh of things, is, Merleau-Ponty says, "an ultimate notion"[1]—one that frees us from the subject-object, monism-dualism bifurcations that permeate the history of Western ontology. Indeed, Merleau-Ponty's reversibility thesis—which is best grasped as an *Ur-thesis*, as a showing of the fundamental interweaving that "theses" tear asunder—is one of the most powerful and provocative elements of his thought.

And yet in recent years the reversibility thesis has become the focus of considerable critique—specifically, that it is not able to account for the phenomena of intersubjectivity and alterity.[2] A first worry is that the reversibility thesis is fundamentally obscure. Indeed, what sense can we make out of Merleau-Ponty's suggestions that non-sentient things "look at me"?[3] A second concern is that the reversibility thesis begs the question as a response to the philosophical problem of other minds: Doesn't, in fact, appealing to reversibility presuppose the very thing of which we need an account? And thirdly, it is charged that talk of "reversibility" and "reciprocity" eliminates *difference* between oneself and others— that it "reduces the other to the same."[4] I will argue in this chapter that these criticisms are unjust—that they depend upon a distinctly ungenerous reading of Merleau-Ponty's late work. More specifically, I believe that they fail to recognize the extent to which the reversibility thesis can and should be grasped through Merleau-Ponty's account of *sensibility* in *Phenomenology of Perception*.[5] I will argue that when we do justice to that account, and read the reversibility thesis through it, the above criticisms can be seen to dissolve.

## GESTALT SENSIBILITY IN PERCEPTION AND BEHAVIOR

Toward the end of undermining empiricist and intellectualist theories of perception, Merleau-Ponty opens Part One of *Phenomenology of Perception* with the following expression of the perceptual gestalt:

> [A] "figure" on a "background" [e.g., a colored patch on white paper] contains . . . much more than the [sense-]qualities presented at a given time. It has an "outline," which does not "belong" to the background and which "stands out" from it; . . . the background on the other hand having no bounds, being of indefinite colouring and "running on" under the figure. The different parts of the whole . . . possess, then, besides a colour and qualities, a particular *significance* [*sens*]. (1962, 13; 1945, 20)

For Merleau-Ponty (following the core insight of gestalt psychology) perception, as we live it, always and irreducibly has an internally related figure-background structure: to perceive a thing just is to select it *out of* and *against* a background (or field) from which it is distinct. If so, then—Merleau-Ponty argues—all empiricist and intellectualist accounts of complex perception as the cognitive compilation of discrete sensations, sense-data, or *qualia* are unsound, since the identification of discrete "sensations" can only be achieved against a background irreducible to them.[6] In sum, complex perception—understood in terms of the figure-background structure—is not built up like "a house out of bricks" as modern philosophy and classical psychology has it;[7] rather, living perception provides the ontological basis (and hence disconfirmation) of all such accounts.[8]

But for Merleau-Ponty the perceptual gestalt is more than a figure against a background; it also involves the oblique meaning, or "*sens*," that "transfuses" them.[9] Consider again the colored patch on white: One doesn't *see* the background "running on" behind the figure; rather one has the *sense* that it does—a sense that, as it were, *radiates* from or *inhabits* the difference or gap between the patch and the paper. This is why Merleau-Ponty refers to this nascent, latent meaning as both "behind" the figure and "independent of the background."[10] Neither positively given nor transcendentally signified,[11] perceptual meaning for Merleau-Ponty is not "significance" (as Colin Smith's translation repeatedly has it), but *sens*—an irreducible, yet oblique sense that impregnates the gestalt:

> The sensible configuration of an object . . . is not grasped in some inexpressible coincidence, it "is understood" through a sort of act of appropriation. . . . Once the prejudice of sensation has been banned, a face, a signature, a form of behaviour cease to be mere "visual data" whose psychological meaning is to be sought in our inner experience, [and instead become] whole[s] charged with immanent meaning. (Merleau-Ponty 1962, 57; 1945, 70)

While this quote makes clear Merleau-Ponty's view that the *sens* of a gestalt is not some fundamentally "inner" or "private" event, he more fully demonstrates elsewhere that the gestalt as a whole or in its "parts"—figure, *sens*, background—defy propositional analysis, i.e., cannot be coherently maintained as the occurrence or product of cognitive judgments.[12] For Merleau-Ponty then, perceptual experience—far from being "a veil of representations"—is better grasped as the ongoing configuration of the world by a living body that underlies and informs propositional thought. But as a configuring of the world by my body, as the corporeal selecting of perceptual figures out amidst a field, it is impregnated with a latent sensibility—a sense of what gets hidden both from and by my perspective. As Merleau-Ponty puts it:

> [P]erception is just that act which creates at a stroke, along with the cluster of data, the meaning which unites them—indeed which not only discovers the meaning *which they have*, but moreover sees to it *that they have a meaning*. (1962, 36; 1945, 46)

And since the *sens* of a gestalt is one that emerges because of my corporeal immersion in a world of things, it also serves as an oblique guide for my orientations, for other perspectives I might take up. It is the double aspect of this "primary" meaning—as both sense (of what's hidden) and guide (to other possible perspectives) that the French word *sens* retains. Hence, with this rich and multiple *sens* at the heart of it, the perceptual gestalt is not best understood as the "figure-ground structure," but rather as a meaning-laden complex beyond the form-content distinction altogether.

While much could be said about the importance of the perceptual gestalt so understood, e.g., how it frees theory of meaning from the bifurcated cognitivist categories of philosophical modernism and transcendental phenomenology, what we must see is that it leads Merleau-Ponty to a philosophically rich understanding of behavior. Indeed, far from being the sum result of prior and discrete excitations, behavior for Merleau-Ponty is more richly and most basically understood as a complex relation between local "figuration" against global "background," shot through with *sensibility:*

> If I stand out in front of my desk and lean on it with both hands, only my hands are stressed and the whole of my body trails behind them like the tail of a comet. It is not that I am unaware of the whereabouts of my shoulders or back, but these are simply swallowed up in the position of my hands, and my whole posture can be read so to speak from the pressure they exert on the table. If I stand holding my pipe in my closed hand, the position of my hand is not determined discursively by the angle which it makes with my forearm, and my forearm with my upper arm, and my upper arm with my trunk, and my trunk with the ground. I know [*sais*] indubitably where my pipe is, and thereby I know where my hand and my body are, as primitive man in the desert is always able to take his bearings immediately without having to cast his mind back, and add up the distances covered and deviations made since setting off. (Merleau-Ponty 1962, 100; 1945, 116–117)

A first thing to seen in this quote is its evocation of even the simplest behavior as an internally related figure-ground. Indeed, when I lean on the desk, my hands bear the weight of my body and become the culmination, the "figure" of it—with my back, my shoulders, the muscles in my arms rippling into place. But I could only locally project my hands on the desk against my body's global configuration, and so that "background" both conditions and is conditioned by the former. This is why Merleau-Ponty says that the behaving body is a projective being: its most basic function is to project out of and against itself toward things, to perpetually resolve itself into figure-ground structure, to be itself a perspective toward the world at the same time it conditions perspective through its perceptual figurations.[13]

And just as the perceptual figure-ground is infused with prepropositional meaning—the *sens* of hidden perspectives and possibilities—Merleau-

Ponty's "corporeal schema" is a precise analogue to it. Neither presently given nor fully absent, neither propositional in character nor the product of judgment, this "corporeal schema" is best grasped as a kinesthetic sense of my body that is held out in my behavioral gestalt—lodging as it were in the difference between my local projection and global orientation. Indeed, for me to reach out and grip the table—a local action both conditioning of and conditioned by the whole of my body—*means* that my arms, shoulders, legs have also assumed some relatively determinate position. Tracing this *sens* is how I "know" the position of my hand and body when focused on my pipe, why "my whole posture can be read . . . in the pressure [my hands] exert on the table," why I can rub a sore muscle in my back without having to either look to find it or judge that it hurts. As an oblique prepropositional sense of my body that is no more or less basic than the behaviorial figure-ground that occasions it, Merleau-Ponty argues that it is precisely the corporeal schema that undermines the reductive machinations of physicalism: "For its part the organism presents physico-chemical analysis not with the practical difficulties of a complex object, but with the theoretical difficulties of a meaningful being."[14]

In this section we have briefly seen Merleau-Ponty's account of latent, oblique sensibility in living perception and behavior. What we must now do—on our way to the reversibility thesis—is see the fundamental importance of this account to Merleau-Ponty's work on alterity and intersubjectivity. It is to these arguments that we now turn.

## GESTALT SENSIBILITY AND ALTERITY

Recall what we have seen so far: Beyond my propositional concepts and judgments I occasion perceptual gestalten. And the "I" in question here is a behavioral gestalt, a being-in-the-world that projects out of and in virtue of itself. A first thing to be stressed is what could only be alluded to above—namely, that for Merleau-Ponty specific perceptual figurations and behavioral projects are themselves internally related, two mutually conditioning modalities of one system: wherever perception occurs so too does behavior.[15] It follows from this, and our earlier discussion of the *sens* peculiar to each, that my perceptual-behavioral life is shot through with multiple meanings—a sense not only of my corporeality and its position, but also of other possible perspectives I might effect. We see then that alterity in one sense is already there in the simplest perception: as an oblique *sens* of other possible comportments it is at the heart of every figure-ground, lodging as it were in the "ontological difference" between the terms of gestalt.

But consider what happens when a behaving body arrives on the scene:

> No sooner has my gaze fallen upon a living body in [the] process of acting than the objects surrounding it immediately take on a fresh layer of significance: they are no longer simply what I myself could make of them, they are what this other pattern of behaviour is about to make of them. . . . Already the other body has ceased to be a mere fragment of the world, and become [sic] the theatre of a certain process of elaboration, and as it were, a certain "view" of the world. (Merleau-Ponty 1962, 353; 1945, 406)

Just when "I"—my projective behavior—was having the oblique sense of other possible perspectives on a thing, along comes a body that also projects toward it. That possible perspective that was merely an ambiguous sense for me has now been taken up by a behaving being, a projective gestalt. And it is here—in my perceptual figuring of this behavior—that I sense (*sens*) this "entity" as another perspectivally perceiving being, a being with a sense (*sens*) of its own corporeality. As Merleau-Ponty puts it:

> I experience my own body as the power of adopting certain forms of behaviour . . . now, it is precisely my body which perceives the body of another, and discovers in that other body a miraculous prolongation of my own intentions, a familiar way of dealing with the world. (1962, 353–54; 1945, 406)

And also:

> [E]ach one of us [is] pregnant with the others and confirmed by them in his body [; this] baroque world is not a concession of mind to nature; for although meaning [*sens*] is everywhere figurative, it is meaning which is at issue everywhere.[16]

For Merleau-Ponty then, one doesn't judge by analogy, or apodicticly know the other qua other; rather, behavior before, toward, or with me is infused with a sense (*sens*) of alterity—seeing behavior prepropositionally *means* to my perceiving, behaving body that here is another, similar in kind.

A first thing to be seen about this account of intersubjectivity is that it doesn't beg the question to "the problem of other minds." After all, it might be charged that one already needs to know the other as such in order to grasp this movement before me as *behavior*. But we can clear Merleau-Ponty on this score if we recall his view of behavior as a projective gestalt: my reaching out for a pen is only achieved against a specific orientation of the rest of my body—an orientation that both conditions and is conditioned by the local project. Indeed, to move or remove one part of the living body *just is* to occasion movement or change in the rest. And this means that we do in fact perceive behavior as *behavior*—since rocks, machines, and fields of wheat do not have parts that interrelate in this highly specific way.[17] In sum, behavior as an internally-related, sense-manifesting "system" is not only something that I prepropositionally live, it is also something I can *perceptually figure* and in doing so *sense* that this is another perceiving being, another corporeal schema.

Understanding Merleau-Ponty's account of intersubjectivity in terms of this sensibility is both clarifying and powerful. For one thing, it helps us, with significant precision, correct the shortcomings of certain phrasings that appear occasionally in Merleau-Ponty, but more frequently in secondary literature. For example, it is simply too loose to say that on this account "one perceives the other"; rather one perceives *behavior* that, against the double background of the world and my corporeality, bears the *sens* of other perceiving being. This is not, I insist, a merely technical distinction: not only does Merleau-Ponty himself insist time and again on the fundamental role of perceiving *behavior* as such in our intersubjective experience,[18] but—as we just saw—without the perception of behavior as a specific and fundamental kind of phenomenon in our experiential field, the whole account is threatened by circularity.[19]

Understanding Merleau-Ponty's account of intersubjectivity through the phenomenon of sense (*sens*) also reveals the error of referring to "prepersonal" intersubjectivity as *anonymous*. For while it is true on Merleau-Ponty's view that I am already bound up with others in a way prior to and informing of my propositional *concepts* (of self and others), it is an intervolvement that is shot through with different *senses*—the *sens* of my corporeal schema, the *sens* of other perspectival openings onto the world relative to my position. As Merleau-Ponty decisively puts it:

> I perceive the other as a piece of behaviour, for example, I perceive the grief or the anger of the other in his conduct, in his face or his hands, without recourse to any "inner" experience of suffering or anger. . . . But then, the behaviour of another, and even his words, are not that other. *The grief and the anger of another have never quite the same [sens] for him as they have for me.* For him these situations are lived through, for me they are displayed.[20]

Merleau-Ponty argues here that one's prepropositional relations with others are, far from an experience of "anonymity" or nondistinction, shot through with an irreducible and inassimilable distance, a gap between my lived sense of self and the emergent sense of other. Insisted on time and again by Merleau-Ponty (certain passages notwithstanding), this irreducible difference between self and others not only coheres with the latest psychogenetic observations, but also grounds and explains the relative stability of the self-other conceptual pair across cultural, historical, and linguistic domains.[21]

Another strength of grasping intersubjectivity through the phenomenon of sense (*sens*) is that it fully squares with our everyday notion that we can be mistaken about whether or not some real or imagined entity actually is an other. Indeed, since my experience of the other qua other is as a *sens* that impregnates some comportment (against the double background of the world and my corporeality), it follows that the other is not "given," "present," nor "signified," but rather irreducibly "traced" or *meant* before me, and thus "read" as it were by my living body. And this means that my fundamental experience of alterity is less an apodictic intuition than a *corporeal interpretation*, and so a priori open to misreading.

Having said that however is not to reopen the door of Cartesian narcissism—leaving one to wonder whether there are any other existing egos—for as Merleau-Ponty explicitly argues, formulating that thesis already presupposes the living *sens* of others:

> [M]y experience must in some way present me with other people, since otherwise I should have no occasion to speak of solitude, and could not begin to pronounce other people inaccessible. . . . I can evolve a solipsist philosophy but, in doing so, I assume the existence of a community of men endowed with speech, and I address myself to it. (1962, 359; 1945, 412–13)

The upshot here is that while it is possible for me to prepropositionally "misread" some *specific* X before me as an instance of behavior, doubt about whether there are any such "things" does not legitimately follow, since framing that thought, and even the possibility of "misreading" could only occur against the background of intersubjective experience. Indeed, it is never a matter of me, ex nihilo and prepropositionally, facing the spectacle of the world trying to figure out which if anything is *An Other* (a Sartrean image my presentation has possibly perpetuated); rather, I quite literally "find myself" amidst and against a family or community of specific others who inform my behavioral projects and perceptual figurations. In short, for Merleau-Ponty the sense-manifesting gestalt of alterity is as ontologically fundamental as its perceptual and behavioral analogues—as mutually conditioning of them as they are of it.

There are other things about Merleau-Ponty's account of the fundamental role of sense (*sens*) in intersubjective phenomena that might be developed by way of support. For example, how consistent it is with our experience of animals, and how it powerfully coheres with Merleau-Ponty's arguments that language plays "a crucial role" in living intersubjectivity. But perhaps the best measure of its force is that attending to it can undo those recent criticisms of the reversibility thesis. In order to make those arguments, we must first see that the phenomenon of gestalt sensibility informs Merleau-Ponty's late thought on reversibility. These two projects are the concern of the final section.

## GESTALT SENSIBILITY AND REVERSIBILITY

There is no one place in any of Merleau-Ponty's late writings where he explicitly states that reversibility is to be understood through the phenomenon of gestalt sensibility. And yet I will argue here that Merleau-Ponty's reflections on reversibility reveal this specific connection, that is, that the terms of gestalt inform those reflections in a most important way.

To begin this case, let's consider a quote from the late essay, "The Philosopher and His Shadow":

> There are certainly more things in the world and in us than what is perceptible in the narrow sense of the term. . . . Sensible being is not only things but also everything sketched out there, even virtually, everything which leaves its trace there, everything which figures there, even as a divergence and a certain absence. . . . This is what *animalia* and men are: absolutely present beings who have a wake of the negative. A perceiving body that I see is also a certain absence that is hollowed out and tactfully dealt with behind that body by its behavior. (*Signs* 1964, 171–72; *Signes* 1960, 216–17)

One thing evident here is an explicit and much discussed element in Merleau-Ponty's late writings: namely, the phenomenon of "a certain absence," of "divergence," of what is elsewhere called *écart*, as an irreducible "separation" or "openness" that makes possible the positivity of things.[22] Setting aside Merleau-Ponty's use of this "separation-openness" in *The Visible and the Invisible* to undermine a host of Western ontologies, what's crucial for our purposes is that it was already explicated in his earliest writings on gestalt. For, as Merleau-Ponty insists in *Phenomenology of Perception*, it is only in virtue of such a "difference" or "depth" that a figure can be selected *against* its background:

> The [figure-background] structure, or the perspective, is no obstacle to me when I want to see the object: for just as it is the means whereby objects are distinguished from each other, it is also the means whereby they are disclosed. To see is to enter a universe of beings which *display themselves*, and they would not do this if they could not be hidden behind each other. (1962, 68; 1945, 82)

Moreover, just as we have seen Merleau-Ponty's early position that a figure-background configuration is "impregnated" with sense (*sens*) in virtue of that "difference"—a sense of what is hidden, of other possible perspectives and comportments—so too does the quote from "The Philosopher and His

Shadow" convey the oblique meaning in the "hollows" of sensibility and behavior. Others are not *given* to me, Merleau-Ponty insists in that quote, not
positively present, but rather "sketched" before me, trailing behind this body
like a "wake." Indeed, neither wholly present nor wholly absent this "trace" of
the other "as a divergence," this "certain absence" precisely echoes the living
sense (*sens*) of the other that lodges between my corporeality and this bit of behavior before me, in the irreducible difference between us. Nor is this connection between *écart* and the *sens* of a gestalt unique to this passage; Merleau-
Ponty evokes it time and again throughout the late writings and with utter
explicitness in a number of working notes. Consider, for one example, the following note from May 1959:

> It is in better understanding perception (and hence imperception)—
> i.e.: understand perception as differentiation. . . . Understand that
> the "to be conscious" = to have a figure on a ground . . . the figure-
> ground distinction introduces a third term between the "subject"
> and the object." It is *that separation (écart)* first of all that is the per-
> ceptual *meaning* [le *sens* perceptif]. (1968, 197; *Le visible*, 250)

So what we have discovered through this textual work is that *écart* and
perceptual *sens* are inextricably linked in Merleau-Ponty's late thought. And
this means that Merleau-Ponty's reversibility thesis is fundamentally informed
by the phenomenon of gestalt sensibility. Why is that? *Because Merleau-Ponty
explicitly holds that écart lodges at the heart of reversibility:*

> [W]e spoke summarily of a reversibility of the seeing and the visi-
> ble, of the touching and the touched. It is time to emphasize that
> it is a reversibility always imminent and never realized in fact. My
> left hand is always on the verge of touching my right hand touch-
> ing the things, but I never reach coincidence. . . . [M]y flesh and
> that of the world therefore involve clear zones, clearings, about
> which pivot their opaque zones . . . (1968, 147–48; *Le visible*, 194)

*Écart*, then, for Merleau-Ponty is the "open pivot," the "hinge" around which
reversibility swings. But it is, we have just seen, a *sense-laden* pivot.[23] And this
means that the "folding back," the "coiling over," the *reversibility* of the seen
upon the seer, the touched upon the touching is, in a phrase, *a phenomenon of
sens:* to see *means* for me—obliquely and prepropositionally—I can be seen; to
touch my left hand with my right *means* (as a possible comportment) I can
touch my right with my left, and we understand why Merleau-Ponty often
refers to the inverse movement as *virtual.*[24] In sum, reversibility fundamentally
involves the phenomenon of sensibility—a living *sens* of being visible and
touchable that emerges through some perceptual or behavioral "figuration."

It is here, with this recognition of sense (*sens*) at the heart of reversibility, that the recent objections to the reversibility thesis can be seen as flawed. First of all, we can see that Merleau-Ponty is not being fundamentally obscure when he endorses Klee's comments that the trees of a forest seem to see him, or when he speaks of "feel[ing] looked at by the things."[25] For we now understand that this "feeling of" or "seeming to" be seen is the *sens* of one's own visibility—the sense of alterity, of other perspectives on the world and on me—which inhabits and informs my every sight. And in no way does this make the "folding back," the "being seen," the *sens* of alterity epiphenomenal or derivative. For just as the perceptual, behavioral, and intersubjective gestalten "hang together" at the ground, so too does seeing and sensing; they are two mutually informing leaves of the same book. This is precisely why Merleau-Ponty insists in *The Visible and the Invisible* on calling this lived interfolding of sight and *sens* "the Sensible"—drawing on the word's multiple implications. Given the main argument of this chapter, much more might well be developed about this "Sensibility," this chiasmic *flesh*, this paradoxical "generality . . . innate to myself"—for instance, how it promises a compelling, nontranscendental solution to "the problem of universals." Nonetheless, we have seen what we need to for our immediate purpose. Namely, that grasping gestalt sensibility in the movement of reversibility dissolves the criticism that Merleau-Ponty's late writings forward some obscure and implausible anthropomorphism about inanimate things.

For all that lived alterity, the "general" sense of other perspectives on the things and on me that resonates in every perceptual figure-ground, it is imperative to recall Merleau-Ponty's view that it achieves particular content when I perceptually figure some *behavior*. And that is because this comportment toward me, or the things in my field, or *with* me in some shared project, *means* something in a quite specific way: namely, that this human or animal entity also perceives, also has a *sens* of its corporeality, and hence is another more or less similar to me. And this allows us to see why talk of "reversibility" and "reciprocity" doesn't beg the question about "knowing other minds." Since, as we saw earlier, Merleau-Ponty's view is that others are prepropositionally *meant* or *sensed* in their behavior as such, and since reversibility is a phenomenon of sense, it turns out that, far from being circular, Merleau-Ponty's reversibility thesis offers a powerful account of living intersubjectivity—a solution to the "problem of other minds."

Finally, and perhaps most pressing, this reading of reversibility through the phenomenon of *sens* also obviates the charge that Merleau-Ponty's reversibility thesis "reduces the other to the same." For, as we have seen, it is precisely the difference, the *écart*, the irreducible "separation" between us that "traces" the *sens* of reversibility. Indeed, far from "destroying the radical alterity of the other,"[26] the reversibility thesis—understood as a phenomenon of *sens*—insists upon it: the other qua other, Merleau-Ponty tells us, is never apodicticly "given," never "comprehended" against some horizon, never assimilable by me; for all our intercorporeality, for all our flesh-to-flesh intervolvement, there is irreducible "separation" between us—an "absence" that obliquely bears your "trace."[27] And so while elaborating and adjudicating the full range of Levinas's critique of Merleau-Ponty is beyond the limits of this chapter, we have seen that one strand of it is deeply questionable. Indeed, when Levinas charges that Merleau-Ponty's thought of reversibility "reduces the other to the same," or is an epistemological positivism,[28] he not only fails to do justice to the radical, differential account of *sens* that is essential to it, but he also fails to acknowledge the debt his own writings on "the trace of the other" bear it.[29]

But perhaps in the end it will be suggested that my reading of the reversibility thesis through the terms of gestalt sensibility mires Merleau-Ponty's late and soaring writings in early, superceeded concepts. However, I would like to suggest by way of conclusion that this criticism forgets that Merleau-Ponty never *ceased* "thinking" the gestalt and its oblique meaning; it is thematized in all his writings, insistently in the late working notes, tied to *écart* and flesh. And this means that while M. C. Dillon and others are right that certain themes in Merleau-Ponty's early work are best understood in terms of the late,[30] the converse is also true in a profound way. Indeed, if the central claim of my chapter here is forceful—namely, that reversibility is most clearly and unproblematically grasped as a phenomenon of *sens*—then we see the severe limits of favoring the "late" writings over "early" ones. For just as self and others are two interwoven, yet fundamentally differentiated modalities of one "system," so too, it would seem, are they.


## NOTES

For Arthur Melnick

This paper was presented at the Seventeenth Annual International Conference of the Merleau-Ponty Circle at St. Joseph College, West Hartford, Connecticut, September 1992. I would like to thank James Morley and Dorothea Olkowski for their support and many helpful suggestions for its improvement.

1. Maurice Merleau-Ponty, *The Visible and the Invisible*, trans. Alphonso Lingis (Evanston: Northwestern University Press, 1968), p. 140; *Le Visible et l'invisible*, ed. Claude Lefort (Paris: Gallimard, 1964). For all substantive quotations I will cite the page(s) from both the English and the French editions (respectively).

2. Galen Johnson makes a fine case that "alterity" is preferable to "intersubjectivity" given the latter term's relation to philosophically modern concerns about *knowing* other minds." "Alterity," he suggests following Levinas, keeps the focus on *ontological* relations with others and differences. Nonetheless, I think it is important, for reasons that will emerge, to have a term that characterizes the specific kind of alterity relation we have with *behaving* beings (humans and animals), and "intersubjectivity," despite its baggage, seems best. For Johnson's argument and an excellent survey of some of the issues that this paper will speak to see his "Introduction" to *Ontology and Alterity in Merleau-Ponty*, ed. Galen A. Johnson and Michael B. Smith (Evanston: Northwestern University Press, 1990), pp. xvii–xxxiv.

3. See, for instance, "Eye and Mind," trans. Carleton Dallery, in *The Primacy of Perception*, ed. James M. Edie (Evanston: Northwestern University Press, 1964), p. 167. Also see *The Visible and the Invisible*, p. 139.

4. This criticism is most famously made by Emmanuel Levinas in *Totality and Infinity*, trans. Alphonso Lingis (Pittsburgh: Duquesne University Press, 1969), Section 1. Also see "Two Texts on Merleau-Ponty," trans. Michael B. Smith, in *Ontology and Alterity in Merleau-Ponty*, pp. 55–66. This criticism is developed in a somewhat different way by Claude Lefort in "Flesh and Otherness," in *Ontology and Alterity in Merleau-Ponty*, pp. 3–13.

5. M. Merleau-Ponty, *Phenomenology of Perception*, trans. C. Smith (London: Routledge & Kegan Paul, 1962); *Phénoménologie de la perception* (Paris: Gallimard, 1945). For all substantive quotations I will cite the page(s) from both the English and the French editions (respectively).

6. "But if the shape and the background, as a whole, are not sensed, they must be sense, one may object, in each of their points. To say this is to forget that each point in its turn can be perceived only as a figure on a background. When Gestalt theory informs us that a figure on a background is the simplest sense-given available to us, we reply that this is not a contingent characteristic of factual perception, which leaves us free . . . to bring in the notion of impressions. It is the very definition of the phenomenon of perception" (Merleau-Ponty 1962, 4; 1945, 9–10).

7. *Phenomenology*, p. 21.

8. To see these arguments in greater detail, see M. C. Dillon, *Merleau-Ponty's Ontology* (Indianapolis: Indiana University Press, 1988), Part One. Also see my "The Antinomy of Perception: Merleau-Ponty and Causal Representation Theory," in *Man and World*, Vol. 24 (1991), pp. 13–25.

9. *Phenomenology*, p. 14.

10. *Phenomenology*, pp. 14, 35.

11. This last insight—that gestalt sensibility for Merleau-Ponty is not some transcendental signified—is absolutely imperative. Most importantly, it shows that Levinas's argument that Heidegger equates Being as horizon with meaning—rearticulated by Derrida in at least one text as a vestige of Heidegger's commitment to the "metaphysics of presence"—simply does not hold against Merleau-Ponty. Indeed, we have just seen Merleau-Ponty's explicit view that the meaning is *not* equivalent to the background (or horizon), but happens or lodges in the irreducible *difference* between the figure and background—"traced" there in the difference that is no concept or thing. Setting aside the question of the force of this criticism to *any* of Heidegger's work after 1930, that it has no bearing on Merleau-Ponty's account of meaning has significant implications. First, it suggests a fundamental

poverty in Levinas's treatment of Merleau-Ponty. But also, and relative to this, it obscures certain profound affinities between Merleau-Ponty's thought and the writings of both Levinas and Derrida. For Levinas's criticism of Merleau-Ponty's alleged account of meaning see "Meaning and Sense," in *Collected Philosophical Papers*, trans. Alphonso Lingis (The Hague: Martinus Nijhoff, 1987), pp. 75–107. For Derrida's specific argument against Heidegger, see *Of Grammatology*, trans. Gayatri Chakravorty Spivak (Baltimore: The Johns Hopkins University Press, 1976), pp. 18–26.

12. For Merleau-Ponty's arguments see, in particular, *Phenomenology*, chapter 3, and "The Film and the New Psychology," in *Sense and Non-Sense*, trans. Hubert L. Dreyfus and Patricia Allen Dreyfus (Evanston: Northwestern University Press, 1962), pp. 48–59. Also see Hubert L. Dreyfus, *What Computers Can't Do*, Revised Edition (New York: Harper & Row, 1979).

13. See, in particular, Merleau-Ponty's *The Structure of Behavior*, trans. Alden L. Fischer (Pittsburgh: Duquesne University Press, 1983), Part II.

14. *Phenomenology*, p. 56; 1945, p. 69.

15. "[I]f my body can be a 'form' and if there can be, in front of it, important figures against indifferent backgrounds, this occurs in virtue of its being polarized by its tasks, of its *existence towards* them, of its collecting together of itself in pursuit of its aims. . . . [O]ne's own body is the third term, always tacitly understood, in the figure-background structure, and every figure stands out against the double horizon of external and bodily space" (Merleau-Ponty 1962, 101; 1945, 117).

16. "The Philosopher and His Shadow," in *Signs*, trans. Richard C. McCleary (Evanston: Northwestern University Press, 1964), p. 181; "Le Philosophe et son ombre," in *Signes* (Paris: Gallimard, 1960), p. 228. For all substantive quotations I will cite the page(s) from both the English and the French editions (respectively).

17. This is not for Merleau-Ponty to claim that we cannot be mistaken about whether or not this particular movement before me is behavior; as will be shown below, misreadings are possible on his account—a feature that I take as a great strength of it.

18. See, for some examples, *Phenomenology*, pp. 57–58 and pp. 352–54, "The Film and the New Psychology," pp. 52–53, "The Philosopher and His Shadow," p. 172, and *The Visible and the Invisible*, pp. 82–83.

19. There is a certain resonance here between Merleau-Ponty's position and Wittgenstein's claims in *Philosophical Investigations* that perceiving behavior is enough for us to "know" other minds. But the connection is merely superficial: not only is Wittgenstein's understanding of behavior repeatedly cast in terms of the internal-external bifurcation—a picture of consciousness that Merleau-Ponty explicitly criticizes—but also Wittgenstein has no recognition of the prepropositional sense (*sens*) that is so crucial to Merleau-Ponty's account. I believe it is precisely the failure to see this perceptual sensibility and the role it plays in intersubjective life that makes Wittgenstein's insistence that "we just *see* the other" so unsatisfying.

20. *Phenomenology*, p. 356; 1945, p. 409, emphasis added. This is another passage—a particularly crucial one—in which Colin Smith's translation of *sens* as "significance" distorts the character and subtlety of Merleau-Ponty's view.

21. On these matters see Daniel Stern, *The Interpersonal World of the Infant* (New York: Basic Books, 1985). Drawing on recent findings in psychogenetic development, Stern

concludes: "Infants begin to experience a sense of an emergent self from birth. They are pre-designed to be aware of self-organizing processes. *They never experience a period of total self/other differentiation.* There is no confusion between self and other in the beginning or at any time during infancy" (10, emphasis added).

22. Also see "Eye and Mind," pp. 180–85, for an important discussion of this phenomenon as "depth."

23. "[I]t would be naive to seek solidity in a heaven of ideas or in a *ground* of meaning—[meaning] is neither above nor beneath the appearances, but at their joints; it is the tie that secretly connects an experience with its variants" (Merleau-Ponty 1968, 116).

24. See, for instance, "An Unpublished Text," in *The Primacy of Perception*, pp. 6–7. Also see "The Philosopher and His Shadow," pp. 171–72.

25. See "Eye and Mind," p. 167, and *The Visible and the Invisible*, p. 139.

26. Levinas, *Totality and Infinity*, pp. 35–36.

27. Merleau-Ponty, "The Philosopher and His Shadow," p. 172.

28. For this last suggestion see Levinas's "Two Texts on Merleau-Ponty," in *Ontology and Alterity in Merleau-Ponty*, pp. 57–58.

29. See, for example, Levinas's "Meaning and Sense," in *Collected Philosophical Papers*, Section 9, "The Trace."

30. For Dillon's forceful arguments in this regard see *Merleau-Ponty's Ontology*.

CHAPTER 7

# Bodily Logos

## JAMES, MERLEAU-PONTY, AND NISHIDA

NOBUO KAZASHI

In this chapter we aim to explore the significance of the striking convergence between the central ideas of the later Merleau-Ponty and those of Kitaro Nishida, a modern Japanese philosopher, against the background of William James's radical empiricism. After providing for some preliminary explanation with regard to Kitaro Nishida, whose name should be quite new to most Western readers, we shall first establish a scene of philosophic encounter between James and Merleau-Ponty so as to better situate and appreciate Nishida's ideas in the context of contemporary phenomenological movement.

Kitaro Nishida was born in 1870, two years after the collapse of the feudal regime, and died in 1945, the year World War II ended. Thus, Nishida belongs to the second generation of Japanese intellectuals who struggled to steer an autonomous course in the face of the overwhelming influx of Western thought and culture, and is generally regarded as the most significant philosopher of modern Japan.[1]

However, what is to be noted first in view of the overall objective of this chapter is the fact that it was in James's idea of pure experience that the young Nishida believed himself to have found a philosophical stand, not only radical enough to ground a new philosophical system on, but also congenial to some of the core features of traditional Buddhist thought. The major tenet of the

Jamesian philosophy of pure experience was the negation of the ontological dualism of subject-object, which entailed such consequential corollaries as the "functional" reinterpretation of the notion of consciousness, the discovery of the ambiguous body as the center for the field of lived experience, the thematization of the phenomenon of "fringes" or "horizon-structure" as essential to any type of experience, and the restitution of affective values as originally pregiven in the ambiguity of pure experience.

These ideas in phenomenology were propounded in James's *Essays in Radical Empiricism* in such a clearly focused manner that Whitehead once considered James's work comparable to Descartes's *Discourse on Method* in terms of the "inauguration of a new stage in philosophy." Alfred N. Whitehead wrote in *Science and the Modern World*: "James clears the stage of the old paraphernalia; or rather he entirely alters its lighting."[2] In view of Nishida's responses to James's philosophy of pure experience, however, we might be tempted to expand on Whitehead's evaluation of James by an addition of the following sort: "At the same time James transforms the very design of the theater of modern Western philosophy in such a way as to, without knowing it, open the stage to the Eastern philosophical tradition."

For Nishida wrote in a letter to one of his friends in 1910 as follows: "These days I have been reading the recently published articles of James. I find them interesting. They seem to bear a clear resemblance to Zen. . . ."[3] Nishida was reading those articles of James's which were later to be included in *Essays in Radical Empiricism*. In brief, Nishida encountered the Jamesian philosophy of pure experience under Buddhist illumination. Thus, Nishida's maiden work, *An Inquiry into the Good*,[4] published in 1911, a year after James's death, starts with a chapter simply entitled "Pure Experience." And the collected works of Nishida, comprising fifteen volumes of philosophical inquiry, are generally considered the products of his persistent and strenuous endeavors, spanning more than three decades, to transform and overcome the psychologistic shortcomings of the Jamesian notion of pure experience by providing it with sociohistorical dimensions.

Now it is well over two decades since a renewed and vigorous interest in the philosophy of James began to emerge among those American scholars concerned with the phenomenological movement. And it is to be noted that as early as 1943 Gordon Allport had already remarked with good reason:

> Radical empiricism had never become integrated with modern psychology. It might have served as the foundations for an American school of phenomenology, but it did not. Instead, the examination of the intent and constitution of experience was left largely to Husserl and his associates in Germany.[5]

Later scholarship on James has abundantly substantiated the legitimacy of All-port's contention. However, it appears to me that, thus far, most of the phenomenological studies on James have been carried out with their major foci on comparisons between James and Husserl. In a sense, this general tendency has been quite natural because there is substantial evidence that James exerted decisive influence on Husserl, particularly through some of the chapters in *The Principles of Psychology*, such as "The Stream of Thought," "Attention," and "Conception."

For the purpose of this chapter it is of little significance to dwell on this point, but let us remind ourselves of a significant passage from Husserl's diary written during his so-called crisis of 1906:

> James's *Psychology*, of which I could read only some and very little, yielded some flashes (*Blitze*). I saw how a daring and original man did not let himself be held down by tradition and attempted to really put down what he saw and to describe it. Probably this influence was not without significance for me, although I could read and understand precious few pages. Indeed, to describe and to be faithful, this was absolutely indispensable. . . .[6]

As a matter of fact, Husserl's involvement with James's thought was, far from being haphazard, a very deep and long-standing one. According to Spiegelberg: "The earliest evidence of Husserl's study of James can be found in an article of 1894 where, in his discussion of the contents of cognitive acts, he refers twice to James's chapter on 'The Stream of Thought' and specifically to his doctrine of 'fringes.' "[7] In his later references to these early studies Husserl seems to have spoken variously of his intention to review James's *Principles* (to Alfred Schutz), of having discontinued the series of the *Monatshefte* in order to study James more thoroughly (to Dorion Cairns), and even of having abandoned his plan of writing a psychology, "feeling that James had *said what he wanted to say*" (to Ralph Barton Perry, my emphasis).[8]

Thus, it is now widely agreed that traces of James's considerable influence can be recognized in such Husserlian notions as "horizon," "object of thought," and even "intentionality." However, most of the studies carried out on this theme of the "Jamesian philosophy set in the context of the phenomenological movement" seem to have settled for the view that, for all his original insights, James stopped short of developing a full-fledged phenomenology.[9] I suppose few would object to such an overall evaluation, which might appear quite reasonable inasmuch as the Jamesian enterprise is set against the elaborate and rigorous endeavors of Husserl's transcendental phenomenology. But it is my conviction that James's attempt at developing a philosophy of pure experience, for the final elaboration of which he ran out of time, would take on new meanings if we juxtaposed it with the notion of the "flesh" delineated by Merleau-Ponty in his also unfinished work, *The Visible and the Invisible*.

"A philosophy of ambiguity" was the name given by de Waelhens to Merleau-Ponty's fundamental stance, at least in the early stage of his philosophical career. The ambiguity of the term *ambiguity* itself epitomizes the point at stake. The "ambiguity" in the sense of the indeterminacy or vagueness that permeates our existence in the world derives ultimately from the "ambiguity" of our embodied being in the sense of its irreducibility either to the transparency of self-consciousness or to the inertia of matter.

Merleau-Ponty begins the chapter entitled "The Intertwining—The Chiasm" in *The Visible and the Invisible* by confirming the necessity for philosophy to:

> install itself in a locus where they [reflection and intuition] have not yet been distinguished, in experiences that have not yet been "worked over," that offers us all at once, pell-mell, both "subject" and "object," both existence and essence, and hence give philosophy resources to redefine them.[10]

Merleau-Ponty gives the name of flesh to this "formative medium (or milieu) of the subject and the object," which, according to him, "has no name in any philosophy."[11]

In turn, James explains his notion of "pure experience" in his article, "Does Consciousness Exist?," included in *Essays in Radical Empiricism*:

> The instant field of the present is at all times what I call the "pure" experience. It is only virtually or potentially either object or subject as yet. For the time being, it is plain, unqualified actuality, or existence, a simple *that*. In this *naïf* immediacy it is of course *valid*; it is *there*, we *act* upon it; and the doubling of it in retrospection into a state of mind and a reality intended thereby, is just one of the acts.[12]

It appears to me rather difficult not to be struck by the clear convergence of the most fundamental concern of both philosophers to bring to light the ontologically primordial layer of experience, only the full recognition of which would enable us to find a way to overcome the dualism of subject and object and that of mind and body as well. Merleau-Ponty's fascination with the phenomenon of what he calls a "sort of reflection" accomplished by the ambiguous body has its major source in a passage in the fifth meditation of Husserl's *Cartesian Mediations*, where he discusses the body's reflexive relationship to itself.[13] However, James anticipates Merleau-Ponty by some decades in concluding quite tersely: "Our body is the primary instance of the ambiguous."[14] Thus, the notion of ambiguity can be regarded as one of the key notions, alongside that of fringes in *Essays in Radical Empiricism*.

James's descriptions of the lived body are characteristically vivid and concise. For instance, he writes in the chapter, "Experience of Activity," in *Essays in Radical Empiricism*: "Sometimes I treat my body purely as a part of outer nature. Sometimes, again I think of it as 'mine,' I sort it with the 'me,' and then certain local changes and determinations in it pass for spiritual happenings."[15] Also in a note to the same chapter, we read:

> The individual self, which I believe to be the only thing properly called self, is a part of the content of the world experienced. The world experienced (otherwise called the "field of consciousness") comes at all times with our body as its centre, centre of vision, centre of action, centre of interest. . . . The body is the storm centre, the origin of co-ordinates, the constant place of stress in all that experience-train.[16]

Where does this convergence in the anti-Cartesian perspective on the body come from? Far from a haphazard coincidence, it surely was one of the major consequences of the phenomenological enterprise to "return to the stream of life"[17] without taking preconceived ideas for granted and to describe our lived experience with utmost "attentiveness and wonder."[18] In a word, both philosophers' critiques of the body-mind dualism were direct corollaries of their common critique of the subject-object dualism. Pure experience and the flesh were the names given respectively by James and Merleau-Ponty to the ontological milieu they discovered to be anterior to the conceptual bifurcation of the immediately given into the subjective and the objective.

In this vein, perhaps after Schopenhauer and Nietzsche and alongside Bergson, James seems to deserve the credit for the phenomenological revaluation of the ambiguity of the body, in addition to the credit given him by Husserl for the discovery of the phenomenon of horizon.[19] However, James's arguments suffer significantly, to borrow an expression of Bruce Wilshire, from "applying unjustifiably Occam's razor to the philosophical content of *Essays* in a way that sets them off substantially from the *Principles*."[20] Thus, it is more often than not the case that we encounter in his other writings more pregnant renditions of the Jamesian philosophy of pure experience in the making.

In the last analysis, the concept of pure experience as presented in *Essays* is too sparse in content to bear the weight of all the ontological and epistemological problems that might arise: on this view, one and the same piece of pure experience is characterized as capable of functioning either as perception itself, or as perceiver, or as perceived, solely by virtue of the different contexts it can form with the continuous series of pure experiences surrounding it. It is this overall problem underlying the Jamesian philosophy of pure experience that limits its understanding of the ambiguity of the body. James's view seems to have stopped short of comprehending the reflexive role the body plays in our prereflective relation with the world, which was to be highlighted by the later Merleau-Ponty under the name of the bodily "chiasm." Consequently, this limit in James could be considered to derive from the rather facile solution he gave to the problem of how to understand the emergence of the subject-object dichotomy out of the stream of pure experience, which is alleged to have no inner duplicity consisting of the knower and the object known.

Introducing his idea of pure experience at the beginning of the essay, "Does Consciousness Exist?," James argues:

> The separation of it [experience] into consciousness and content comes, not by way of subtraction, but by way of addition—the addition, to a given concrete piece of it, of other sets of experiences, in connection with which severally its use or function may be of two different kinds.[21]

Not only does James neglect the problem of where ultimately to ground the origin of the formation of these different experiential contextualities out of the stream of neutral pure experience, he also does not address the problem of how to understand the relationship between the subjective and the objective trains of experience once they have allegedly come to form different modes of connections.

If James had turned his acute eye for observation to this problem, he might have come to sketch out a view fairly close to the one elaborated by Merleau-Ponty under the name of the "I-the world chiasm."[22] For one is only a step away from realizing the perpetual entanglement of the subjective and the objective in the stream of pure experience if one takes note of the fact that, to use one of Merleau-Ponty's expressions, the "dehiscence" of the field of experience and its polarization into the subjective and the objective is a thoroughly continuous affair, rather than something that happens once and for all. Such a realization might have induced James to give a drastic reconsideration to his explanation of the separation of pure experience in terms of addition as mentioned above.

In this regard, it is very suggestive that Kitaro Nishida, a representative philosopher of modern Japan, came to put forth a "dialectical" view of our embodied existence that bears a striking resemblance to Merleau-Ponty's notion of the bodily chiasm through his lifelong endeavor to overcome the psycholo-

gistic character of the Jamesian doctrine of pure experience. One crucial qualification: in juxtaposing Nishida's dialectical view of our embodied existence
and Merleau-Ponty's notion of the chiasmic relationship between the body and
the world, we have no intention to characterize the latter as dialectical in the
ordinary sense of the term. In the first place, Nishida's use of the term *dialectical* is highly misleading, but let it suffice here to point out that what Nishida
called "absolute dialectic" is characterized by its resolute refusal to envision a
final overcoming of contradictory moments. For further characterization, let
us permit Nishida's texts to speak for themselves.

In one of his major essays, "Logic and Life," written in 1936, Nishida
propounds the notion of "acting intuition," one of the central tenets of his
later philosophy. But let me warn you in advance that there is, so to speak, an
awkward abuse of the notion of self-contradiction, which is unfortunately
characteristic of the later Nishida's texts, and Nishida, unlike Merleau-Ponty,
is far from being an excellent stylist. In Japan, Nishida is often said tauntingly
to be more abstruse than Hegel.

> The very life of our selves, which are possessed of *historical bodies*
> and are acting-intuitional, is self-contradictory. Historical life itself
> is self-contradictory. It cannot be the case that what knows is what
> is known. Our self-awareness is self-contradictory. Our body is also
> a thing. Things are what is seen. But our body is what sees at the
> same time *that it is what works*. . . . One recognizes a self-contra-
> diction solely in the thinking self because he starts with the think-
> ing self separating the bodily self from it. But even the thinking self
> cannot exist apart from our *historical body*. Things are *expressive*,
> and things have names. We intuit things acting-intuitionally as
> *bodily being*; our thinking self consists in intuiting things acting-
> intuitionally as names. Apart from the historical body that intuits
> actingly, there would be neither *self-contradiction* nor *self-awareness*.
> Therefore, there would not be a starting-point for the thinking self
> either.[23] (my emphasis)

There are similar passages in some of Nishida's texts where he tried un-
tiringly, over and over again, to formulate what he came to call the position of
"Acting-intuition." Those familiar with Merleau-Ponty's later thought will
find themselves tempted to set Nishida's passage against parts of "Eye and
Mind," where Merleau-Ponty wove a beautiful tapestry out of his vision of
the chiasmic texture of the bodily field, which he came to name the "flesh of
the world":

> The enigma is that my body simultaneously sees and is seen. That
> which looks at all things can also look at itself and recognize, in

what it sees, the "other side" of its power of looking. . . . It is not *a self* through transparence, like thought, which only thinks its object by assimilating it, by constituting it, by transforming it into thought. . . . This initial paradox cannot but produce others. Visible and mobile, my body is a thing among things; it is caught in the fabric of the world, and its cohesion is that of a thing. But because it moves itself and sees, it holds things in a circle around itself. Things are an annex or prolongation of itself; they are incrusted into its flesh, they are part of its full definition; the world is made of the same stuff as the body. This way of turning things around, these antinomies, are different ways of saying that vision happens among, or caught in, things.[24] (my emphasis)

In spite of the different terminologies the two philosophers employ, it would be quite hard, I submit, to fail to notice some highly intriguing intertextual resonances that ring between the passages just quoted. Clearly the common motif from which these textual variations well forth is the ontological notion of the bodily, expressive self as obtaining in and through the chiasmic, in Merleau-Ponty's term, or self-contradictory, in Nishida's term, relationship between the bodily self and the world. In other words, as Nishida's initial position of the philosophy of pure experience was developed, through a process of further self-critique, into a new "dialectical" vision of the self, Merleau-Ponty's early philosophy of ambiguity was transformed into a chiasmic vision of the self.

Now, the ambiguous body is essential to considering our existence in the world, not because the body is ambiguous in the negative sense of ever-oscillating indeterminately between the subjective and the objective poles, but because the ambiguous body is incessantly playing the pivotal role in the self-reflexive structuring of the bodily field of experience. Nishida literally struggled to chisel out such a vision under the titles of acting intuition and the self-identity of the absolute contradictories; and, so did Merleau-Ponty under the titles of the flesh and the chiasm.

Yet, one might wonder, is it not self-evident that we are possessed of a body? Indeed it is. Why then these hyperbolic expressions of enigma, initial paradox, or self-contradiction? Perhaps it is necessary for us to attempt a phenomenological reduction with regard to the embodied nature of our existence and to defamiliarize ourselves with so self-evident and intimate an object as "my body," so that we shall discover the unexpectedly strange countenance the body conceals under the veil of taken-for-grantedness.

Then, and only then, we might begin to catch glimpses of the ever-evading otherness not only in the naturalness of the body's bearings, which are already and always inscribed by the social presence of the "generalized other," but also at the unconscious bottom of what sees, which is our innermost Other-in-the Self.[25] The body as what sees and the body as what is seen are both strange givens, and, hence, can turn out strangers to each other in spite of the seemingly unbreakable intimacy established in and through the everyday interactions with other embodied beings. In this sense, Nishida's awkward expression, "the self-identity of absolute contradictories," might be taken to capture the continual and, at bottom, fragile nature of the integration between the body as what sees and the body as what is seen.

In Merleau-Ponty's thought, the idea of Gestalt turned out to form a creative and organic unity with some of his other key ideas, such as those of incarnate existence and the horizon-structurality of the perceptual field. At the same time, he calls the very notion of Gestalt into question. In one of the working notes for *The Visible and the Invisible*, he writes:

> And who experiences it [a Gestalt]? A mind that would grasp it as an idea or a signification? No. It is a body—In what sense? My body *is* a *Gestalt*. It is co-present in every Gestalt. It is a Gestalt; it also, and eminently, is a heavy signification, it is flesh; the system it constitutes is ordered about a central hinge or a pivot which is openness to . . . a bound and not a free possibility. . . . And at the same time it is a component of every *Gestalt*. The flesh of the *Gestalt* . . . is what responds to its inertia, to its insertion in a "world," to its field biases.[26]

In sum, the *Gestalts* or forms that are visible in the field of perceptual experience emerge only by virtue of the matrix-Gestalt of our bodily ek-sistence, which is, in principle, invisible to us because we *are* the body. The forms or significations of visible objects and the forms of our bodily existence are empirically distinct and separate, but ontologically they form an inseparable whole, which *is* a field of experience.

Paraphrasing the same point, Merleau-Ponty wrote down in another working note:

> I cannot see myself in movement, witness my own movement. But this *de jure* invisible signifies in reality that *Wahrnehmen* and *Sich bewegen* are synonymous; it is for this reason that the *Wahrnehmen* never rejoins the *Sich bewegen* it wishes to apprehend; it is another of the same. But, this failure, this invisible, precisely attests that *Wahrnehmen* is *Sich bewegen*, there is a success in the failure. . . . *Wahrnehmen* and *Sich bewegen* emerge from one another. A sort of reflection by Ec-stasy, they are the same tuft. . . . To touch is to touch oneself. To be understood as: the things are the prolongation of my body and my body is the prolongation of the world, through it the world surrounds me.[27]

This working note shows very clearly not only how tenaciously Merleau-Ponty kept ruminating upon some of the inspiration he drew from Husserl's texts to develop his own ontological vision, but also how close his last formulations of such a vision came to those of Nishida's, carried out under the general heading of acting intuition.

But, to be exact, what did Nishida mean by the notion of "acting intuition" and what philosophic transformations would it entail as further consequences? Let us hear Nishida's own voice to grasp his views; the first two excerpts are taken from "Logic and Life" and the last one from "The World as Dialectic Universal": "We see the world of forms to the extent that our body is formed. Therefore, we can maintain that, without the body, there would be no self. It holds true for animals, too. Therefore, the body is of the logos character"[28] (my emphasis). "True intuition is not, as is usually understood, simply one's losing oneself, or things and the self becoming one. It means that the self becomes creative. . . . There our body becomes what sees as *well as what works. . . . The world becomes the self's body.*"[29] (my emphasis). And finally:

> Intuition does not mean that the whole is seen at one time. It is not merely a *totum simul.* Rather it means that the universal is infinitely self-determining or that the *basho* [place] is self-determining. . . . Man is a relative totality. . . . Even in artistic intuition it [the totality] is not given simply all at once; it is not realized simply as it is. The artist goes through a process of seeing things step by step; a process of improving the totality. Therefore, we can say, with Bergson, that even the artist himself does not know how the work will turn out. *Moreover, as the artist constructs a work which he himself cannot know, so too we proceed to construct history.*[30] (my emphasis)

Nishida applied his notions of "acting intuition" and *basho* [place] so as to grasp the essential forms of relationship between the individual and the sociohistorical world;[31] in other words, here we recognize an "art-model" for understanding sociohistorical reality. Just like Merleau-Ponty who recognized the "best of Bergsonism," not in the well-known Bergsonian idea of "intuitive coincidence" between the subject and the object, but in the "exchange between the past and the present, matter and spirit, silence and speech, the world and us," Nishida recognized the essence of intuition in the anticipatory comprehension of the whole that was alleged to obtain in and through the expressive interpenetration between the individual and the sociohistorical world as the grounding *basho* [place] for his existence. And it was in this sense that both philosophers upheld the artistic, bodily activity as the paragon of such "dialectical" interpenetration between the immanent and the transcendent. We are reminded of a well-known passage in Merleau-Ponty's "Eye and Mind":

> It is by lending his body to the world that the artist changes the world into paintings. To understand these transubstantiations we must go back to the working, actual body—not the body as a chunk of space or a bundle of functions but that body which is an intertwining of vision and movement.[32]

As must be beyond doubt by now, what Nishida tried to describe under the name of acting intuition was nothing but the phenomenon of intertwining between vision and movement on which the later Merleau-Ponty would center his ontological meditations, although Nishida focused his considerations, not on kinetic movement as such, but rather on productive activity in the broader sense of the term. In sum, expressive "acts" are grounded in, and originate from, the sociohistorical horizon of being; in this sense, expression is not so much the product of a particular individual as that of the field of sociohistorical being itself.

In conclusion, it will be in order for us to confirm the innovative thrusts of the Nishidian notion of acting intuition in contrast to the traditional Cartesian notion of intuition. For it concerns the viability of this central notion in Nishida, and has direct and crucial relevance to the evaluation of both James's notion of pure experience and the later Merleau-Ponty's notion of the flesh of the world. For what lies at the root of the philosophical endeavors of all these three thinkers was the common, keen realization of the necessity to rethink and reformulate the notions of experience and of reflection in the light of our bodily existence in the world.

Let us delineate here the points at stake in the most general terms. The cornerstones for the Cartesian philosophy as a methodological meditation for the pursuit of scientific knowledge were, among others, the presupposition of the legitimacy of the body-mind dualism, that of the legitimacy of the subject-object dualism, the centrality of the principle of "clear and distinct ideas," and the resultant vision of the human individual as an "autonomous agent." By contrast, what characterizes the philosophical projects of James, Nishida, and Merleau-Ponty is, roughly speaking, the shared, critical stance taken with regard to each of these four key elements in Cartesianism. That is to say: first, the establishment of the body as the ground for our prediscursive and yet active communion with the world; second, the acknowledgment of the intertwining inseparability of object-knowledge and self-knowledge in our being in the world; third, the thematization of the phenomenon of horizon as an indispensable moment in the constitution of experience of any kind; fourth, the understanding of the self as embedded in and supported by the field of experience.

In sum, it would be in this vein that we can fully appreciate Whitehead's comparison of James's "Does Consciousness Exist?" to Descartes's *Discourse on*

*Method* in terms of the "inauguration of a new stage in philosophy." Also, it is
in this context that the significance of Nishida's notion of acting intuition as
well as that of Merleau-Ponty's notion of the flesh of the world can be drawn
out in a most productive manner. And such realization shall help us to slough
off the usual, facile dichotomy of East and West in philosophy.[33]

## NOTES

This article is based on my paper presented under the title of "Bodily Field of Ex-
perience as the Historical Horizon for Expressive Acts: An Essay toward a Comparative
Study of Merleau-Ponty, James, and Nishida" at the meeting of the Merleau-Ponty Circle at
Canisius College in 1989.

1. As a matter of fact, seven of his major works are now available in English translation, and, not to mention those works on his philosophy written in Japanese, the number of articles on the subject written or accessible in European languages has already gone
well beyond one hundred. See *Nishida Tetsgaku: Shinshiryoh to Kenkyuh no Tebiki* (*Nishida
Philosophy: New Material and A Research Guide*), ed. Yoshio Kayano and Ryosuke Ohashi
(Kyoto: Minerva Shoboh, 1987). This work contains a bibliography of the works on
Nishida's philosophy done in European languages as well as in Japanese.

2. Alfred N. Whitehead, *Science and the Modern World* (New York: The Free Press,
1925), p. 143.

3. *Nishida Kitaro Zenshu* (*The Complete Collection of Works by Kitaro Nishida*), 19
vols. (Tokyo: Iwanami Shoten, 1953–55), vol. 18, p. 132.

4. Kitaro Nishida, *An Inquiry into the Good*, trans. Masao Abe and Christopher
Ives (New Haven: Yale University Press, 1990). The first English translation was made by
Valdo H. Viglielmo under the title, *A Study of Good* (Tokyo: Printing Bureau of the Japan-
ese Government, 1960).

5. Gordon Allport, "The Productive Paradoxes of William James." Quoted in
Hans Linschoten's *On the Way toward a Phenomenological Psychology: Psychology of William
James*, trans. Amedeo Girogi (Pittsburgh: Duquesne University Press, 1968), p.31.

6. Herbert Spiegelberg, *The Phenomenological Movement*, vol. I (The Hague:
M. Nijhoff, 1978), p. 114.

7. See a footnote on p. 113 in Spiegelberg, 1978.

8. Spiegelberg, 1978, pp. 113–14.

9. For example, James Edie discusses the original features of James's understanding
of the intentionality of consciousness in comparison with that of Brentano in a passage in
*William James and Phenomenology* (Bloomington: Indiana University Press, 1987). Edie
maintains: "We are required to say both that he effected the transcendental turn (in
Husserl's sense) and that he remained 'on the way toward a phenomenological psychology'—an initiator and explorer who did not himself enter the promised land he had discovered" (p. 31).

10. Maurice Merleau-Ponty, *The Visible and the Invisible*, trans. Alphonso Lingis (Evanston: Northwestern University Press, 1969), p. 130.

11. Merleau-Ponty, 1969, p. 147.

12. *Essays in Radical Empiricism*, ed. Ralph B. Perry (Gloucester, Mass.: Peter Smith, 1967), pp. 23–24.

13. Edmund Husserl, *Cartesian Meditations*, trans. Dorion Cairns (The Hague: M. Nijhoff, 1960), p. 97.

14. James, 1967, p. 153.

15. James, 1967, p. 153.

16. James, 1967, p. 170.

17. Perry, 1935, p. 106.

18. Maurice Merleau-Ponty, *Phenomenology of Perception*, trans. Colin Smith (New York: Humanities Press, 1962), p. xxi.

19. See Edmund Husserl, *The Crisis of European Sciences and Transcendental Phenomenology*, trans. David Carr (Evanston: Northwestern University Press, 1970) , p. 264.

20. Bruce Wilshire, *William James and Phenomenology: A Study of "The Principles of Psychology"* (Bloomington: Indiana University Press, 1979), p. 170.

21. James, 1967, p. 9.

22. Merleau-Ponty, 1969, p. 264.

23. *Nishida Kitaro Tetsugaku Ronbunshu (A Collection of Articles by Kitaro Nishida)*, vol. II (Tokyo: Iwanami Shoten, 1988), pp. 264–66 (my translation).

24. Maurice Merleau-Ponty, *The Primacy of Perception*, ed. James Edie (Evanston: Northwestern University Press, 1964), pp. 162–63.

25. See Merleau-Ponty's discussion of "double anonymity" in *Phenomenology of Perception*, p. 448.

26. Merleau-Ponty, 1969, pp. 205–206.

27. Merleau-Ponty, 1969, pp. 254–55.

28. Kitaro Nishida, *Nishida Kitaro Tetsugaku Ronbunshuh (A Collection of Philosophical Articles by Kitaro Nishida)*, 3 vols. (Tokyo: Iwanami Shoten, 1987; 1988; 1989), vol. II, p. 233 (my translation). The introduction of the idea that the body is of the Logos-character might sound abrupt here. But Nishida also writes: "Starting from our biological body, we possess things as instruments, and make things our own body technically: therein is constituted our technical body. Thus, when the world becomes one's own body starting from the biological body, it can be thought that the Self loses its own body. And it can be thought as well that thence we enter the world of the merely namable, the world of intentional objects, the world of consciousness. But it is not that our body has become lost, but *our body has become deepened to the speaking body*. Actually, however, when we say that we possess instruments, it already implies that we are those who speak" (Nishida 1988, 244: my translation and my emphasis).

29. Nishida, 1988, pp. 246–47. (my translation).

30. Kitaro Nishida, *Fundamental Problems of Philosophy: The World of Action and the Dialectical World*, trans. David Dilworth (Tokyo: Sophia University Press, 1970), p. 184.

31. In this chapter we cannot afford to take into account all the stages in Nishida's philosophical development, especially the later ones where Nishida came to propound the "logic of *basho* or place."

32. Merleau-Ponty, 1964, p. 162.

33. For further exploration of the contemporary significance of Nishida's philosophy, see my article, "The Musicality of the Other: Schutz, Merleau-Ponty, and Kimura," included in *The Prism of the Self*, ed. Steven G. Crowell (Amsterdam: Kluwer Academic Publisher, 1995), pp. 169–186.

CHAPTER 8

# Body Image Intercourse

## A Corporeal Dialogue between Merleau-Ponty and Schilder

GAIL WEISS

I cannot understand the function of the living body except by en-
acting it myself, and except in so far as I am a body which rises toward the world.

— Merleau-Ponty, *Phenomenology of Perception*

There is no question that there are from the beginning connecting
links between all body-images, and it is important to follow the
lines of body-image intercourse.

— Paul Schilder, *The Image and Appearance of the Human Body*

It is arguable that their respective discussions of the body image are two
of the most important contributions Merleau-Ponty and Schilder have made
to phenomenology and psychoanalysis respectively. Schilder's monumental
work, *The Image and Appearance of the Human Body*, is the first full-length
study of the body image as a physiological, libidinous, and socially structured
phenomenon. While Merleau-Ponty does not devote an entire text to the body
image, his interest in and discussions of this "corporeal schema" extend over

two decades from his earliest book, *The Structure of Behavior*, to his final, un-finished work, *The Visible and the Invisible*.[1]

Both Merleau-Ponty and Schilder stress that the body image changes not only in response to actual, physiological changes in the body and/or physical changes in the situation, but is greatly (and often lastingly) affected by psychi-cal and social changes in the body/situation that need not be grounded in or tied to a current state of affairs. As Merleau-Ponty notes, "the normal person *reckons with* the possible, which thus, without shifting from its position as a possibility, acquires a sort of actuality" (Merleau-Ponty 1962, 109). While Merleau-Ponty is primarily thinking here about future actions and how they can be corporeally anticipated in and through the body image, Schilder em-phasizes the role that fantasies and the imagination play in constructing and re-constructing the body image:

> It is one of the inherent characteristics of our psychic life that we continually change our images; we multiply them and make them appear different. This general rule is true also for the pos-tural model of the body. We let it shrink playfully and come to the idea of Lilliputians, or we transform it into giants. (Schilder 1950, 67)

Indeed, Schilder goes on to claim that each individual has "an almost unlim-ited number of body-images," a startling and provocative claim whose impli-cations have been largely undeveloped and one that could be especially useful in feminist theorizing about the body.

By developing the lacunae and critically extending the implications of Merleau-Ponty's and Schilder's accounts of the body image, a richer feminist understanding of how racial, gender, class, age, ethnic, and cultural differences are *corporeally* registered and reproduced can be achieved. Without an ade-quate understanding of the crucial role that the body image plays in reflecting and sustaining individual, social, and political inequalities, there is a danger that positive social and political changes will not address the individual's own corporeal existence in the intimate manner necessary to move successfully to-ward the eradication of sexism, racism, classism, ageism, and ethnocentrism. Although this chapter does not seek to suggest the course for such changes, I do believe that the plasticity and stability of the body image can serve to main-tain an oppressive "status quo" and that a greater awareness of the "body power" we have at our disposal through this very plasticity and stability can re-sult in new, perhaps subversive, body images that can be used to fight oppres-sion on a corporeal front.

## THE BODY IMAGE AS A GESTALT

According to Merleau-Ponty, the body image exhibits an intersensory, spatial, and temporal unity that is not "the straightforward result of associations established during experience, but a total awareness of my posture in the intersensory world, a 'form' in the sense used by Gestalt psychology" (Merleau-Ponty 1962, 99–100). This unity is not founded upon an inner or internal unity of the body's organs, muscles, bones, nervous system, and skeletal structure (although these latter are indeed incorporated within the body image) rather, it derives from the world within which the body is always situated and in reference to which the body continually orients and reorients itself: "the body not only flows over into *a world whose schema it bears in itself* but possesses this world at a distance rather than being possessed by it."[2]

To say that the body bears the schema of the world in itself is to indicate that the body does not impose any sort of pregiven structure upon the world, but is itself structured by its world, which in turn implies that the body image reflects from the start the particularities *and* generalities of a given situation, not merely the idiosyncracies of its own physiological or genetic makeup and psychical constitution. Nonetheless, Merleau-Ponty is careful to avoid any characterization of the world as a "body-constituting" force, since it is the body that "possesses this world at a distance rather than being possessed by it."[3]

The primary means by which the body "possesses" the world are through perception and the bodily motility that makes our perceptual "grasp" on the situation possible, and it is through perception and bodily motility that the body itself "flows over into a world." This reciprocal, reversible *intra*relationship of body and world whereby the body "flows over" into a world whose "schema it bears in itself," gives rise to an increasingly complex understanding of the gestalt and the role(s) it plays in perception. For, according to Merleau-Ponty, not only is the body image itself a gestalt but what we perceive are also gestalten, that is, forms, which produce "a certain state of equilibrium, solving a problem of maximal coherence and, in the Kantian sense, making a world possible." Unlike Kant's understanding of form as an a priori, Merleau-Ponty's form

> is the very appearance of the world and not the condition of its possibility; it is the birth of a norm and is not realized according to a norm; *it is the identity of the external and the internal and not the projection of the internal in the external.* (Merleau-Ponty 1962, 61, emphasis added)

The schematic organization of both the body image and perceived objects does not predate the phenomena themselves but their schematic organization does not come about on an ad hoc basis either. Rather, the body image and the perception of discrete objects are progressively developed and refined, with the body image first appearing during the "mirror stage" (from six to eighteen months of age) as a corporeal schema that requires, but cannot be reduced to, the infant's awareness of her/his specular image as an image of her/his own body. The developmental nature of perception is in turn clearly implied in the latter's dependency on the efficacy of the body image, since, as Wallon recognized:

> [Perception] presupposes a minimal bodily equilibrium. The operation of a postural schema—that is, a global consciousness of my body's position in space, with the corrective reflexes that impose themselves at each moment, the global consciousness of the spatiality of my body—all this is necessary for perception. (Merleau-Ponty 1964, 122)[4]

Regarding the development of the body image, Merleau-Ponty stresses that: "the consciousness of one's own body is thus fragmentary [lacunaire] at first and gradually becomes integrated; the corporeal schema becomes precise, restructured, and mature little by little" (Merleau-Ponty 1964, 123). The visual image of the body presented to the child in the mirror cannot, Merleau-Ponty asserts, be equated with the child's own experience of her/his body but the perception of the specular image as a discrete, unified image of the child's body is precisely what facilitates the necessary restructuring and maturation of the child's own bodily awareness into a unified postural schema.[5] To understand properly the significance of the mirror stage for the development of the body image (and consequently, as we have seen above, for perceptual development), we must turn to Merleau-Ponty's own account of the mirror stage, an account that displaces (rather than disavows) Lacan's emphasis upon the mirror stage as leading "to the assumption of the armour of an alienating identity, which will mark with its rigid structure the subject's entire mental development."[6]

## THE MIRROR STAGE

Lacan characterizes the development of the child in the mirror stage as a complex transition from a nonunified body image to the construction of the body image as an orthopaedic totality. "The *mirror stage* is a drama whose internal thrust is precipitated from insufficiency to anticipation—and which manufactures for the subject, caught up in the lure of spatial identification, the succession of phantasies that extends from a fragmented body-image to a form of its totality that I shall call orthopaedic" (Lacan 1977, 4). Merleau-Ponty, like Lacan, recognizes that there is a process of self-alienation that paradoxically accompanies the move from a fragmented body image to the body image as a "gestalt." What is paradoxical is that the necessarily alienating acceptance of the specular image as an image of oneself, somehow facilitates rather than disrupts the development of a coherent body image out of two, seemingly disparate experiences: seeing one's body "from the outside" in the mirror, and being introceptively aware of one's body "from the inside." For Merleau-Ponty, there are two spatial problems that must be resolved in order for the child to work through this paradox:

> [I]t is a problem first of understanding that the visual image of his body which he sees over there in the mirror is not himself; and second, he must understand that, not being located there, in the mirror, but rather where he feels himself introceptively, he can nonetheless be seen by an external witness *at the very place at which he feels himself to be* and with the same visual appearance that he has from the mirror. In short, he must displace the mirror image, bringing it from the apparent or virtual place it occupies in the depth of the mirror back to himself, whom he identifies at a distance with his introceptive body. (Merleau-Ponty 1964, 129)

The first problem is rendered even more complicated for the child because the initial failure to recognize the specular image as an image of oneself must eventually give way to a recognition of the specular image as being of oneself, yet not identical to oneself.[7] It is precisely this schism between the "of oneself" and "to oneself" that is internalized in the resolution of the second problem and which henceforth becomes an integral (alienating) aspect of the body image. Although this schism is not overcome and remains a source of alienation throughout an individual's life (insofar as the specular image will never be equivalent to one's own, more fluid body image), both Lacan and Merleau-Ponty emphasize that it is this very schism that makes it possible for the child to project and extend her/his own bodily awareness beyond the immediacy of her/his introceptive experiences by incorporating the perspective of the other on one's own body—a perspective one actively participates in—rather than having it thrust upon one from the outside. Thus, for Merleau-Ponty:

> The specular image, given visually, participates globally in the existence of the body itself and leads a "phantom" life in the mirror, which "participates" in the life of the child himself. What is true of his own body, for the child, is also true of the other's body. The child himself feels that he is in the other's body, just as he feels himself to be in his visual image. (Merleau-Ponty 1964, 133–34)

While Lacan invokes the "paranoic alienation, which dates from the deflection of the specular I into the social I" (Lacan 1977, 5), Merleau-Ponty acknowledges the alienation without viewing it as a source of paranoia since the specular I is not "deflected" into the social I but the two are one in the same. That is, the specular image offers the child a new perspective not only on her/his own body and her/his being-for-others (what we may call an "outside-in" perspective) but simultaneously allows the child to project her/himself outside of her/his body into the specular image and, correspondingly, into the bodies of others (an "inside-out" perspective).[8] Although the former may indeed be a source of profound alienation, it is the latter, especially, that provides the ground for strong identifications with others, identifications that expand the parameters of the body image and accomplish its transition from an introceptive, fragmented experience of the body to a social Gestalt.[9]

These identifications, however, do not offer an alternative to alienation since they are themselves made possible only on the basis of the self-alienation produced by the specular image. According to Merleau-Ponty:

> This forces me to leave the reality of my lived *me* in order to refer myself constantly to the ideal, fictitious, or imaginary *me*, of which the specular image is the first outline. In this sense I am torn from myself, and the image in the mirror prepares me for another still more serious alienation, which will be the alienation by others. For others have only an exterior image of me, which is analogous to the one seen in the mirror. Consequently others will tear me away from my own immediate inwardness much more surely than will the mirror. (Merleau-Ponty 1964, 136)

Paradoxically, the self-alienation that arises out of the "schism" between the specular and the introceptive body images, not only serves as a prelude to the "more serious alienation" Merleau-Ponty describes above, but also makes possible "the acquisition of a new function as well: the narcissistic function" (Merleau-Ponty 1964, 136). While Merleau-Ponty does not provide an account of the significance of this narcissistic function in the development of the body image, it is Schilder who both asks and ultimately answers the crucial question: "What is the relation of narcissism to the image of the body?" (Schilder 1950, 196).

## THE NARCISSISTIC STRUCTURE
## OF THE BODY IMAGE

Schilder, like Lacan and Merleau-Ponty, stresses the developmental nature of the body image and the virtue of his account is his particular concern with the impact of individual experiences and the psychical response to those experiences on the body image as well as his refusal to view the psychical and physiological influences on the body image as independent of one another:

> Concerning the image of the body, we have to suppose that there is a factor of maturation which is responsible for the primary outlines of the postural model of the body. But the way in which these outlines develop, the tempo of development, will be largely dependent on experience and activity; and we may suppose that the finer trends of the body-image will be still more dependent on the life experiences, the training, and the emotional attitudes. There is no reason why one should join either of the extremist groups, for one of which experience, learning, and conditioning are in the foreground (Watson), while for the other experience means little or nothing (Köhler, Koffka, Wertheimer and Wheeler). . . . There will be functions which are merely determined by anatomy and physiology. But even in those the psychic influence and the influence of experience will, according to our latest observations, play some part. In other experiences, especially in those concerning the libidinous structure of the postural model, experience will play an outstanding part, but even so experience will be connected with anatomy and physiology. (Schilder 1950, 196–97)

Although Schilder bases his account of the libidinous structure of the body image on the primary narcissism whose significance was discussed at length by Freud, he is critical of Freud's understanding of primary narcissism as centered on the body of the newborn. Since, Schilder claims, the newborn is unable to differentiate her or his body from the rest of the world (i.e., since s/he does not experience the body as a discrete entity), it is

> senseless to say that for the newborn child only the body exists and the world does not. Body and world are experiences which are correlated with each other. One is not possible without the other. When Freud states that on a narcissistic level only the body is present, he must be mistaken. The newborn child has a world, and probably even the embryo has. It is true that on such a primitive level the borderline between world and body will not be sharply defined, and it will be easier to see a part of the body in the world and a part of the world in the body. (Schilder 1950, 123)

In his essay, "On Narcissism: An Introduction," however, Freud does acknowledge that there are, from the start, not one, but two sexual objects that form the basis for primary narcissism, namely the infant and "the woman who nurses him."[10] Ultimately, for Freud, the woman who breastfeeds the child plays a very active role in the process by which the infant becomes erotogenically invested in her/his own body, since she is the one who first stimulates the newborn's mouth through the nourishment provided by her breasts, a stimulation that results in a more generalized sexual pleasure that comes from the very act of sucking.

During this oral stage of development, the narcissistic libido is clearly concentrated in the infant's mouth, and as the child moves on to the anal and phallic stages of development, the intensity of libidinal investment in the mouth will shift first to the anus, then to the clitoris or penis. For Schilder, the object of the narcissistic libido is not the mouth, anus, penis, or clitoris per se, but the image of the body that arises out of the sexually pleasurable sensations associated with them. Thus, as the child passes through the various stages of psychogenic development, "the narcissistic libido will be attached to the different parts of the image of the body, and in the different stages of libidinous development the model of the body will change continually" (Schilder 1950, 123).

To say that the narcissistic libido has as its object the image of the body rather than the body itself, does not imply for Schilder that this image is at all distinct nor, as we have seen above, does it imply that this image is focused upon the body independently of the world. To talk about an "experience," as far as Schilder (and Merleau-Ponty) are concerned, already implies an intimate exchange between body and world that results in a lack of boundaries between the two. This is true not only of the pre–mirror stage infant, but also, Schilder notes, of adults as well for whom "body and world are continually interchanged. It may be that a great part of experiences will not be finally attributed either to body or world" (Schilder 1950, 123).

Pimary narcissism, then, for both Freud and Schilder, never involves an infant's unmediated relationship with her or his own body, but from the start implies a complex series of interactions between the infant and others in an ongoing situation, and the image the infant forms of her/his body through primary narcissistic investments in different bodily zones or regions will already reflect the influences of others and the situation long before the child can recognize her/himself or others as discrete entities (i.e., long before the child enters the mirror stage).[11] As Schilder affirms, "the touches of others, the interest others take in the different parts of our body, will be of an enormous importance in the development of the postural model of the body" (Schilder 1950, 126).

Although Schilder is claiming that the body image is the "object" of the narcissistic libido well before the mirror stage, this does not mean that he disagrees with Lacan's and Merleau-Ponty's view of the body image as "fragmented" prior to the mirror stage. Both Schilder and Merleau-Ponty are in agreement that the body image cannot exhibit the quality of stability that experimental psychologists identified so early on, if it does not exhibit an equilibrium; this equilibrium cannot be achieved, however, if too much libidinal energy is concentrated on a single region or zone of the body, for, as Schilder observes: "whenever one part obtains an overwhelming importance in the image of the body, the inner symmetry and the inner equilibrium of the body-image will be destroyed" (Schilder 1950, 126).[12]

It is through primary narcissism, then, that the newborn first begins the construction of her/his body image, a process that is never completed, but that continually evolves throughout an individual's life. While Schilder accepts Freud's characterization of the stages of libidinous development, he also emphasizes (as does Freud) that no two individuals proceed through these stages in the same way. And, although Schilder does claim that "in the whole structure of the schema of the body, the erogenic zones will play the leading part" (Schilder 1950, 123), the physiological development of the body also contributes greatly to the "building-up" of the body image, not through an internal, biological process but through "continual contact with the outside world" (Schilder 1950, 137). Finally, Schilder wants us to realize that the body image of one individual cannot be understood as radically distinct from the body image of other individuals since:

> The child takes parts of the bodies of others into its own body-image. It also adopts in its own personality the attitude taken by others towards parts of their own bodies. Postural models of the body are closely connected with each other. . . . Body-images of human beings communicate with each other either in parts or as wholes. (Schilder, 1950, 137–38)

The ongoing communication between body images that Schilder describes need not involve two different individuals, or even two different bodies. Through the development of an ideal body image, an internalized body image that arises out of the young child's identifications with particular and generalized others, body image intercourse is always taking place, even in our most private moments.[13] To understand the normative role played by the ideal body image in everyday life, we must turn to Freud's conception of a related phenomenon, the ego-ideal.

## THE EGO-IDEAL AND ITS COUNTERPART: THE BODY IMAGE IDEAL

According to Freud:

> The development of the ego consists in a departure from the primary narcissism and results in a vigorous attempt to recover it. This departure is brought about by means of the displacement of libido to *an ego-ideal imposed from without*, while gratification is derived from the attainment of this ideal. (Freud 1957, 121, emphasis added)

The "self-love" of primary narcissism is both reinforced and disturbed by the child's recognition of her/his specular image during the mirror stage. It is reinforced because the unique disclosure of one's corporeality provided by the specular image offers a new source of erotic intensity, namely, through libidinal investment in the image of oneself that reveals one's being-for-others. At the same time, however, the specular image, precisely by disclosing one's being-for-others, introduces the self-alienating dimension that Lacan has discussed in such detail, a dimension that marks the point of departure from primary narcissism, an irrecoverable loss that in turn motivates the formation of the ego-ideal. Merleau-Ponty directly acknowledges the crucial role the specular image plays in the construction of this ideal image (which both he and Freud conflate with the superego) in the following passage:

> The personality before the advent of the specular image is what psychoanalysts call, in the adult, the ego (*soi*), i.e., the collection of confusedly felt impulses. The mirror image itself makes possible a contemplation of self. With the specular image appears the possibility of an ideal image of oneself—in psychoanalytic terms, the possibility of a super-ego. *And this image would henceforth be either explicitly posited or simply implied by everything I see at each minute.* (Merleau-Ponty 1964, 136, emphasis added)

One of the most salient features of the ego-ideal, as Freud has described it, is its status as a projection of a (lost) perfection, a "substitute for the lost narcissism of his childhood—the time when he was his own ideal" (Freud 1957, 116). Thus, the ego-ideal offers an image of completeness and self-sufficiency that substitutes, I would argue, not for the real thing (since the child never had this completeness and self-sufficiency to begin with) but for an illusion, the illusion that supports primary narcissism.[14] In Heideggerian language, we may say that the ego-ideal offers the (ever-elusive) promise of *Dasein*'s grasping itself in its totality, the promise of *Dasein*'s "being-a-whole." For Heidegger, the ontic impossibility of realizing such a totalizing project is due to human temporality, that is, to the ontological structure of human existence. To "freeze" our possibilities once and for all in a given actuality would be, in effect, to die, to no longer be *Dasein*. As Heidegger observes, "as long as *Dasein is* as an entity, it has never reached its 'wholeness.' But if it gains such 'wholeness,' this gain becomes the utter loss of Being-in-the-world."[15]

The perspectival nature of perception also ensures that the ego-ideal can never be presented or grasped as a genuine "object" of perception, for, as Merleau-Ponty notes:

For there to be perception, that is, apprehension of an existence, it is absolutely necessary that the object not be completely given to the look which rests on it, that aspects intended but not possessed in the present perception be kept in reserve. A seeing which would take place from a certain point of view and which would give us, for example, all the sides of a cube at once is a pure contradiction in terms; for, in order to be visible all together, the sides of a wooden cube would have to be transparent, that is, would cease to be the sides of a wooden cube. (Merleau-Ponty 1967, 212–13)

As an image of perfection, wholeness, completeness, the ego-ideal has characteristics that radically distinguish it from any and all perceptual objects. Our inability to understand the ego-ideal on perceptual terms, makes it also difficult, in Merleau-Ponty's account, to understand the level on which it functions in our everyday experience. Clearly, it would be inaccurate to depict the ego-ideal as a wholly unconscious phenomenon, since many of us, to a greater or lesser extent, are able to consciously articulate and even deliberately construct features of our own ego-ideal(s). And yet, the ego-ideal also resists being made into a facticity; its very nature as an "ideal" projection guarantees that in order for it to be efficacious as such, it cannot be realized at any given point in time.

To complicate matters further, Freud's understanding of the ego-ideal as developing not independently of the ego but in and through the (bodily) ego, suggests that it, too, should "be regarded as a mental projection of the surface of the body," a projection that "is ultimately derived from bodily sensations."[16] The ego-ideal, then, must not be seen as disembodied, as a mere phantom, but must be recognized as having its own materiality, a materiality that is directly tied to our own corporeal experience and which provides the very means for our libidinal investment in it. And one way of understanding the ideal body image, I would suggest, is as a corporeal enactment of the ego-ideal, an enactment whereby all of the normative force of the ego-ideal is directed upon the individual's own body image.

## THE MATERIAL EFFECTS OF
## A HISTORICO-RACIAL SCHEMA

In *Black Skin White Masks*, Frantz Fanon[17] suggests that the problems faced by the young girl in the development of an ego-ideal/body image ideal are negligible in comparison with the difficulties black men and women face in their efforts just to construct a coherent body schema. For these latter individuals, "consciousness of the body is solely a negating activity. It is a third-

person consciousness. The body is surrounded by an atmosphere of certain uncertainty" (Fanon 1967, 110–11). This "corporeal malediction," Fanon attributes to the peculiar nature of the "dialectic" that unfolds between the black
body and its world, a dialectic that is mediated from the outset by a not-so-
invisible third term, namely, white society with its white values, white norms
(both moral and aesthetic), and white expectations. Fanon argues that there is
another schema operative not above but below the corporeal schema.[18] This
schema Fanon calls a "historico-racial schema" and its elements are provided
not by "'residual sensations and perceptions primarily of a tactile, vestibular,
kinesthetic and visual character,' but by the other, the white man, who had
woven me out of a thousand details, anecdotes, stories" (Fanon 1967, 111).
The additional "task" faced by men and women of color is one of reconciling
their own "tactile, vestibular, kinesthetic, and visual" experiences with the
structure imposed by this historico-racial schema, a structure that provides the
"racial parameters" within which the corporeal schema is supposed to fit. "I
thought," Fanon poignantly notes, "that what I had in hand was to construct
a physiological self, to balance space, to localize sensations, and here I was
called on for more" (Fanon 1967, 111).

Fanon goes on to describe his own experience of finding his corporeal
schema "assailed at various points . . . crumbled, its place taken by a racial
epidermal schema" (Fanon 1967, 112). Rather than being able to relinquish
responsibility for a schema not of his own making, Fanon discovers that this
racial epidermal schema, which constructs him as The Black Man, also
makes him "responsible at the same time for my body, for my race, for my
ancestors" (Fanon 1967, 112). And, through assuming this responsibility
foisted upon him, Fanon tellingly reveals the only response possible for the
"moral" individual who accepts the condemnation of white society for his or
her "degraded" state: "Shame. Shame and self-contempt. Nausea" (Fanon
1967, 116). He too internalizes, to use Fanon's language, the "myth of the
negro," a myth that proclaims all blacks to be "savages, brutes, illiterates,"
and he describes the price of "defying" the myth as a black physician, as
follows:

> It was always the Negro teacher, the Negro doctor; brittle as I was
> becoming, I shivered at the slightest pretext. I knew, for instance,
> that if the physician made a mistake it would be the end of him
> and of all those who came after him. What could one expect, after
> all, from a Negro physician? As long as everything went well, he
> was praised to the skies, but look out, no nonsense, under any con-
> ditions! The black physician can never be sure how close he is to
> disgrace. I tell you, I was walled in: No exception was made for my

refined manners, or my knowledge of literature, or my understanding of the quantum theory. (Fanon 1967, 117)

The narrative movement of this passage from first to third to first person, visibly demonstrates the invisible social processes at work in the construction of a racially-coded corporeal schema and emphasizes that social ob-
jectification should not be viewed as a subsequent influence upon the
construction of an individual body image (i.e., coming into play only in the
development of an ego—or body image ideal), but is always already operative,
and, for those societally designated as "minorities," the internalization of this
racial epidermal schema (whose inscriptive force penetrates the psyche through
the skin) results in a (psychophysical) inferiority complex that no body image
ideal, however positive, can ever completely overcome. One corporeal consequence, according to Fanon, is that the black man "suffers in his body quite
differently than the white man." It is on the basis of this difference, and more
importantly, the reasons for this difference, that Fanon critiques Sartre's understanding of the Other when applied to a black consciousness since "the
white man is not only The Other but also the master, whether real or imaginary" (Fanon 1967, 138).

Fanon, like Merleau-Ponty and Schilder, draws upon both the phenomenological and psychoanalytic traditions to develop his own understanding of
the racialized body image. Although his account offers a morphological description of the (unbearable) tension between a body image and the historico-
racial schema out of which it develops that is lacking in either Merleau-Ponty or
Schilder, he too, quite explicitly, focuses on the situation of the male, the colo-
nized black man in particular, leaving the unique situation of black women almost entirely out of account.[19] This failure to account for the unique development of the woman of color's body image, the differences in the historico-racial
schema that underlies it, and the consequences of these latter for the internalization of a body image ideal that is both gendered and racialized in problematic ways, can and must be addressed, but can only be indicated here.

As far as the corporeal schema of the white man is concerned, Fanon argues that his "Negrophobia" is not merely a social attitude or psychical dispo-
sition, but is rather,

> to be found on an instinctual, biological level. At the extreme, I
> should say that the Negro, because of his body, impedes the clos-
> ing of the postural schema of the white man—at the point, natu-
> rally, at which the black man makes his entry into the phenome-
> nal world of the white man. (Fanon 1967, 161)

Moreover, Fanon calls for an investigation of

the extent to which the *imago* of his fellow built up in the young
white at the usual age would undergo an imaginary aggression with
the appearance of the Negro. When one has grasped the mechanism described by Lacan, one can have no further doubt that the
real Other for the white man is and will continue to be the black
man. And conversely. Only for the white man The Other is perceived on the level of the body image, absolutely as the not-self—
that is, the unidentifiable, the unassimilable. For the black man, as
we have shown, historical and economic realities come into the
picture. (Fanon 1967, 161)

While the white man experiences the image of the black man as a
phobogenic object, a stimulus to anxiety insofar as he is a corporeal reminder
of how precarious is the illusion that sustains the "completeness" of the body
image and its (perfect) idealizations, Fanon suggests that the black man experiences not whiteness but *his own blackness* as the not-self, as that which resists
all attempts to achieve corporeal closure. Whereas the Jew, for Sartre, is overdetermined from within, through her/his internalization of the antisemite's normative assessment of her/his psyche, Fanon claims that the person of color is
overdetermined from without, on the basis of her/his skin color alone (Fanon
1967, 115–16). The Jew can remain (in many but certainly not all cases) invisible in her/his Jewishness; the individual of color has no such "choice."[20]
And yet, it is more accurate, I would argue, given Fanon's own analysis, to see
the person of color as overdetermined both from within and without insofar as
racist attitudes and actions clearly penetrate the skin and are incorporated into
both white and black body images.

To understand the impact of the historico-racial schema on the development of the body image and the body image ideal(s) and to understand how
gender, class, age, and cultural norms and expectations are also internalized, interwoven, and expressed in each, it is necessary to explore further the contributions that other people make to the construction of one's body image. Both
Schilder and Merleau-Ponty emphasize the importance of others in the
processes of construction/destruction/reconstruction that characterize the ongoing development of the body image. Both are especially interested in the
nonverbal communication that plays such a crucial role in what Schilder calls
"body-image intercourse." Schilder stresses again and again that "the body-
image is a social phenomenon," that "there exists a deep community between
one's own body-image and the body-image of others," that the "body-images
of human beings communicate with each other either in parts or as wholes"
(Schilder 1950, 217, 138). For Merleau-Ponty, to develop a body image is to
develop an image of my body as visible to others. There is no body image with-

out this visibility of the body. As a result, the "synthesis" of the specular image and the introceptive feelings I have about my body that occurs (at the end of) the mirror stage is less, Merleau-Ponty claims, "a synthesis of intellection than it is a synthesis of coexistence with others." (Merleau-Ponty 1964, 140).

## THE INTEGRITY OF THE BODY IMAGE

Through the processes of introjection, projection, and identification described by Schilder, the body image continually incorporates and expels its own body (parts), other bodies, and other body images. Moreover, as the phantom limb phenomenon amply demonstrates, the body parts that may be incorporated or expelled in the body image need not be actually present to have an active role in the constitution of the body image. Although the experience of a phantom limb can be partially accounted for by attributing it to the body image's memory of the amputated limb, a memory that is essential for the formation of the habit body and which helps to provide the necessary stability that makes integrated and complex bodily movements possible, Schilder argues that there is a strong emotional investment in the missing limb that must be taken into consideration as well. Thus, the role that memory plays in the construction of one's present body image(s) can only be understood if the emotional contexts that situate (and stimulate) these memories are also illuminated and addressed. As Schilder observes:

> We are accustomed to have a complete body. The phantom of an amputated person is therefore the reactivation of a given perceptive pattern by emotional forces. The great variety in phantoms is only to be understood when we consider the emotional reactions of individuals towards their own body. (Schilder 1950, 67)

Schilder's reference to the amputee as an "amputated person," is itself revealing, because there is a sense in which the phantom is produced not only to maintain the coherence or completeness of the body image but, in doing so, to maintain the individual's own sense of self.

Merleau-Ponty characterizes the body image's resistance to absorbing the reality of the missing limb in terms of a (positive) desire to retain our active engagement in a social world that defines us as individuals:

> What it is in us which refuses mutilation and disablement is an *I* committed to a certain physical and inter-human world, who continues to tend towards his world despite handicaps and amputations and who, to this extent, does not recognize them *de jure*. The refusal of the deficiency is only the obverse of our inherence in a

world, the implicit negation of what runs counter to the natural momentum which throws us into our tasks, our cares, our situation, our familiar horizons. To have a phantom arm is to remain open to all the actions of which the arm alone is capable; it is to retain the practical field which one enjoyed before mutilation. (Merleau-Ponty 1962, 81)

The memory of the body image, which is revealed so poignantly through the experience of the phantom limb and which guarantees the stability of the postural model of the body from one moment to the next, is itself schematically organized and exhibits the same flexibility as the body image does. The tension between the amputee's body and her/his body image, which struggles to maintain its integrity by refusing to incorporate the missing limb into its corporeal schema, is not an isolated or unique phenomenon. Rather, for both Schilder and Merleau-Ponty, the phantom limb is only a more extreme form of a phenomenon that all of us experience on a daily basis, namely, the attempt to maintain a certain bodily equilibrium in the face of continual changes in both our body and our situation. Schilder, especially, emphasizes that the continual changes occurring both within and outside of our bodies necessitates the construction of not one, but several body images.

To the extent that one may posit an "original shape" to the body image, it must be remembered that "this original shape is based upon continual transformations from the postural model of the child into the postural model of the adult. There is a long series of images" (Schilder 1950, 67). This series of images, Schilder maintains, must not be understood linearly, with each new body image replacing the previous one as we move from infancy to adulthood. Rather, previous body images remain accessible and can be reenacted in a moment as when we return to a childhood "haunt" and find ourselves simultaneously haunted by an earlier body image that was able to negotiate the childhood space with ease. These earlier body images are also projected onto our own children as we watch their fascination with/dread of their bodies and as we find ourselves inhabiting their way of living their bodies as the emotional center of the world.

Thus, it is not just the amputee who refuses to "give up" an earlier body image in order to retain the emotional, physical, and social possibilities that resonated within that earlier situation. In the conclusion of *The Image and Appearance of the Human Body*, Schilder makes this point quite clear and leaves the reader with a rather startling, parenthetical observation:

Vestibular experiments and observations of amputated people have shown that every body contains in itself a phantom (*perhaps the body itself is a phantom*) in addition. It is obvious that the phantom character of one's own body will come to a still clearer expression

in dreams, which, like phantasies, show a particular variability.
(Schilder 1950, 297, emphasis added)

To say that the body itself may be a phantom, is to suggest that "the body" is itself a type of projection, a possibility ready to materialize itself in any number of shapes or forms. Moreover, just as the amputee incorporates the phantom into her/his body image in order to preserve bodily integrity, so too, we incorporate the body as a Gestalt, as a "heavy signification," to use Merleau-Ponty's words, into our own body images, in order to ground our sense of agency and to establish our "real" presence in the world as a material force to be reckoned with. The body image, then, enables us to identify not only with the bodies and body images of others, but also can express a desire to achieve a stable identity by projecting that very stability onto our own bodies.

## CONSTRUCTING THE BODY THROUGH THE BODY IMAGE

In *Bodies that Matter*,[21] Judith Butler discusses the role that identifications play in the assumption of a particular sex, and the point she makes about assuming a sex is directly applicable to the identification that materially supports identification with a sex, namely, a sexed *body*:

> Identifications, then, can ward off certain desires or act as vehicles for desire; in order to facilitate certain desires, it may be necessary to ward off others: identification is the site at which this ambivalent prohibition and production of desire occurs. If to assume a sex is in some sense an "identification," then it seems that identification is a site at which prohibition and deflection are insistently negotiated. To identify with a sex is to stand in some relation to an imaginary threat, imaginary and forceful, forceful precisely because it is imaginary. (Butler 1993, 100)

The imaginary threat that stimulates the desire for identification with something that will provide us with existential stability, is the threat that this stability will itself be revealed to be a phantasmatic construction, viable only to the extent that it is corporeally sustained at each and every moment of our existence. Butler goes on to observe that the "place" of identification can never be secured:

> Significantly it never can be said to have taken place; identification does not belong to the world of events. Identification is constantly figured as a desired event or accomplishment, but one which finally is never achieved; identification is the phantasmatic staging of the event. In this sense, identifications belong to the imaginary; they are

phantasmatic efforts of alignment, loyalty, ambiguous and cross-cor-
poreal cohabitation; they unsettle the "I"; they are the sedimentation of the "we" in the constitution of any "I," the structuring presence of alterity in the very formulation of the "I." Identifications are
never fully and finally made; they are incessantly reconstituted and,
as such, are subject to the volatile logic of iterability. They are that
which is constantly marshaled, consolidated, retrenched, contested,
and, on occasion, compelled to give way. (Butler 1993, 105)

To say that the body image posits "the body" as a given entity, as the
locus for specific desires and forms of identification, is not to deny the materiality of the body or to claim that the body is merely a figment of our (cultural) imagination. The imaginary, unlike the imagination, does not designate
a particular realm or faculty, but permeates our entire perceptual life in so thor-
oughgoing a fashion that Merleau-Ponty asks the question, "Is vision, the sense
of spectacle, also the sense of the imaginary?" (Merleau-Ponty 1964, 138).

That for most individuals, the phantom limb eventually does disappear,
(often, as Schilder observes, shrinking first) with or without therapy, should
not be understood as the "triumph" of the body (or the specular image of the
body) over the body image, but rather, as the construction of a new morphological imaginary, one that offers new sites of projection and identification and
new bodily possibilities. And yet, as Elizabeth Grosz reminds us, we must also
recognize that it is not the case that "anything goes":

The body is not open to *all* the whims, wishes, and hopes of the
subject: the human body, for example, cannot fly in the air, it cannot breathe underwater unaided by prostheses, it requires a broad
range of temperatures and environmental supports, without which
it risks collapse and death. On the other hand, while there must be
some kinds of biological limit or constraint, these constraints are
perpetually capable of being superseded, overcome, through the
human body's capacity to open itself up to prosthetic synthesis, to
transform or rewrite its environment, to continually augment is
powers and capacities through the incorporation into the body's
own spaces and modalities of objects, that, while external, are internalized, added to, supplementing and supplemented by the "organic body" (or what culturally passes for it), surpassing the body,
not "beyond" nature but in collusion with a "nature" that never really lived up to its name, that represents always the most blatant
cultural anxieties and projections.[22]

While Merleau-Ponty and Schilder provide a rich point of departure for
considering the complex, constitutive interrelationships between the body, the
body image, libidinous development, neurophysiological organization, the self,

other selves, other bodies, objects, and the situation as such, feminist theorists such as Butler, Grosz, Irigaray, Young, and Bordo have offered their own interventions into this particular corporeal dialogue. Through an exploration of the specula(riza)tions provided by these latter theorists, we can extend Merleau-Ponty's and Schilder's respective discussions of the body image to address the series of political, economic, racialized, sexualized, and gendered cultural/corporeal exchanges that set the terms for, and continually interrupt, body image intercourse.

## NOTES

1. It is noteworthy that references to Schilder's work on the body image can be found throughout Merleau-Ponty's texts including *The Structure of Behavior*, trans. Alden Fisher (Boston: Beacon Press, 1963), *Phenomenology of Perception*, trans. Colin Smith (London: Routledge & Kegan Paul, 1962) and even in a November 1959 Working Note from *The Visible and the Invisible*, trans. Alphonso Lingis (Evanston: Northwestern University Press, 1968), p. 220.

2. Maurice Merleau-Ponty, "The Indirect Language," in *Prose of the World*, ed. Claude Lefort, trans. John O'Neill (Evanston: Northwestern University Press, 1973), p. 78, emphasis added.

3. This is precisely the type of claim that gets Merleau-Ponty into trouble from a feminist standpoint since the sexual neutrality of the body, which Merleau-Ponty endeavors to maintain, is completely undermined by this masculinist project of possessing without being possessed in turn. Moreover, it is interesting to note the way in which the world suddenly takes on the "feminine" characteristics of the seductress, from whose "clutches" the body successfully manages to preserve its distance. The body becomes a male protagonist engaged in a perpetual "flirtation" with a female, "worldly" antagonist, and not surprisingly, it is the male who wins the round.

4. Maurice Merleau-Ponty, "The Child's Relations with Others," in *The Primacy of Perception*, ed. James Edie, trans. William Cobb (Evanston: Northwestern University Press, 1964), p. 122.

5. Merleau-Ponty is quite clear about the nonequivalence between the visual image and the child's awareness of her/his body. To demonstrate the impossibility of reducing the latter to the former, he makes the strong claim that:

> The child's visual experience of his own body is altogether insignificant in relation to the kinesthetic, cenesthetic, or tactile feeling he can have of it. There are numerous regions of his body that he does not see and some that he will never see or know except by means of the mirror. There is no point-for-point correspondence between the two images of the body. . . . If he comes to identify as bodies, and as animated ones, the bodies of himself and the other, this can only be because he globally identifies them and not because he constructs a point-for-point correspondence between the visual image of the other and the introceptive image of his own body. (Merleau-Ponty 1964, 116)

The point Merleau-Ponty is at pains to bring home is that the body image cannot be understood as a specular construction that somehow arises through the comparison/subordination of bodily sensations with/to the specular image; this does not mean, however, that the specular image fails to play a significant role in facilitating the development of the body image as a coherent construction.

6. Jacques Lacan, "The Mirror Stage as Formative of the Formation of the I," in *Écrits: A Selection*, trans. Alan Sheridan (New York: W.W. Norton & Co., 1977), p. 4.

7. In his essay, "Cezanne's Mirror Stage," in *The Merleau-Ponty Aesthetics Reader*, ed. Galen Johnson, trans. ed. Michael Smith (Evanston: Northwestern University Press, 1993), pp. 262–77, Hugh Silverman describes the process the child must go through as follows:

> Identification with the specular image only occurs after the child has treated the image as an image of another and after that assumption of alterity breaks down and a radical distancing from the image as other takes place. Thus when the child sees the image as an image of him or herself, it is not so much that it is the self as that it is *not other*. The "I" (je) is formed out of a dialectic in which the image is postulated as other, denied, and then affirmed as the self. One could say that it is a process of incorporation of otherness into the self. (Silverman 1993, 272)

While Silverman's account provides a lucid description of the "progress" the child makes in the mirror stage, he goes on to claim that "naturally this occurs only in the case of the recognition of self in the mirror. Objects and other people remain other," and it is these latter claims that I take to be problematic because I do not think that Merleau-Ponty wants to make such a strong distinction between the otherness of the self and the otherness of others in his own discussion of the mirror stage. In fact, as I will go on to argue, Merleau-Ponty supports his claim that "the specular image seems to be the threshold onto the visible world," precisely by viewing the otherness revealed in the specular image as an otherness of the self that is made possible by others and one that provides an opportunity to internalize the otherness of others in such an intimate fashion that they no longer remain simply "other."

8. The "outside-in perspective" has been used in a much different context by bell hooks (see "marginality as site of resistance" in Russell Ferguson, Martha Gever, Trinh Minh-ha, Cornel West, eds., *Out There: Marginalization and Contemporary Cultures* [Cambridge: MIT Press, 1990], pp. 341–43) and Patricia Hill Collins (see *Black Feminist Thought: Knowledge, Consciousness, and the Politics of Empowerment* [New York: Routledge Press, 1990] to discuss the marginalized perspective of black women, a perspective that can be both oppressive and empowering. In her essay, "marginalization as site of resistance," hooks also emphasizes the "inside-out" perspective of black domestic workers who look from their white employers' homes and through their white employers' eyes "across the tracks" to their own homes and their own lives. She discusses the unique position these women find themselves in since they occupy both the "outside-in" and "inside-out" perspectives, perspectives that enhance their intimate knowledge of gender, race, and class as, in Collins's terms, "an interlocking system of oppression." The relationship between the perspectives on oneself and the other offered by the specular image and the perspectives on oneself and the other offered by co-inhabiting the "outside-in" and "inside-out" perspectives as a black domestic worker needs to be explored in more depth in order to see how the alienation that accompanies the incorporation of the specular image can serve to reinforce and consolidate oppressive attitudes and actions.

9. What distinguishes Merleau-Ponty's account of the mirror stage from Lacan's is clearly not the former's understanding of the specular image as a source of identification, since this identification is a central aspect of Lacan's account. Rather, Lacan views the mirror stage primarily in terms of the child's deceptive (yet necessary) identification with her/himself as a totality via the "complete" picture offered by the specular image, and he goes on to focus on the ramifications of this deceptive understanding of the "I" throughout an individual's psychic life. Merleau-Ponty, on the other hand, while agreeing with Lacan that "when the child looks at himself in the mirror and recognizes his own image there, it is a matter of identification (in the psychoanalytic sense of the word)—that is, of 'the transformation occasioned in the subject when he assumes,'" and while acknowledging that "the passage from the introceptive me to the visual *me*, from the introceptive *me* to the 'specular I' (as Lacan still says), is the passage from one form or state of personality to another" (Merleau-Ponty 1964, 135–36), stresses the child's new understanding of what it means to be visible, for oneself and for others, and the corresponding recognition, on the part of the child, of an ideal space, which "can occur only in passing to a higher level of spatiality that is no longer the intuitive space in which the images [introceptive and specular] occupy their own place" (Merleau-Ponty 1964, 130).

In emphasizing the child's new understanding of visibility and spatiality, Merleau-Ponty displaces Lacan's emphasis on the temporal conflation of a future, complete "I" with the present incomplete sense of self, a fundamental *méconnaissance* that is, for the latter, the source of the deception that provides the necessary basis for the constitution of the "I." What he offers instead is the development of an *intra*corporeal spatiality accomplished through the mirror stage that provides a more positive and productive account of the formation of the body image (and of the I) as an intersubjective phenomenon that need not be grounded in deception.

10. Sigmund Freud, "On Narcissism: An Introduction," in *A General Selection from the Works of Sigmund Freud*, ed. John Rickman, trans. Cecil M. Baines, rev. Joan Rivière (New York: Liveright Publishing Corp. 1957), p. 88.

11. *In Powers of Horror: An Essay on Abjection*, trans. Leon S. Roudiez (New York: Columbia Press, 1982), Julia Kristeva emphasizes that the "edenic image of primary narcissism" is one that can be maintained only by the neurotic subject (and, therefore, at great expense) since there is a real threat to the ego-in-formation that is invoked in and through primary narcissism, which perpetually "shatters" its mirror of perfection. This threat, as Kristeva describes it, is none other than the threat of the dissolution of the ego into its non-object, the abject. Not only is the body image fragmented in primary narcissism, but the ego of primary narcissism is equally precarious: according to Kristeva, it is: "uncertain, fragile, threatened, subjected just as much as its non-object to spatial ambivalence (inside/outside uncertainty) and to ambiguity of perception (pleasure/pain)" (Kristeva 1982, 62). Moreover, Kristeva maintains that the fragility of the ego of primary narcissism and the threat of its undifferentiation from all that is not-ego, does not disappear once and for all as the individual moves on to a later developmental stage: "for the subject will always be marked by the uncertainty of his borders and of his affective valency as well" (Kristeva 1982, 63). It is precisely how the subject responds to this ever-present threat of undifferentiation and the loss of equilibrium that it involves, that helps to determine what comes to constitute the abject for that individual. And, it is through the incorporation or refusal to incorporate the abject into the psyche that the (lack of) boundaries of the body image come to be constituted as well.

12. It is precisely this lack of equilibrium, in fact, that marks what are often referred to as "distorted" body images. In anorexia, for instance, the excessive libidinal energy concentrated upon the mouth, disgestive tract, and anus, constantly belies the anorexic's efforts to separate herself from her body, an impossible dilemma that leads directly to the unbearable angst that "Ellen West" so poignantly describes in Ludwig Binswanger's existential psychoanalytical account, "The Case of Ellen West," in *Existence: A New Dimension in Psychiatry and Psychology*, ed. Rollo May, Ernest Angel, and Henri Ellenberger, trans. Werner M. Mendel and Joseph Lyons (New York: Basic Books, 1958), pp. 237–364.

13. I am borrowing the expression, "generalized other" from George Herbert Mead, who defines it as the internalized attitude of "the organized community or social group which gives to the individual his unity of self." (George Herbert Mead, *Mind, Self, and Society from the Standpoint of a Social Behaviorist*, ed. Charles Morris [Chicago: University of Chicago Press, 1962], p. 154).

14. Although Freud would perhaps disagree with this interpretation of primary narcissism as founded upon an illusion, Schilder's understanding of primary narcissism does support such a position.

15. Martin Heidegger, *Being and Time*, trans. John Macquarrie and Edward Robinson (New York: Harper and Row, 1962), p. 280.

16. Sigmund Freud, "The Ego and the Id," in *The Freud Reader*, ed. Peter Gay (New York: W.W. Norton & Co., 1989), p. 637.

17. Frantz Fanon, *Black Skin White Masks*, trans. Charles Lam Markmann (New York: Grove Weidenfeld, 1967).

18. I am using the terms *above* and *below*, as Fanon does, to figuratively describe how both the ego-ideal and body image ideal may be viewed as "above" the ego and body image insofar as they come later developmentally, and insofar as they perform a normative (the ought) function with regard to these latter. In claiming that there is another schema "below" the corporeal schema, Fanon is claiming that the body image is not the first schematic morphological construction but that there is another one that precedes it and that is imposed from the outside; an earlier schema that constructs the very "elements" that in turn form the basis for the construction of the corporeal schema. Moreoover, this schema, like the ego—or body image ideal, also serves as a strong normative force in the development of the body image, but unlike these latter, it is (internalized) and operative even before the body image is fully functional.

19. Fanon (1967, 41–62) does devote a chapter to the erotic dynamic between the woman of color and the white man, but aside from this chapter, he almost completely ignores the ways in which this historico-racial schema is also coded according to sex and gender since he takes the corporeal experiences of black men as the norm for the race as a whole. Later on in the book, Fanon does seem to acknowledge sexual difference in the response of whites to black men, in particular, insofar as the black male becomes a phobogenic object through his reduction to his penis, an identification that reinforces the white male's own castration anxiety and, in turn, enhances his own sense of (corporeal) inferiority.

20. Fanon also points out that whereas the Jew poses an *intellectual* threat for the antisemite (due to her/his putative acquisitiveness and business acumen), the black man poses a *biological* threat as a "penis symbol." Thus, while the Jew is a threat because s/he is too smart, the black man (and, Fanon acknowledges, the black woman as well) is a threat be-

cause he (she) is too sexual. This sexuality is not only separated from intellectuality but is even viewed as opposed to it which reinforces all the more the morphological differences that characterize what David Theo Goldberg has aptly termed "the anatomy of racism" (See *The Anatomy of Racism*, David Theo Goldberg, ed. (Minneapolis: University of Minnesota Press, 1990).

21. Judith Butler, *Bodies that Matter: On the Discursive Limits of "Sex"* (New York: Routledge Press, 1993).

22. Elizabeth Grosz, *Volatile Bodies: Toward a Corporeal Feminism* (Bloomington: Indiana University Press, 1994), pp. 187–88.

CHAPTER 9

# Merleau-Ponty and Irigaray in the Flesh

## ELIZABETH GROSZ

How can one . . . attribute the *existence* of the hymen *properly* to woman? Not that it is any more the distinguishing feature of man or, for that matter, of the human creature. I would say the same for the term "invagination" which has, moreover, always been reinscribed in a chiasmus, one doubly folded, redoubled and inversed, etc.

—Jacques Derrida, *The Ear of the Other*

Is Merleau-Ponty's notion of the flesh—"folding back, invagination, or padding"[1]—simply another masculine appropriation of the metaphors of femininity to ground an ontology, epistemology, or theoretical system? Is it simply another way of asserting the sexual neutrality (i.e., the implicit masculinity) of theoretical paradigms and systems, which, as Irigaray so astutely observes, has characterized Western philosophy since its inception.[2] Is woman simply covered over, rendered the invisible underside of a global or neutral "humanity," a bare universal subject whose psychical and neurophysiological interactions Merleau-Ponty has so thoroughly explored throughout his writings but whose sexual specificity he leaves uninvestigated, not even noted in passing? Is he participating in that centuries-old practice of recuperation and unacknowledged reliance on femininity, which is the defining characteristic of phallocentric thought?

145

It takes only the slightest shift in perspective to see Merleau-Ponty's writings in mutually exclusive terms, as either misogynist—misogynist through neutralization, through a refusal to see women's specificities and their differences from men rather than through intent, through a strategic blindness to the status of sex rather than through explicitly sexist remarks—or as profoundly useful for feminist purposes. It is certainly possible, in fact likely, that his work has elements of both. It will not be my task in this chapter to provide a definite solution or a final summary of the relevance of Merleau-Ponty's work, especially his notion of the flesh, for feminist purposes; or to provide a critique of his claims from a feminist perspective. I cannot presume that easy, ready-made judgments are possible with the writings of as subtle a thinker as Merleau-Ponty. My purpose is more limited to exploring the possible points of intersection—whether of resonance or dissonance—between his understanding of the flesh and feminist conceptions of subjectivity, to see if and how he participates in phallocentric presumptions, and if and how his work may help undermine or problematize these presumptions. In short, my goal will be to explore possible alignments between Merleau-Ponty's particular version of phenomenology and feminist theory, which is perhaps best exemplified by the writings of Irigaray.

My chapter is divided into four parts: in the first I will discuss in rather broad and general terms the apparent relations of overlap between Merleau-Ponty's concerns and those of feminist theory, looking at the ways in which his work may consolidate, augment, or supplement feminist theory; in the second section, I will focus more on one paper, "The Intertwining—The Chiasm,"[3] and especially on his radical and transgressive notion of the flesh, with the aim of, in the third section, assessing Irigaray's reading and critique of this paper, through which, in the final brief section, we can return to the question of the relations between Merleau-Ponty's phenomenology and feminist theory.

1.

Merleau-Ponty's stated project involves, among other things, destabilizing the pervasive structure of binary oppositions that characterize the history of Western philosophy. Rather than valorize one or the other side of a dichotomous pair of terms, rather than either affirm their fundamental unity or oneness in some kind of holism (which necessarily implies a reduction of one term to the other) or accept the bifurcation and mutually exclusive and exhaustive status of binarized terms, Merleau-Ponty, in ways that strikingly anticipate Derridean deconstruction, refuses the very terrain and founding presuppositions of dualisms.[4] His work is a resumption or reclamation of the space *in between* binary pairs, that apparently impossible no-man's land of the excluded middle, the gulf separating the one term from its opposite or other. This indeterminate middle ground must, as Derrida has also argued, predate and make possible the binary terms, for it precedes and exceeds them, it is uncontainable in either the one term or the other, and remains symptomatic of the impossibility of their separation. This may explain his preoccupation with the question of how to rethink perception outside the paradigms presupposed by either empiricism or rationalism. Perception is, as it were, midway between mind and body or subject and object, requiring the terms of both categories to be comprehensible. Neither empiricism nor idealism, neither pure psychology nor pure physiology, has been able to provide an adequate explanation either on its own, or in conjunction with its other, for the complex and reciprocal implications of each in its opposite.[5]

His defiance of and challenge to binary polarizations places his interests very close to those of many feminists, especially those who regard logocentrism as fundamentally implicated in and complicit with phallocentrism.[6] Like Derrida, or for that matter, Foucault or Deleuze, Merleau-Ponty struggles against the requirements of canonical philosophy for disjunctive, oppositional either-or decisions, for constrained and tightly controlled definitions of terms and theoretical grounds, for the right to define itself as a discipline without in turn being defined by its others. In this sense, his work warrants careful scrutiny by feminists for its ability to serve as a technique in feminist attempts to displace and transform phallocentric presumptions. It seems to share a common enemy, a common tradition, against which it defines itself: for this reason alone, it seems that Merleau-Ponty's particular brand of phenomenology may prove of great utility for feminists.

Merleau-Ponty and feminists such as Irigaray share common "enemies," common targets to be challenged and overcome, common sources of mistrust or suspicion, common goals of moving beyond or displacing binary structures. But clearly, this in itself is not enough to provide a persuasive link between Merleau-Ponty's work and that which interests feminist theorists. It is significant, however, that in the case of Irigaray at least, her comments regarding Derrida and Deleuze are scathingly critical. She seems deeply disturbed by the metaphorics of becoming-woman that is pervasive in their writings, functioning as it does as a general emblem of political and theoretical radicality, untethered from any connection with women in their concreteness, in terms of femininity as it is lived by women.[7] Her relation to Merleau-Ponty is considerably more "amorous," more in keeping with her stated project of "having a fling with the philosophers."[8]

What Merleau-Ponty seems to offer feminists such as Irigaray is not simply a common theoretical struggle, but, in more positive terms, elements useful for enriching and augmenting key features of feminist theory. In particular, his emphasis on the notion of *lived experience*, on the question of what is phenomenologically given, of what the body-subject experiences, has resonances with probably the most crucial and unique contribution of feminist theory—its capacity to use lived experience and experiential acquaintance (*connaissance*) as a touchstone or criterion in the evaluation, not only of theoretical paradigms and propositions, but also of day-by-day and mass politics. The problem is that many feminists, especially in the 1960s and 1970s, tended to hold rather naive views of experience, taking it as the unquestionable and final arbiter in disputes, seeing in it access to a pure femininity or some kind of incontrovertible truth, rather than (as psychoanalytic theory suggests) regarding it as a symptom or starting point of analysis. Experience cannot be understood as an unproblematic criterion for the assessment of knowledges, for it is clearly implicated in the dominant cultural and theoretical terms through which it is produced and by which it is framed. With the onslaught of antihumanism, Marxism, and poststructuralism in the late 1970s and 1980s, experience then tended to become something of a dirty word, at least in certain feminist circles. Women's experiential accounts seemed from this time on to function more as a form of testimony than as theory or explanation. Nevertheless, I would contend that without some acknowledgment of the major, indeed, formative, role of experience in the establishment and functioning of theoretical systems, sociopolitical and aesthetic constructs, and moral and political values, feminism has no grounds for disputing patriarchal norms. Merleau-Ponty, as one of the few more or less contemporary theorists committed to the primacy of experience, is thus in a unique position to help provide a depth and sophistication to feminist understandings, and uses, of experience in the tasks of political evaluation.

Merleau-Ponty's understanding of lived experience has, in my view, at least three crucial insights from which feminists could well afford to learn: in the first place, he refuses to understand experience, as some feminists have, as ineffable, unquestionable, or simply given: experience cannot thus be claimed as a source of truth, an arbiter in decisions, a neutral vantage point in establishing judgments—although clearly it must play *some* role in them. Experience is not outside social, political, historical, and cultural forces, and in this sense, cannot provide an outside position from which to establish a place for judgment, a pure perspective from which to judge theory or culture. What Marxists have understood as the ideological nature of experience, its fundamental untrustworthiness, is overcome in Merleau-Ponty's understanding of the constructed, synthetic nature of experience, its simultaneously active and passive functioning, its role in both the inscription and in the subversion of sociopolitical values. In counterbalancing the Marxist stress on the socially and ideologically fabricated nature of experience, Merleau-Ponty emphasizes a kind of reciprocal dialectic in which experience is constituted by the social, and which, in turn, effects and is capable of transforming the social.

In the second place, by way of a counterweight to the bracketing off of experience in most versions of poststructuralism and antihumanism, and while remaining wary of the purity of experience, in acknowledging the fundamental complicity of experience as his starting point and as the "object" of his analysis, Merleau-Ponty takes it "seriously," not as something to be explained away as simply untrustworthy, as "ideological," but as something to be explained. In doing so, in a rare stroke within the history of philosophy, he renders philosophy of immediate relevance to day-by-day life. He refuses to allow experience to remain untheorizable. It cannot be understood as ineffable, as purely private, of only psychological relevance. It is not only, in his conception, the starting point of analysis, but also a kind of measure against which the vagaries of theory can be tested, checked, assessed—and in this sense, his use of the notion of experience must be closely allied to similar attempts by feminists to use women's experience to judge the universality and plausibility of masculinist or phallocentric theoretical paradigms.

In the third place, and perhaps most relevant for our purposes here, Merleau-Ponty locates experience at the midway point between mind and body. He links the question of experience not only to the privileged locus of consciousness, but demonstrates that experience is always, necessarily embodied, corporeally constituted, located in and as the subject's incarnation. Experience can only be understood between mind and body (or across them), in their lived conjunction, rather than, as Cartesianism implies, in their logical disjunction. It is this understanding of experience as inherently and ineliminably embodied that Iris Young, for example, regards as Merleau-Ponty's major contribution to feminism and the history of philosophy:

> The unique contribution of . . . Merleau-Ponty . . . to the Western philosophical tradition has consisted in locating consciousness and subjectivity in the body itself. This move to situate subjectivity in the lived body jeopardizes dualistic metaphysics altogether. There remains no basis for preserving the mutual exclusivity of the categories subject and object, inner and outer, I and world.[9]

The centrality of a (nonreductionist) account of the body is part of the attraction that Merleau-Ponty has held for those (relatively rare) feminists who have been influenced by or interested in his work.[10] In refusing to reduce the body to mere physicalism or to a crude materialism, while at the same time insisting on its psychical interiority, its fundamental reliance on psychical schemas, projects, and desires in behavior, movement, and perception, Merleau-Ponty's insights have fed directly into recent feminist projects to rethink the bases of knowledges, the frameworks of the disciplines and dominant or canonical forms of discourse, and to create new forms of social, political, and ethical relation by asserting the specificity and irreducibility of female subjectivity, no longer on the model of ideological determination, but in terms of the specificities of sexed bodies. The necessary embodiment of the subject entails its perspectival and limited or partial access to the objects of knowledge, perception, or behavior; moreover, it allows feminists to ask the crucial question of knowledges: is the history of (embodied) knowledges thus far developed the product of *all kinds* of embodied subjectivity? or is it sexually specific? In other words, does it represent the results of men's perspectives and interests?

If what has passed itself off as universal, human or neutral knowledge is sexually specific, this entails the possibility of the development of other forms of knowledge, social interrelations, ethics, systems of representation, based on different perspectives and interests—those also representing the points of view of women (and indeed others). Moreover, the notion of an inherently embodied subjectivity also implies the possibility of reconceiving the ways in which subjectivity itself is generally understood: instead of seeing subjectivity as the product of a bare, generalizable human form, which has specific details (sex, race, age, historical context, class, etc.) as secondary attributes, the specificities of the subject, these particular "variables" of the universal are integral to the type of "bare humanity" presumed: in short, given the embeddedness of subjectivity in its corporeality, the subject's corporeal specificities in-form the type of subject it is, constituting the very contours, nature, and features of that subject.

Clearly, there is now, in the 1990s an enormous investment on the part of feminist theorists in rethinking the question of sexual difference in terms of notions of corporeality, and Merleau-Ponty's various researches may prove to be of prime significance in this project. His work, though, is not without its problems in feminist terms. Indeed, it is significant that the feminists I have mentioned—Irigaray, Butler, Young, etc.—while utilizing his work, nonetheless remain suspicious of the apparent sexual neutrality of his claims, the ways in which his work provides perhaps an accurate account of the specificities of men's lived experiences, and men's relations to their corporeality, but is unable to account for the specificities of women's experiences—their experiences of sexuality (Butler), their experiences of pregnancy and breasted embodiment (Young), their experiences of the senses (Irigaray). Even if it is true that the validity of his work is restricted to men, this means that it still remains useful in feminist terms, or for some feminist projects; it must be reevaluated, read differently, not as a new account of human being, but as a new account of masculine modes of human being—a major revision of its scope and relevance.

2.

Toward the end of his life, and particularly in his unfinished text, *The Visible and the Invisible,* Merleau-Ponty shifted the terms in which he had understood perception, embodiment, and experience, not so much changing his earlier views entirely, but reorienting them with a different inflection, and on the basis of a different ontological framework.[11] In this last text, Merleau-Ponty's object of theoretical speculation is the concept of "the flesh," which provides the preconditions and grounds for the distinction between mind and body, subject and object, inside and outside, and self and other.

The concept of the flesh is developed by Merleau-Ponty as an "ultimate notion" (Merleau-Ponty 1968, 140), "not the union or compound of two substances, but thinkable by itself," an "elementary or foundational term which has 'no name in philosophy'" (139, 147), which is strictly unthinkable in the governing terms of Western thought. While it does not displace perception as the thematic object of his investigations, the flesh is a more elementary or primary term, the condition of both seeing and being seen, of touching and being touched, of their intermingling and necessary interaction, the commonness in which both subject and object participate, a single "thing" folded back on itself.

Not unlike Irigaray, he wants to return to a prediscursive experience, experience before the overlay of reflection, the imposition of a meta-experiential organization, its codification by reason, language, or knowledge.[12] A "return" to or reconstitution of such prediscursive experience, a "wild being," an uncultivated or raw sensibility, is necessary for the creation of a nondualist, nonbinarized ontology. In returning to a prereflective sensible, however, he is not seeking a pure datum uninfluenced by the social: instead his goal is to find precisely the preconditions within sensibility itself, within the subject (as well as the world), that make the subject open up to, be completed by, the world, things, others, objects, qualities, interrelations. Neither subject nor object can be conceived as cores, atoms, little nuggets of being, pure presence: not bounded, unified entities, they "interpenetrate," they have a fundamental openness to each other.

Merleau-Ponty illustrates this with reference to the relations between the visible (the sensible) and the invisible (the intelligible), the seer and the seen, although it is significant—a point we will return to in the next section—that at crucial points in his argument, Merleau-Ponty turns to the relations between the toucher and the touched. The visible is a kind of palpitation of being, never self-identical, nor absolutely dispersed, a series of fluctuations, differences:

> [The visible] . . . is a concretion of visibility, it is not an atom . . . in general a visible is not a chunk of absolutely hard, indivisible being, offering all naked to a vision which could only be total or null, but is rather a sort of straits between exterior horizons and interior horizons ever gaping open, something that comes to touch lightly and makes diverse regions of the colored or visible world resound at the distances, a certain differentiation, an ephemeral modulation of this world—less a color or a thing, therefore, than a difference between things and colors, a momentary crystallization of colored being or of visibility. Between the alleged colors and visible, we would find anew the tissue that lines them, sustains them, nourishes them, and which for its art is not a thing, but a possibility, a latency, and a *flesh* of things. (Merleau-Ponty 1968, 132–33)

The flesh is the term Merleau-Ponty uses to designate being, not as plenitude, self-identity, or substance, but as divergence or noncoincidence (*écart*). For him, the notion of the flesh is no longer associated with a privileged (animate) category of being, but is being's most elementary level. Flesh is being as reversibility, being's capacity to fold in on itself, being's dual orientation inward and outward, being's openness, its reflexivity, the fundamental gap or dehiscence of being that Merleau-Ponty illustrates with a favorite example—the notion of "double sensation," the capacity of one hand to touch another that is itself touching an object—an example that clearly illustrates the various "gradations" between subjectivity and objectivity: between feeling (the "subjective" dimension) and being felt (the dimension of objectivity) is a gulf spanned by the indeterminate and reversible phenomenon of the being-touched, the ambiguity that entails that each hand is in the (potentially reversible) position of both subject and object, the position of both phenomenal and objectual body:

> My hand, while it is felt from within, is also accessible from without, itself tangible, for my other hand, for example, if it takes its place among the things it touches, is in sense one of them, opens finally upon a tangible being of what it is also a part. . . . Through this crisscrossing within it of the touching and the tangible, its own movements incorporate themselves into the universe they interrogate, are recorded on he same map as it; the two systems are applied upon one another as the two halves of an orange . . . where the "touching subject" passes over to the rank of the touched, descends into things, such that one touch is formed in the midst of the world and as it were in the things. (Merleau-Ponty 1968, 133–34)

It is on the basis of the double sensation as it is articulated in the field of tangibility that Merleau-Ponty frames his arguments about the seer and the visible: it is in an analogy between and an interlocking of the tangible and the visible that Merleau-Ponty presents the implication of the seer in the visible, the shared participation of the "subject" and the "object" is a generalizable visibility. The example of touch is a more convincing example, one where the gulf between the subject and the object is never so distant as in vision, one where the crossing of the subject into the object is more easily recognizable because access to either the inside or the outside is simply a matter of shifting focus rather than literally changing positions. Merleau-Ponty wishes to apply the same principle of folding back, of the "invagination" of being that marks his discussion of the double sensation. While it is clear that in the case of touch, the toucher is always touched, in traditional philosophical models of vision, the seer sees at a distance, and is unimplicated in what is seen. For Merleau-Ponty, the seer's visibility conditions vision itself, is the ground the seer shares with the visible and the condition of any (perceptual, motor) relation between them. To see is also the possibility of being seen, the fundamental interchangeability of the "stuff" of the subject with that of the object:

> He who looks must not himself be foreign to the world that he looks at. As soon as I see, it is necessary that the vision . . . be doubled with a complementary vision or with another vision: myself seen from without, such as another would see me, installed in the midst of the visible, occupied in considering it from a certain spot . . . he who sees cannot possess the visible unless he is possessed by it, unless he is of it, unless . . . he is one of the visible, capable by a singular reversal, of seeing them—he who is one of them. (Merleau-Ponty 1968, 134–35)[13]

Merleau-Ponty's claim is stronger than that everyone who sees is capable of being seen (by someone else). His point is ontological: the painter sees trees; but the tree also, in some sense, sees the painter (his example from "Eye and Mind" 1968, 167). This attribution of visibility to the visible as well as the seer is not an anthropomorphism, but rather, a claim about the flesh, about a (nonidentical, nonsubstantive) "materiality" shared by the subject and objects of perception.

Rather than a kind of animism or anthropomorphism in which he attributes vision to trees, Merleau-Ponty claims that this reversibility is always only potential or immanent: "my left hand is always on the verge of touching my right hand touching things, but I never reach coincidence" (Merleau-Ponty 1968, 147). Although flesh is the principle of reversibility, this reversibility is *asymmetrical*. It is only in this sense that the trees can be said to "see" the painter: as visible, trees and the painter are of the same visibility, the same flesh. The trees are a mirror or measure of my visibility. Flesh brings to the world the capacity to turn the world back on itself, to induce its reflexivity, to fold over itself, to introduce that fold in which subjectivity is positioned as a perceiving, perspectival mobility. To explain this near self-identity, this asymptotic self-coincidence, Merleau-Ponty plays with the metaphor of intercalated leaves, reversible, folded, coiling, fission. Subject and object, mind and body, the visible and the invisible are intercalated: the "rays," the lines of force indelibly etch the one into the other. The flesh is composed of "leaves" of the body and "leaves" of the world: it is the chiasm linking and separating the one from the other, the "pure" difference whose play generates persons, things, their unions and separations.

The subject and object are inherently open to each other, for they are constituted in the one stroke dividing the flesh into its various modalities. They are interlaced one with the other not externally but through their reversibility and exchangeability, their similarity-in-difference and their difference-in-similarity. Things solicit the flesh just as the flesh beckons to and as an object for things. Perception is the flesh's reversibility, the flesh touching, seeing, perceiving itself, one fold (provisionally) catching the other in its own self-embrace.

3.

Feminists have long found inspiration and support for at least some of their projects in utilizing Merleau-Ponty's particular brand of phenomenology, but it is significant that, of all the feminist literature on Merleau-Ponty's writings with which I am familiar, even those feminists who are strongly influenced remain, if not openly critical then at least suspicious of his avoidance of the question of sexual difference. Judith Butler, for example, while strongly praising some facets of Merleau-Ponty's understanding of sexuality as he develops it in *The Phenomenology*—praising him for his commitment to seeing sexuality, not as a drive, nor as a cause of behavior, but as a modality of existence, infusing all aspects of the ways we face and act in the world, part of our situation in the world—at the same time, and particularly in his analysis of Schneider's sexuality, accuses him of phallocentrism: the body and structure of desire he presumes is not in fact "human" but always and only masculine.[14]

Iris Young, although developing a quite different account of embodiment than that represented by Butler's analysis of sexuality in Merleau-Ponty's work, also seems to come to a similar conclusion: that while he provides a number of crucial insights about the forms and structure of human embodiment, nevertheless, he also excludes, or at the least, is unable to provide an explanation for those specific experiences undergone only by women. (Young elaborates in considerable detail the specificities of female embodiment and lived experience in her explorations of women's corporeal comportment and ways of compartmentalizing bodily unity to undertake physical tasks; the experiences of breasted existence, in which, in sexist society, breasts are both an inherent bodily attribute subjectively lived, but at the same time, function as objects, both for men, and for herself; and in the ambiguous and unbounded experiences of pregnancy, where we can no longer definitely specify whether it is one subject and body, or two, that is in question.) The relations between immanence and transcendence, between owning and being a body, between subject and object or between one subject and another, are not the same for women as they are for men, in ways that Merleau-Ponty seems to be unaware of.[15] In short, Merleau-Ponty's position in *The Phenomenology* and other texts is regarded as contentious, even if of value. But it is significant that, apart from Irigaray's reading of *The Visible and the Invisible*, his notion of the flesh has not (yet?) been subjected to feminist critique.

Merleau-Ponty does not explicitly address the question of sexual difference in *The Visible and the Invisible*, yet, if Irigaray's reading is appropriate, it is clear that his work derives much from a kind of implicit sexualization of ontology, the utilization of a whole series of metaphors embedded within and derived from relations between the sexes. These metaphors are the conditions of possibility of his understanding of the flesh, which is itself the condition of possibility of the division and interaction of subjects and objects. In this sense, the feminine may be said to be the unspoken, disembodied underside of the flesh: the flesh has a point-for-point congruence with the attributes of femininity. Such at least is the basis of Irigaray's careful reading of "The Intertwining . . ." in *An Ethics of Sexual Difference*.

Like Butler, Young, and other feminists, Irigaray remains highly sympathetic to Merleau-Ponty's project (indeed, she only ever seems to engage with those philosophers with whom she has a sort of love-hate relation—Freud/Lacan, Nietzsche, Heidegger, Hegel), seeing in it many affinities with her own work. Like other feminists, she remains suspicious of the alleged sexual neutrality or indifference of his writings. To be rather reductively oversimplified regarding her elliptical style, her objections to Merleau-Ponty's reworking of being in terms of the notion of flesh revolve around three major claims: first, the privileged position, indeed the dominance, of vision in Merleau-Ponty's writings, which, in overpowering and acting as the model for all other perceptual relations, submits them to a phallic economy in which the feminine has always figured as a lack or blind spot; second, that the notion of the flesh (in ways similar to more conventional descriptions of nature) is based on its implicit codification with the attributes of femininity; and third, that Merleau-Ponty has covered over, or disavowed the debt of all flesh to maternity: that the flesh not only has the attributes of femininity, but, more particularly, the attributes of maternity. Not only, as Young affirms, is Merleau-Ponty unable to account for the specificities of the maternal body, but further, although it cannot be articulated and theorized as such, nevertheless a notion of maternity and maternal debt underlies and conditions the notion of the flesh—precisely that which is disavowed in his manifest pronouncements is the unspoken condition of his theoretical system.

Irigaray suggests that his privileging of vision occurs in terms of metaphors of fluidity and absorption: he does compare the intimacy of the relations between the seer and the visible to the indeterminacy of the relations between "the sea and the strand" (1968, 131). This fluid connection in Irigaray's writing—and most particularly in her reflections on Nietzsche in *Marine Lover*[16]—has signified not simply the "formlessness" of a feminine *jouissance* but more particularly the amniotic element that links, houses, the child in the mother's body, and which continues to be a "watermark" etched into the subject's body. In this sense, the womb, and the earliest relations between mother and child, those relations, as it were, before the operations of a coordinated and fully constituted vision, must remain in darkness, a kind of nocturnal state that precludes but preconditions vision, an invisible that Merleau-Ponty leaves unacknowledged:

> If it was not the visible that is in question here, it would be possible to believe that Merleau-Ponty alludes here to intra-uterine life. After all, he employs the "images" of the sea and strand. Of the immersion and the emergence? And he speaks of the risk of disappearance of the seer/seeing and the visible. What doubly corresponds to an existence in the intra-uterine nesting: who is still in this night does not see and remains without any visible . . . especially without memory of that first event where he is enveloped-touched by a tangible invisible out of which even his eyes are formed but which he will never see: without seeing, neither visible nor visibility in this place. (Irigaray 1984, 144–45)

This darkness or invisibility of the "dark continent" of maternity nevertheless conditions and makes possible vision and the visible: this darkness cannot simply be understood as the lack of light, the absence of vision, for it too is a positivity and not simply a lack. This invisible condition of existence is a tactile positivity. This tactility is not entirely obscured by Merleau-Ponty's account of vision, for it infiltrates into his very first example, the case of seeing colors. In confronting a color, the subject is again confronted, as Merleau-Ponty acknowledges, not with a "pellicle," an atom, of being, but with a field of differences—differences between colors that enable any single color to be specified, differences between colors, shapes, and textures, and differences between colors and that which is colored. Even here, however, as Irigaray notes, color functions as a fluidity, it presumes a metaphorics of the tactile, of the feminine:

> [Color] pours itself out—stretches itself out, escapes itself...imposes itself upon me as a recall of what is most archaic in me, the fluid. That through which I have received life, have been enveloped in my prenatal sojourn, have been surrounded, dressed, fed, in another body. That by the grace of which I could see the light, could be born, and, moreover, see: the air, the light. . . . Color resuscitates, in me, the whole of that anterior life. (Irigaray 1984, 147)

Perhaps even more significant for her is the claim that the visible and the tactile are not in fact in a relation of reciprocity and mutual dependence, nor in a relation of similarity vis-à-vis the flesh. Merleau-Ponty, as I noted earlier, turns to the tactile to illustrate the thesis of reversibility even though he had thus far in his arguments restricted his claims to the visual. This reversion to the tactile is not simply a lapse, or a more convenient and straightforward example than the visible: Merleau-Ponty needs to invoke the tactile at this point because its characteristics are not generalizable for all the senses—vision operates differently. To illustrate this claim, Irigaray ever so slightly transforms his example. If we recall, Merleau-Ponty invokes the phenomenon of the double sensation, the case of one hand feeling the other which is itself feeling an object. Refashioning these two hands, Irigaray instead invokes the image of the two hands, joined at the palms, with fingers stretched—a relation of symmetry between the two hands, rather than the kind of "structural domination" or hierarchy Merleau-Ponty describes in giving one hand access to the other without in its turn being touched by the other. For him, there is always a slippage in the double sensation: they remain irreducible to each other (the left hand feeling the right hand is of course not the same as the right hand feeling the left). At best, the subject can experience the transformation of one position into the other, but never their identity or simultaneity. This other kind of touching, Irigaray suggests, cannot presume the dominance of one or the other hand, for it is a mutual and reciprocal touching, one, of course, not unlike the touching of the "two lips," which serves as her most consistent description of female sexuality:

> The hands joined, palms together, fingers stretched, constitute a very particular touching. A gesture often reserved for women . . . and which evokes, double, *the touching of the lips* silently applied

upon one another. A touching more intimate than the one of a
hand grabbing another. (Irigaray 1984, 151)[17]

The reversibility of the double sensation, the reversibility of the positions
of touching and touched is the basis of what Merleau-Ponty will also understand as the reversibility of the relations between the visual and the tactile, their
mutual implication. As he says:

> We must habituate ourselves to think that every visible is cut out
> in the tangible, every tactile being in some manner promised to vis-
> ibility and that there is encroachment, infringement, not only be-
> tween the touched and the touching but also between the tangible
> and the visible, which is encrusted in it, as, conversely, the tangible
> itself is not a nothingness of visibility, is not without visual exis-
> tence. . . . Every vision takes place somewhere in the tactile space.
> There is a double and crossed situating of the visible in the tangi-
> ble and the tangible in the visible; the two maps are complete and
> yet they do not merge into one. The two parts are total parts and
> yet are not superposable. (Merleau-Ponty 1968, 134)

In opposition to Merleau-Ponty, Irigaray claims that the map provided
by the tactile is not congruous with nor transposable onto that provided by
the visual. In her understanding, the visual and the tactile function according
to different logic and rhythms, although it is clear that there is much overlap
between them: nevertheless, there is, she claims, a surreptitious reclamation
and reordering of the tactile by the visual, which acts to subordinate all the
senses to its exigencies and forms. Irigaray denies that the visible can be situated within the tangible or that the tangible is situated through the visual: for
her, their relation is not one of reciprocity, insofar as the tangible provides the
preconditions and the grounds of the visible: Her claim, in brief, is that the
visible requires the tangible, but the tangible is perfectly capable of an existence autonomous from the visible (a case perhaps best demonstrated by the
existence of blindness—one cannot conceive of a case of a tangible equivalent
to blindness, where touch no longer functions for the subject but all of the
other senses remains intact: rather, if the tangible does not function, the subject is in a state of unconsciousness). In her understanding, the tangible is the
unacknowledged base or foundation, the source of the visible that renders
any comparison, any congruity between them false: they are not comparable
for they occupy different logical positions—the one is the foundation and
origin of the other. The tangible is the invisible, unseeable milieu of the visible, the source of visibility; it precedes the distinction between active and passive, subject and object: "I see only through the touching of the light" (Irigaray 1984, 155).

The visible and the tactile do not obey the same laws or rhythms of the flesh. And if I can no doubt ally their powers, I cannot reduce the one's to the other's. I cannot situate the visible and the tangible in a cross-shaped reversal chiasmatically. The visible needs the tangible and not reciprocally? Besides, the double and crossed situating of which Merleau-Ponty speaks, if it forgets the sensible medium, it also forgets the mucous of the carnal. That there is (a) situating [*relèvement*] of the visible in the tangible and the tangible in the visible. But the two maps are incomplete and are not to be confused: the tangible is primal, and remains so in its openness. Its touching of, at and through, the other. Its dereliction of never being able to retouch this first touching. (Irigaray 1984, 152)

Most particularly, Irigaray suggests, along lines similar to her critique of the psychoanalytic privileging of vision in the story of Oedipus, that the visual is the domain in that lack is to be located; it is the order of plenitude, Gestalt, and absence: the order that designates female genitals as missing, an order that is incompatible with the plenitude, enfolding, and infinite complexity of the tactile and the tangible. What remains invisible within phallocentrism is both the prenatal condition of corporeal existence, the child's inability to see the mother as source or origin of its existence and the existence of the other sex, a sex different from and incommensurable with the subject: "If I cannot see the other see me, my body no longer sees anything in the difference. I become blind as soon as it is about a body that is sexed differently" (Irigaray 1984, 157).

For Irigaray, it is significant that Merleau-Ponty, perhaps without being aware of what he commits himself to in this maneuver, describes the reversal of the seer and the visible in terms of the two lips. These lips invoked by Merleau-Ponty are not those lips lived and experienced by women as such, although his metaphor may be an attempt to reappropriate this carnal intimacy of female corporeality: his lips remain each within its own identity and place, one on the side of the seer, the other on the side of the visible: neither can touch itself through touching the other—the point of Irigaray's self-enfolding metaphor—for neither is able to dissolve its boundaries through its intimacy with the other:

The singularity of the body and of the flesh of the feminine comes from the fact that the lips are doubled here: the lips above and the below; and from the fact that the sensible that is the feminine retouches the sensible from whence he or she emerges. The woman being woman and potentially mother, the two lips of which Merleau-Ponty speaks can retouch themselves in her, between them, without getting through the seeing. These two dimensions of which Merleau-Ponty speaks are *in* her body. (Irigaray 1984, 155)

More primordial than vision, the tangible is also the necessary accompaniment of the earliest sensations, those in the blackness of the womb, those to do with hearing, a hearing ineliminably bound up with the maternal voice. Chronologically between touch and seeing, hearing, while relying on tactility, cannot hide its earliest feminine/maternal origins: the music of the womb, the precondition of both sound and of meaning. The tactile is always related by her to the concept of the *mucous*, which always marks the passage from inside to outside, which accompanies, and "lubricates" the mutual touching of the body's parts and regions. The mucous is neither the subjective touching of the toucher, nor the objectivity of the touched, but the indeterminacy of any distance between them. It escapes control, not being subject to the kind of voluntary slippage by which the touching hand becomes the touched. She suggests that the mucous may represent the toucher/touched indeterminacy more precisely than when one hand grabs the other.

Irigaray never suggests that Merleau-Ponty is, in any simple sense, "wrong," that his claims are inaccurate or false: rather, her claims are of a different order. They are that, in keeping with her analysis of a selective history of philosophy in *Speculum* and *An Ethics*, Merleau-Ponty's theoretical paradigm owes an unacknowledged debt, indeed its conceptual foundations, to femininity and maternity—a debt whose symptoms reside in the kind of language of pregnancy he continually invokes to articulate the emergence of that torsion within the flesh that constitutes and unites the seer and the visible. The world remains isomorphic with the subject, existing in a complementary relation of reversibility. The perceiving, seeing, touching subject remains a subject with a proprietorial relation to the visible, the tactile: *he* stands over and above, while remaining within his world, recognizing the object and the (sexed) other as inversions of himself, reverse three-dimensional "mirrors," posing all the dangers that mirror-identifications imply:[18]

> If there is no cutting of the cord and of osmotic exchanges with the maternal world and its substitutes, how could sublimation of the flesh take place? It continues becoming in closed circuit, within sorts of nourishing relationships to the other. Does it sublimate itself in order to accede to the alliance with the other? It does not seem so. It perpetuates a state, entertains it in its permanence, absorbing its cutting and shocks? What is called reversibility here is perhaps also that by which the subject producing some mucous at the exterior re-envelops itself in it. Some elaboration of the carnal takes place there. But always in its solipsistic relationships to the maternal. There *is not a single trace of a carnal idea of the other woman nor of a sublimation of the flesh with the other.* At most an alchemy of substitution of a placentary nourishment. (Irigaray 1984, p. 168)

4.

Let us now briefly return to the questions with which I began, those centering around the possible relations between Merleau-Ponty's understanding of the flesh and the interests and concerns of feminist theory to articulate sexual difference. Is Merleau-Ponty's work complicit in phallocentrism, despite his goals of circumventing what might be called logocentrism, and the prevailing structures of binary thinking? If it is, does it nevertheless remain of value to feminist thought? If it does not, does it offer a paradigm that feminists may find useful in exploring the question of sexual difference?

On the basis of various feminist readings of *The Phenomenology* and Irigaray's reading of "The Intertwining—The Chiasm" it seems to me that Merleau-Ponty's work, in its broad outlines occupies much the same position as many apparently misogynist or phallocentric texts occupy in feminist theory— I am thinking here of the writings of Marx, Freud, Lacan, Nietzsche, Heidegger, Derrida, Foucault, Deleuze, and others. In spite of—or perhaps because of—their particular ways of posing *and* eliding the question of sexual difference, these writers have occupied a particularly privileged place in the production of feminist theory, because their work enables feminists to understand both how apparently gender-neutral theoretical or representational systems work, what their unspoken assumptions and unacknowledged costs might be, and how they function to efface their masculinity. This knowledge is prerequisite to, or perhaps the necessary accompaniment of, the development of alternative accounts, accounts able to articulate other points of view, other (sexual) perspectives and interests. Merleau-Ponty's understanding of the flesh, like Lacan's notion of the phallus, Derrida's concept-metaphor of *différance*, and Deleuze and Guattari's becoming-woman, provides an intense and ambiguous locus for feminist investigation insofar as each challenges prevailing (phallocentric, metaphysical) postulates, destabilizing them, providing more open-ended alternatives which may well suit feminist goals of transforming the structures of knowledge. These advantages may outweigh the disadvantages that their complicity in phallocentrism entails: the danger that, in appropriating and utilizing their conceptual schemas, women become participants in their own effacement. In my view, however, these are dangers worth facing, for by means of these various conceptual schemas—Merleau-Ponty's being one of the least developed by feminists—feminists may not only displace the privilege of phallocentrism, but may also find more appropriate terms in which to develop their own self-representations.

To signal, then, in the briefest possible terms—and by way of reiterating my claims at the beginning of this chapter, it seems to me that Merleau-Ponty's

writing, particularly on the flesh, have the following potential value or useful-
ness for feminist theory:

1. In undermining or problematizing the structure of binary oppositions, and particularly the mind-body oppositions, Merleau-Ponty provides a
way for feminists to reconceptualize notions of subjectivity so that sex (or race,
but less clearly, class, and sexual orientation) can be understood, not as an aspect, feature, quality, or attribute of a subject—something he or she has in its
facticity (like eye color). Rather than add to the form of the body-subject, the
sex of the subject provides an entire orientation, a framework from which the
body-subject lives and acts in its world;

2. A closely related point: Merleau-Ponty develops a powerful and important notion of the body-image as a psycho-physiological hinge, which can
enable feminists to rethink subjectivity, mind, and even reason itself, as sexually specific. In other worlds, it can position epistemology and ontology as sexually specific, it can suggest in ways that feminists up to now have resisted, that
women not only have different bodies from men (a point no one would con-
test) but therefore, they must also have different minds from them (a contro-
versial and sensitive point, one that needs very careful elaboration). Perhaps the
only other major thinker taken up by feminist theory who enables us to rethink the "inside," the lived, psychical significance of the body is Jacques
Lacan.[19] It remains to be seen, however, whether Merleau-Ponty's understanding of the body-image is as complicit in phallocentrism as Lacan's—whether,
that is, the female body must be understood on the model of castration or lack;

3. Merleau-Ponty's understanding of the flesh as an inherent intertwining of subject and world founds a new ontology, one that supersedes the ontological distinction between the animate and the inanimate, between the animal and the human, scientist and object of investigation, in ways that might
also suit the interests of feminists (the "hierarchy of being" in which the inanimate lies at the bottom and mind or reason at the top of the pyramid of matter is fundamentally complicit with the hierarchy that positions one kind of
subject (male, white, capitalist) in the position of superiority over others; it
provides a way of reconceiving materiality so that it includes rather than op-
poses the psychic and the sexual); and

4. Feminists are able to read Merleau-Ponty's texts from any perspective
they choose (this of course is true of any text); in this case, feminists may find
it fruitful to read his work as an analysis and explanation, not of human subjectivity, but of male subjectivity (the project of undoing phallocentrism): it
would in this case show the ways in which men come to be "centered," unified,
integrated subjects, active in the world, able to make decisions and undertake

projects—it remains an open question for feminists to ask whether the same is true for women. In other words, many of Merleau-Ponty's key questions can be asked of women ( as women)—which may result in a recognition of the inappropriateness of these questions, or it may result in understanding female subjectivity in richly rewarding ways, using the complexity of Merleau-Ponty's methodologies and the sophisticated detailed insights he develops.

## NOTES

This paper was originally published in *Thesis Eleven*, No. 36, 1993, pp. 37–60.

1. Maurice Merleau-Ponty, *The Visible and the Invisible*, trans. Alphonso Lingis (Evanston: Northwestern University Press, 1968), p. 152.

2. See Irigaray's *Speculum of the Other Woman* (Ithaca: Cornell University Press, 1985) and *L'Ethique de la différence sexuelle* (Paris: Minuit, 1984); trans. as *An Ethics of Sexual Difference* (Ithaca: Cornell University Press, 1993). This chapter will rely on my translations of this text.

3. Which is the fourth chapter of *The Visible and the Invisible* (1968).

4. On the relations between Derrida and Merleau-Ponty, See Flynn, "Textuality and the Flesh: Derrida and Merleau-Ponty," *Review of Existential Psychology and Psychiatry* 18, 1–2–3 (1982/3).

5. Clearly, "perception" is not the only such term in Merleau-Ponty's writings: other undecidable terms, terms that imply the inextricable intermingling of opposites within his writings, include a concept that is closely bound up with that of perception, the "body image," which is both conceptual and physical, psychical and neurological, mind and matter undecidably.

6. Clearly, Merleau-Ponty shares this interest with a number of other poststructuralists, most notably Derrida and Deleuze: on this argument, feminists would have as much in common with Deleuze and Derrida as they do with Merleau-Ponty—a claim with which I would not disagree, but one that goes well beyond the scope of this chapter.

7. There are some men, at the moment . . . who wouldn't be afraid of returning to the pre-oedipus. They ask themselves certain types of questions which, as such, must not be confused with women's questions because many men at the moment say "Now we are becoming women. . . . [T]hat shows the power of the question of difference. As soon as something worthwhile manifests itself concerning women, men want to become women. What interests me is the difference. . . . Above all, don't become women, sirs! (Irigaray *Le Corps-à-corps avec la mere* [Montreal: Le Pleine Lune, 1981]).

8. This is her own phrase for describing her work in *Speculum* and in *This Sex Which is Not One* (1985a). Her argument, in the briefest possible terms, is that in the history of Western philosophy, women have no position to occupy as either subjects or objects of knowledge: to position themselves a subjects means in effect that women must masquerade as men, becoming "honorary men," sexually neutral subjects; and to position themselves as objects is to remain within the positions of passivity located for women by phallo-

centric knowledges. For her, in breaking out of this patriarchal double bind, women only have access to the "tools" of their "feminine wiles," the tools of seduction, mimesis, and hysteria, to articulate their positions as women:

> Thus it was necessary to destroy [phallocentric theory], but . . . with nuptial tools. The tool is not a feminine attribute. But woman may re-utilize its mark on her, in her. To put it another way: the option left to me was *to have a fling with the philosophers*, which is easier said than done. (Irigaray 1985, 150)

9. Iris Marion Young, *Throwing Like a Girl and Other Essays in Feminist Philosophy and Social Theory* (Bloomington: Indiana University Press, 1990), p. 161.

10. See, for example, Whitford's excellent account of the effects of Merleau-Ponty on Irigaray's work, in Margaret Whitford, *Luce Irigaray. Philosophy in the Feminine* (London and New York: Routledge, 1991); Judith Butler, "Sexual Ideology and Phenomenological Description; A Feminist Critique of Merleau-Ponty's *The Phenomenology of Perception*," in J. Allen and I. Young, eds., *The Thinking Muse. Feminism and Modern French Philosophy* (Bloomington: Indiana University Press, 1990).

11. In *The Phenomenology of Perception* (Evanston: Northwestern University Press, 1962), the senses interact, form a union and yield access to a singular world. Sight and touch are able to communicate with each other because they are the senses of one and the same subject, operating simultaneously in a single world. The senses not only communicate with each other, adding to and enriching each other, they are transposable, at least within certain limits, onto each other's domains, although they remain irreducible in their differences. Sight, touching, hearing, smell function contemporaneously and are cumulative in their effects. The senses are transposable only because each lays claim to a total world, a world defining the subject's sensory relation, each of which is able to mesh with, be gridded in terms of, other "sensory worlds":

> The senses communicate with each other. Music is not in visible space, but it besieges, undermines and displaces that space. . . . The two spaces are distinguishable only against the background of a common world and can compete with each other only because they both lay claim to total being.
> The sight of sounds and the hearing of colors comes about in the same way as the unity of the gaze through the two eyes: in so far as my body is not a collection of adjacent organs, but a synergic system, all the functions of which are exercised and linked together in the feneral action of being in the world, in so far as it is the congealed face of existence. . . . When I say that I see a sound, I mean that I echo the Vibration of the sound with my whole sensory being, and particularly with the sector of myself which is susceptible to colors. (Merleau-Ponty 1968, 136 fn 2)

12. Far from providing "proof" or evidence of Merleau-Ponty's, or Irigaray's, ensnarements in essentialist notions of subjectivity, this recourse to prediscursive experience (which Irigaray elsewhere describes, following Lacan, as the imaginary) provides an account of resistance, given a "social constructionist approach": the thickness, the recalcitrance or resistance of experience to social inscriptions and inculcations is a necessary postulate if we are to retain the hope of transgressive resistances and refusals of the kinds of inscription that would otherwise fully constitute us as subjects. Moreover, such a prediscursive experience must, like the flesh itself, provide the "starting points", the fictional presumptions of 'raw materials', necessary for any social constructionist model—hence the complicity of constructionism in its apparent opposite, essentialism.

13. Merleau-Ponty's notion of the reversibility of the seer and the seen is strikingly similar to Lacan's account of the 'double dihedral of vision' he posits as crucial to the functioning of the gaze. Lacan, like Merleau-Ponty affirms that to see implies the possibility of being seen:

> I must, to begin with, insist on the following: in the scopic field, the gaze is outside. I am looked at, that is to say, I am a picture.
>
> This is the function that is found at the heart of the institution of the subject in the visible. What determines me, at the most profound level, in the visible, is the gaze that is outside. It is through the gaze that I enter light and it is from the gaze that I receive its effects. Hence it comes about that the gaze is the instrument through which light is embodied and through which . . . I am *photo-graphed.* (Lacan 1977, p. 106)

However, Lacan disagrees with Merleau-Ponty insofar as the gaze is not reducible to perception: the model of vision does not rely on the functioning of desire in the same way as the gaze does. Merleau-Ponty ascribes to the painter's vision the same perceptual attributes he uses to characterize perception: but for Lacan, the construction of the frame or boundary renders the gaze of the artwork, the gaze or desire as a divergence from or within vision:

> Indeed, there is something whose absence can always be observed in a picture— which is not the case in perception. This is the central field, where the separating power of the eye is exercised to the maxium in vision. In every picture, this central field cannot but be absent, and replaced by a hole—a reflection, in short, of the pupil, behind which is situated the gaze. Consequently, and in as much as the picture enters into a relation to desire, the place of a central screen is always marked, which is precisely that by which in front of the picture I am elided as subject of the geometral plane. (Lacan 1977, p. 108)

14. Butler develops what seems to me a most convincing case against the apparent sexual neutrality of Merleau-Ponty's claims. For example, she argues that:

> Indeed, it is difficult to understand how Merleau-Ponty . . . makes general claims about bodies, unless by 'the body' he means the male body, just as . . . . the 'normal subject' turned out to be male. . . . If the female body denotes an essence, while bodies in general denote existence, then it appears that bodies in general must be male. (Butler, 1990, p. 94)

15. See in particular, the papers "Throwing like a Girl. A Phenomenology of Feminine Body Comportment, Motility and Spatiality", "Pregnant Embodiment: Subjectivity and Alienation"; and "Breasted Experience: The Look and the Feeling" all in Young, 1990.

16. She also seems to utilize many of Merleau-Ponty's insights regarding the body-schema in her understanding of the concept of morphology; her conception of 'the elemental', a new ontology, also shares clear affinities with his use of the term. On these notions, see Grosz 1989.

17. As Irigaray notes, this gesture is, of course, the gesture of prayer: her use of this example of a touching of the touching also evokes the women's liberation movements' use of the two hands to represent the two lips—a double reference to the sexual specificity of women, and to women's particular, if disavowed, relation to God and the divine:

> . . . God is always entrusted to the look and never imagined enough as tactile well-being [*bonheur tactile*] . . . Lacking this well-being, God will always be thought of as a god that touched in the suffering but never in the joy of well-being . . . Never a God who envelops me, surrounds me, cradles me . . . Loves me carnally, erotically. (1984, p. 153)

18.  From her other writings, most notably *The Sex Which is Not One* she makes clear some of these perils, most notably, the fact that the mirror only ever reveals a picture of the subject—the other remains at best an imperfect double, always defined by the parameters of the subject's self-attributions; and secondly, the fact that mirror-identifications must remain blind to the plane that constitutes the mirror—a kind of 'invisible', different from Merleau-Ponty's conception, which conditions the visible, in this case, the specular.

19.  Lacan's understanding of the imaginary anatomy is closely akin to Merleau-Ponty's—which is hardly surprising given a series of common sources in theorists of the body-image (Schilder, Gelb and Goldstein, in particular). For further details of Lacan's notion of the imaginary anatomy or body image, see "The Mirror Stage . . ." (Lacan, 1977a); and my discussion of it in Grosz, 1990.

CHAPTER 10

# Segmented Organisms

## ALPHONSO LINGIS

Justice is such an elusive thing to get any kind of concrete idea of. In fact, it seems to be a notion marginally invoked, almost never at the center of any discussion. One first talks about how a system works, a particular kind of market economy, the assignment of values to abstract things such as intellectual property, the kinds and availability of education and health care, access to and manipulation of the organs of information and the expression of opinion, the different migrations of peoples into a region, and the different economic niches the various ethnic groups have come to occupy. Justice seems to be both marginal and for tomorrow; something to keep in mind somehow as the present economic and technological situation works itself out or evolves.

And then, one day, you see justice, it materializes in front of your eyes.

The day before, I had been released from the hospital in Rio de Janeiro; I got up just before sunrise and decided to go out for a little walk down the promenade of Avenida Atlantica in Copacabana where I was staying. I took my wallet, thinking I would treat myself to a good breakfast at the Meridien Hotel three blocks up. I was shuffling along, bent over due to the sutures.

"*Senhor, que horas sao?*" I heard. I looked up, an adolescent kid was pointing to his wrist and asking the time. I looked at my watch; it was six, and then suddenly I knew what was going to happen. Five or six of them closed in; I thought to protect my sutured abdomen and sunk to the sidewalk, trying to close my body upon itself. One of them held a knife to my throat. I really did not feel them taking my watch and clearing my pockets. Then they pulled back. As I started to get up again, one of them tossed me my hotel key before prancing off. They crossed the avenue and vanished into the city. The timing, the rhythm of the act seemed flawless to me, certainly more interesting than any play in a football field watched from the bleachers. It was like a well-choreographed scene in a cabaret, the actors appearing from the backstage, closing in about the gleaming prop or fetish, the knife, the group unfolding and vanishing without missing a beat. The question itself was part of the scenario, as I felt as soon as I looked at my watch to answer it. Who after all is strolling along the sea at daybreak and wants to know exactly what time it is? The kid meant: Hey mister you got a fine watch there! There was also something erotic in the whole play. Nobody walks Copacabana beach at any hour of the day or night with anything but lust in his or her heart. It just isn't possible, the most serious joggers cast prurient glances at one another's sweat-molded shorts as they pass one another. I had had glimpses only of the face of the one who asked me the time and of the other who held the knife to my throat, both had big gleaming eyes; the others had blankets like capes about them, and no doubt had spent the night sleeping on the beach. Keeping my eyes fixed on the phallic knife at my throat, they, reduced erotically to gleaming eyes and blankets, had taken my watch and wallet with fingers light as caresses.

While it was happening, I was intensely aware of the stylized perfection of the operation and its erotic pulse. But as soon as it happened another idea completely occupied my head: justice. It was the organizing theme, the intelligible schema. An eighty-dollar watch, a cobra-skin wallet with maybe seventy-five dollars in cruzeiros in it; a white tourist, well dressed in fashionable shorts and a T-shirt, on the way to the Meridien; six adolescents running now across the boulevard to return to the *favela* from which they came. But the notion of justice did not come out of my making that reflection, intelligibly assembling these elements of a morning on Avenida Atlantica. It came right in the conjunction of knife with throat. The throat of any one of those idle rich old farts that come from thousands of miles away to bask on the beach at Copacabana, eat lobster, read newspapers, and go back again. And you—you are there, you got born, you with this young and hungry body, you who don't have coins for rice and black beans. The knife, it turned out, was a tourist souvenir knife that had been grabbed off one of the stands that vendors were already setting up, and was tossed back to the vendor by my departing assailants. A souvenir knife and a throat; suddenly justice materialized there, under the pink-tinted dawn clouds of Copacabana. (The fact that it happened to be the knife at my throat was a detail that naturally could not make it occur to me that there was anything objectionable in what they did; morality, Kant told us long ago, can be identified simply as the kind of reasoning in which one does not make oneself the exception.)

Heading back to my hotel, I realized that my credit card was in that wallet, and, noticing now a police post, I stopped to get the police report I would need when going to American Express for the replacement. The cop bounded up, headed to where I was attacked, and then pulled his gun and ran across the sands. I tried in vain to signal to him that it was not on the beach but here on the sidewalk that I had been attacked. It took me a while, bent over as I was, to catch up with him. On the way back to the police post, he pulled off the shirts from the faces of sleeping people on benches and on the sands and turned them over and demanded if this was one of them, even though I told him in my crude Portuguese and with gestures that my attackers had run off into the city. "They come back," he muttered. I said I had to file a report, I would go to the precinct office, "No," he said, "you wait." I went to have coffee at my hotel. Fifteen minutes later the hotel desk clerk came to tell me the police had captured my attackers. They had three street kids and the police explained they had changed clothing in the meantime, but it was these, they had been identified by witnesses. I realized I could not identify the attackers, they were not wholes, I had seen only hands, eyes, knife that fitted together in a rapid melodic line. The cops made each of the three kids stand up, turn around, take off his clothes, so that I could see all there was to them as they insisted it was these three. Suddenly it occured to me to say no, to insist it was not these three and to wait there until finally the police let them go. Rio de Janeiro is the city where the police, who have the guns, are hired by the shopping centers as night guards. They shoot the street kids, throw the bodies in dumps, attribute them to gang killings among themselves. Some five hundred children were killed in the city that way last year.

How little a tourist, who does not even know Brazilian Portuguese, understands of the city spread out about him! Yet justice itself had materialized, integral and indisputable. Justice is not the distributive arrangement of "persons" but a couplings of body parts. The sense of justice is the sense that certain pairings of body parts are right. The tourist's aging white throat and the knife in the adolescent fist, for example.

Justice, as a notion of practical reason, and rightness, as a notion of pure or theoretical reason, seem indeed inseparable. When you suddenly see justice in front of your eyes, you have a unit that makes sense, that eminently makes sense, that you use to make sense of other things. Even if the concept in it, the notion of justice, does not seem to be definable in some general and categoreal way.

Maurice Merleau-Ponty's first project was to refute the analytic thinking that breaks up behaviors into couplings of an organ with an implement or resistance. First he promoted the Gestalt as a notion of structure: there is in an

organism an organization that continually determines the position and function of the parts. I don't think he ever thought much about the original form
of organisms—segmented worms. The primitive one-celled forms of life first
expanded into forms where all the functions were there in each of the segments; any segment that gets severed from the rest can move, nourish itself,
grow, and reproduce. Merleau-Ponty instead took up Kurt Goldstein's saying
that the body can do but one thing at a time. And perceive but one thing at a
time; a figure against a background is, he wrote, the very definition of perception. Then he adopted the formulation of existence-philosophy, and applied
it to bodily behaviors: whereas animals perceive and respond to environments,
humans perceive and act in the world. Later he made the notion of posture
central. There forms one unitary diagram, oriented upon an objective, which
both coordinates the positions and displacements of the parts and members of
the body, and coordinates the sensory surfaces so as to perceive one thing at a
time. A single movement, of a hand, of a face, or a leg is supported by the
whole posture, and expresses it. That is why, in the cinema, Eisenstein can
show all the anxiety and all the indignation of a woman in a closeup of her
hand tightening on her handkerchief. Later, the phenomenon of expression became a central theme of Merleau-Ponty's thinking; his abandoned manuscript
*The Prose of the World* was concerned with the moment when infantile bab-
bling becomes speech, when strokes of paint begin to represent something,
when isolated reactions dispersed throughout social space begin to form a political movement and class consciousness.

Merleau-Ponty's polemic against analytic physiology is paradoxical; the
reflex arc cannot be taken as the unit of intelligibility, he argues, because it is
found either in pathological cases or in highly intelligent subjects. Schneider is
an existential arc that adheres to its environment. He can function effectively
when the tasks and the tools are laid out before him; he holds a job in a shoe
factory. But he cannot take any initiative, cannot even merely point to things
or parts of his own body without taking hold of them. He cannot detach himself from the concrete enough to imagine a variant of it. Merleau-Ponty says
that Schneider, like an animal, lives in an *Umwelt* without extending his existential arc unto the *Welt*. The *Welt* would not be the constellation of partial
and imaginary situations that could evoke gestures of pointing without grasping; it would be the entire field, the array of all variants of the *Umwelt*. It is the
behavior bracketed on the *Welt* that is intelligible of itself and makes intelligible the defective cases. One produces reflex arcs in the laboratory by immobi-
lizing the subject, disconnecting him from active involvement in a situation; it
is then that a tap of the mallet on the knee provokes an immediate local reaction. But also highly intelligent subjects are capable of the quasi-automatic re-

flex behaviors. Merleau-Ponty explains that it is their global grasp of the *Welt* that leaves them free to isolate a sensory-motor segment that then responds to a purely local stimulus.

There might be times when one is there as a whole, all one's faculties engaged and integrated with one another, one's presence wholly lined up with one's future goals and one's past experiences. The experience is paradigmatic for thinkers such as Heidegger and Merleau-Ponty, but it is rare. When one learns how to type or swim the butterfly correctly or run a punch-press, these behaviors become closed segments, virtual automatisms, and very little of oneself is engaged in them. Merleau-Ponty invokes Saint-Exupéry, who speaks of rare moments when all one's sensibility, all one's faculties are awakened and concentrated on the task. It makes night flying an incomparably intense and incomparably personal experience. Certain kinds of tasks, certain dangers demand this kind of total presence.

But there is also a demand to be there as a whole that is formulated, or is latent, in society. Society demands that a woman act like the mother she is, not just go to a motel for the night with some pickup and forget about her children at home. Society demands that a twenty-six-year-old male dress and act and talk like a man, and not dress up like a teenage girl one day and try out for the cheerleader squad.

Language works the unification, the integration by which one stands there as a whole. To be in society is to speak, that is, to respond to others. One not only has to respond to their greetings and their questions, but one has to answer for what one says or has said. The others always face you as the one present here and now who has to answer for things said five minutes ago and yesterday and last year. "But you said . . . But you promised . . ." To speak, to say "I," is not simply to designate oneself as the one now making this utterance; it is to reiterate the same term and attribute to it again utterances and deeds predicated of it before. If one has changed, one has to reinstate what one was as the motive for what one has now become. "Yes I promised to go with you this year, but out of my more long-term commitment to my parents, I am staying home to care for them . . ."

To be there as a whole seems to be an ethical demand. A demand to be responsible, to answer for what one sees and says and does. Irresponsibility and amorality or immorality are segmenting the flow of one's life, letting things said or done pass without being explained or accounted for, letting bygones be bygones. Something happened, a circuit formed briefly between parts of me, the pistol rose in my hand and fired, the Arab fell. I must integrate this even into the total diagram of my existence: I am a murderer, I shall be a murderer for forty years in prison until I die, a reformed and repentant murderer but a murderer.

One makes oneself a whole by continually answering for what was seen through one's eyes, said by one's mouth, done with one's hands. To be a member of society is to exist and act under accusation. The temptation to not answer for something that was seen or said or done through one's organism yesterday, to attribute it to another psychic agency, to begin to break up into discontinuous psychic sequences is the very formula for antisocial existence. The schizophrenic is a sociopath. Multiple personality disorder is the ultimate psychosis psychiatry has to deal with, and society sees the sociopath not so much in violence—violence can be, as in policemen or professional boxers, perfectly socialized—but rather in someone who leads a double or triple life.

At the same time that the social field seems to be the locus of a continual demand that each constitute himself as a whole and stand there as a whole, it seems to be locus of continual dismemberment. Marx eloquently analyzed the industrial capitalist society that purchases men as hands without decision-capacity, as labor force without understanding, as calculative faculties without imagination, as ambition without heart, as ordering faculties without whim or caprice. The soldier is detached from his understanding and decision; the assembly-line worker from his imagination; the capitalist himself from his fancy and his tastes. For industry, people are hair that gums up, that looses its luster, its bounce, that gets gray, that falls out; people are teeth that get yellow, brown with smoking or tobacco chewing, that accumulate plaque and acids and foul odors; people are feet whose arches fall, which develop odors, whose toes develop fungus between them; people are stomachs that get acidic, that develop cramps, that bloat after Thanksgiving and Christmas meals, that develop gas that awakens the body at night. To pay for shampoo and jeans, foot powder and work shoes, toothpaste and beer, antacids and hamburgers, the workers sell their manpower, their skilled hands or just the brute force of their arms and back, their 20-20 vision, their brainpower, or their imagination.

Modern society is a society of alienation, not only alienating man from the instruments and resources of his labor and from the fruits of his labor, but also alienating him from his own body parts, forcing him to sell his arms, his back, his brain, his imagination to another. The notion of alienation invokes the notion of the integral man who would belong to himself, possess his own arms and legs, have a brain of his own and have his own imagination and fancy and will.

This notion of the integral man is problematic; he is found neither in feudal society, where the serf belonged to the lord, nor in savage society, where the sense of the individual distinct from the clan cannot be found. What is troubling is that this notion seems to be a theme precisely of capitalism. Bourgeois society, by drowning the most heavenly ecstasies of religious fervor, chivalrous

enthusiasm, and Philistine sentimentalism in the icy water of egotistical calculation, by pitilessly tearing asunder the motley feudal ties that bound man to his
"natural superiors" and leaving remaining no other nexus between man and
man than naked self-interest, has made the notions of possession, appropriation, acquisition coextensive with the person. To exist as a self is to maintain all
one's properties and attributes. Sacrifice, abnegations, sumptuary expenditures,
generosities are definitively consigned to the feudal past.

Yet Marx will paradoxically show that the more the capitalist is driven by
self-interest the more he dismembers himself, the more he drowns his heart
and his fancy in the icy waters of egoistic calculation, the more he himself is
possessed by his possessions. Since he cannot possess himself as lord of production without acquiring possession of the resources and the instruments of
production, he trades the family home for industrial property, he invests the
family reputation in a commercial logo, he invests all his brainpower in the factory, he capitalizes on his virility to acquire the kind of wife that will be a cor-
porate asset, he sells himself as surely as do the laborers. The theme of prostitution since Marx dominates all the critique of industrial capitalism, the
consumer society, contemporary culture, the media, the ideologies, sexuality.

Prostitution is conceptualized as "selling oneself." Instead of maintaining
oneself whole and wholly there, one sells one's kisses and caresses, one sells
one's labor power, one's skills, one's talents, one's intellect, one's imagination.
At a certain point it is oneself that one has sold with these separable faculties,
body parts, or segments of time. There is no longer any oneself involved in the
irrigations and discharges in one's genitals; these paid orgasms are nowise a part
of one's own erotic existence. Or rather there is a self, but it is another: the
client does not just want wet meat to masturbate against, he wants a Brazilian
mulatta, a Parisian tart, and it is these selves that organize the kisses, the caresses, lubrications, and discharges and materialize them. The young law
school graduate gives over his intelligence, his imagination, his thespian skills,
his cordiality to the company, and there forms a self that answers for the things
seen, said, and done for the company. Another self that may form, after hours,
on weekends, finds itself more and more absorbed into the self that was sold to
the company.

I wonder if the notion of prostitution, in the pens of philosophers, is not
like their notion of God. These terms in fact have different meanings for lib-
ertines and for mystics, who have experience of these things, and for philosophers, who do not.

If one buys a prostitute it is a strange purchase, buying a whole individual for an hour or a night. One wouldn't call it buying if you paid a couple of
thousand dollars to the car dealer and he gave you a Chevrolet for an hour and

told you you could play with all the knobs and dials but could not turn on the ignition and drive off. The real prostitutes, those who have the talent for it, are rather those who rent parts of their bodies, segments of their time, segments of their rap, at exorbitant prices. In fact one can hardly call it prices. A prostitute is not someone one buys; it is someone one throws one's money away on. To get hooked on a prostitute is to throw one's money away, and throw away one's good sense, one's honor, one's family, one's reputation, one's self-esteem. It is in this dispossession, this expropriation that increasingly devours everything that one acquires something like a unitary sense of oneself—romantic, accursed one, fool. The prostitute for her or his part is not a cynic who doles out her or his parts and substance in portions meant to represent the whole self. It is, it has always been after all very rare that prostitutes, with all the money that passes through their hands, end up chairpersons of the boards of directors of corporations; they typically lose their heads as often as their clients, over some undivorceable doctor or senator or some penniless and tubercular student or some faithless dandy or some brute continually in and out of jail.

Marx educated us to see real society under the juridic representation of it, to see the social field, a field where one is dismembered, alienated, sold, under the juridic representation of it as a multiplicity of persons who stand as wholes and answer for all that is seen, said, and done in their psychophysiological organisms. But if some modicum of real experience with prostitutes makes the concept of being sold problematic, and a survey of history makes the concept of alienation appear dependent on the utopian and indeed capitalist notion of integral man, then we can come to see, without these culpabilizing notions, the social field as made of couplings of body parts.

One arrives at a city and one sees a lot of tall buildings, which are labelled bank, corporation office, department store, post office, train station, hotel, and one sees a lot of people moving about and doing a lot of things that one recognizes—driving cabs, shopping, waiting on tables, shampooing and cutting hair, drilling teeth, etc. This itemizing of the contents of the city, however far it is pursued, does not give one a sense of the social fabric, the distinctive reality of the human association—I mean, what one is talking about when after a short or long stay in Paris one uses the term *the Parisians*... When one talks about "the New Yorkers" or "the Bostonians," "the Neapolitans" and "the Milanese."

A Brooklyn, Cairo, or Tokyo cabby all have their hand on the wheel and their feet on the accelerator and brake pedals and drive you to the destination you say, but as you sit there you notice the arm out the open window ready to make the fuck-you sign at any irate non-cabby, or playing, like the hand of a stoned drummer, on the horn, or clad in white gloves. It's noticing these things that is noticing how the people concretely connect in this society. When you've been away for awhile, you step from the airport and settle into the cab, and you grin to yourself: white gloves—this is Japan. Just arrived the night before in Singapore, I stepped out of my hotel early in the morning and saw a dribbling of grade school kids, sallow-faced and short-panted, issuing out of air-conditioned high rises and heading for the waiting air-conditioned taxis that would deliver them to their schools full of computers. As they trotted across the yard to the waiting taxis, each of these beady-eyed kids held up alongside of his face a small battery-operated fan. Singapore . . .

One sees couplings of body parts, and couplings of body parts with parts of things. You really don't relate to the cabby as a whole person, nor he to you; however much a gentlemen he is, to the point of speaking gently and carrying your bags to your door when he senses you are in some personal distress, most of your life and preoccupations are not going to be involved. You don't relate to the desk clerk at the hotel as a whole person, nor to the waitress, nor to the bartender, the barber, nor the massage girl that night. Recently there is a generalized recognition that talk of relating to the person as such is a confused extension of juridic discourse, and people are insisting you have to relate to the cabby, the desk clerk, the bartender as a man—or more often that you have to relate to the waitress, the hotel manager, the massage girl as a woman. But to envision someone as a man, or as a woman, rather than as a cabby, a desk clerk, a waitron, is to envision them as abstract wholes, wholes that can somehow be wholes even when one does not specify the couplings of their body parts with the steering wheels of cars, computers, trays of dishes, or massage oil. Just as the place where one envisages someone as a person is the witness stand of a court of law, so the place where one envisages someone as a man, or as a woman, is the darkness of singles bars.

It is in noticing those white gloves, or that hand outside the open window with the ready fuck-you sign, that one begins to get a concrete sense of a Japanese, or a Brooklyn cabby, and a concrete sense of the Japanese, and the New Yorkers. It's when you have got down that serious and sure movement of the hand that lifts the wine glass into which the waiter has poured an inch, that pouting of the lips and shrugging of the shoulders, and when you without thinking pick up the fork and knife to peel the banana or the orange, that you are not only getting a sense of the French, but are becoming one of them yourself.

One of the most endearing gestures of the Cariocas is the thumbs-up. They do it all the time. A taxi driver, when you give him the fare; a shoeshine boy when you pick up for him something he dropped; the maid when you hold the elevator door for her; the clerk at the post office when you bring the package you want registered to the right window, a girl on the beach whose eyes yours cross when both of you have seen a fine leap made by a surfer. We would say "thank you," or, "fine," in such circumstances, but how empty and hollow these expressions usually are! We so often say those words to take a distance from someone. The Carioca flip of the thumb is unequivocally, physically affirmative! It is customarily accompanied with a wink of the eye.

In the highlands of Papua New Guinea and Irian Jaya, it's the handshake. The Europeans shake hands all the time, and their handshake is very conventionalized; the American handshake, not a routine gesture when meeting and when parting, is much more expressive. But the handshake among the Papuans is altogether distinctive, and all the stereotypes you have ever read about them—headhunters, Stone Age men in the twentieth century, primitives, etc.—is completely shaken out of your head when you first experience the handshake. This great naked and greased warrior offers you his hand, and passes it over yours with the most indescribably, astonishingly silken caress. When you see them greeting one another that way, it gives you an insight into the way they relate to one another that blows your mind. If, before you went, you outfitted yourself from L.L. Bean or Safari in the local garb, and, taking a walk in the bush, you come upon a warrior with boar's tusks in his nostrils and holding spears, he offers you this delicate and sensual silken handshake, and at the same time passes his other hand around your waist with the same silken touch, and gently strokes your penis sheath . . .

It is not that these small moves are expressive, that the whole condenses in them, like one of Cézanne's apples where the daubs of paint had to contain not only the color, the contour, but also the pulp, the juice, the savor, and the smell of the inexhaustible reality. Rio de Janeiro is not a more affirmative society, structure, multitude than New York or Calcutta, cities equally praised for their vitality; it is just that the Cariocas make this thumbs-up gesture that is full unto itself, fills up the space. What is so satisfying about it is that the cabby fills up the space between you with his gesture which terminates your relationship; there is closure. The doctor peels off the dressings, peers at your sutures, and his hand by itself gives you the thumbs-up. The knife at the throat as the watch and wallet are being lifted is not expressive of something big and universal like Justice, the universal distributive law that must reign throughout society in order to be real anywhere; the knife at the throat and the watch and wallet that are being lifted is a little choreographed number complete and perfect in itself, expressive of nothing further, terminating any relations there were or shall be between you. Since they have the knife you are not going to run after them yelling for the cops. They will vanish. Luis Buñuel liked to mock the notion of Christian charity, where an individual makes an isolated gesture, momentarily relieving the misery of another individual, while the whole system, intact, perpetuates itself. This act is of the same kind; the white man will be as laden with his ill-gotten gain as before, the street kids of Rio will be as desperate as before. If it does not express a generalized state of such acts of individual initiative. Kant would demand that we apply the test of universalizability to their initiative that morning, and the critique of practical reason would demonstrate that this act is perfectly self-defeating; in the measure that street gangs hold knives to the throats of rich tourists to that exact proportion they cease to come at all. The next time they want some sun and sand they will go to Kuwait, where if the rich are abused George Bush will have a half million combat troops on the beach in a month.

But the rightness of the coupling is generally evident in the coupling itself. White gloves on the hands of the cabby, who is after all going to charge you $135 to drive you into Tokyo from the airport, seems right. No conceivable objection to the thumbs-up sign from the cabby in Rio de Janeiro occurs to you, and it indicates to you the right way to connect with Cariocas. It makes sense, it helps you make sense of the social field. How right it seems that the handshake among fearless warriors be without defenses, not conventionalized, that it be silken and sensual. Rightness, as a notion of practical reason, and intelligibility, as a notion of pure or theoretical reason, seem indeed inseparable. When you see the rightness of a coupling of body parts, in this society, such as such a handshake, or in human association universally, such as the throat of the rich fuck and the knife, you have a unit that makes sense, that eminently makes sense, that you use to make sense of other things.

One could be puzzled by the extreme divergence between the experience of thinking or writing and the way writers are spoken of, the ways they end up speaking of themselves. Thinkers end up having ideas. They are praised for, and questioned about books or articles they wrote twenty years earlier. One supposes they have a system of their own in which all their thoughts fit in and intermesh with one another and form a continuous construction or organic growth. Like Schopenhauer, who, in the Preface to his *World as Will and Representation* explained that all the concepts in his book form a system such that the meaning of each presupposes the meaning of all the others, and that therefore the reader will not understand the first concept in the book until he has come to the last one, and so will have to read the whole book twice. The notion of the life of the mind being a whole, a seamless fabric, is shored up with the notion of an author, a notion that is primarily juridic, depending for its concreteness on the notion of intellectual property, copyrights, royalties., etc.

All that contrasts violently with the experience of thinking and writing, the experience of being thoughtful. A living mind is not a field integrated by an overall system, but a segmented worm, where pieces break off and wriggle off on their own. Thought begins when one comes upon something, some event, apparition, predicament that singularly engages one's own powers. Typically it is not some insight that one has, that one then works on, but rather an angle, a peculiar way to see something bizarre about that event, apparition, predicament, or just a hunch that one could think up, composing something singular on it. One thinks, one composes, one writes, indistinguishably. Some days in a fever, other days one looks over what one has written like so much straw. One day a sentence that seemed stable looks awkward, skewed, and one works on it, and one ends up with a string of a new, vibrant, and luminous sentences. It is so often said that writing, thinking, is a craft, but one cannot work on one's sentences like a carpenter continually planing and sanding a piece of furniture until it is perfect. After looking at it too much it loses all relief. Thoughts too much thought no longer think anything, Merleau-Ponty wrote, they can think only as tacking threads in the unknown. One puts the whole essay aside for a few days, a few months, then takes it out, rewrites whole chunks of it, throws it all away, or finds it unimprovable. If so, it is finished, or anyhow ended. A month or six months later one might read it to a conference, but the thinking is all over then, what one is now doing is trying to read it with the right eloquence, performing it.

What one then finds is that it is not a thought one has, but rather one of which one has expropriated oneself. You wanted to write about the enigma of Inca architecture, all the days, weeks, months that you were working on this piece you were thinking about it, worrying it, marvelling over it, absorbed and mesmerized by it. You wrote the essay, and one day realized it was as perfect as you could ever make it. Now you can no longer think of the enigma of Inca architecture. If someone asks you what you meant when you said this or that in your essay, you have to ask—where? what page? and then go back, and, just like him, try to figure out what the words themselves say. You do not have in reserve something more, better, clearer, than what you were able to say then. You realize that for someone else your essay might be a path into the enigma, the wonder, of Inca architecture; it can no longer be that for you.

Once, in New Guinea, I had gotten caught up in an essay I was writing, spent every day working on it for more than a month, single-mindedly, fascinated, exhilarated. I had gone over it many times, recasting sections of it, crafting every sentence. It was a month spent in steadily growing clarity; I felt more and more illuminated and found my essay more and more limpid. Then, I lost it. When I realized it was really gone, I thought, well, before I start occupying my mind with anything else I will rewrite it, right away. I had gone over every section and every sentence of the essay so often I thought I must have pretty much memorized the whole thing by now. So I immediately set out in the days to follow to recreate the essay. In fact it turned out to be a different essay, not only different in the composition but in the turns the thought took and the place it ended up at. The essay was lost definitively. I had thought that it was like nothing I had ever written, so completely it had possessed me for a month, and then found that by writing it I had dispossessed myself of it completely.

But, one will object, isn't it true that everything one thinks through, everything one works on until one finds the composition that holds together leaves traces in one? Hypnosis convinced Freud very early that nothing is ever lost from the river of experience. That is true; thinking through an insight and working on it until it reaches its own proper form, its own coherence and co-hesion, is like working on a dance number or the butterfly stroke until all the parts and members of one's body come together in doing it; one then contracts a schema, which is, Merleau-Ponty explained, both a power to reenact it and an indefinite power to renew, to vary it. The only thing is that this schema that then gets implanted in one's cerebral circuitry is the worst obstacle there is to thought. As soon as one wants to think, or write an essay, it emerges, like a par-adigm that commands normal science according to Thomas Kuhn. From then on one is no longer only preoccupied with trying to keep alert for the peculiar angle, the insight, the enigma lurking there that one's own brain is singularly wired for, but one has to fight off the schema, the paradigm that slides over it from the last problem, event, apparition one thought and wrote about. One finds more and more that the problem, the toil, the struggle to think is to keep one's mind vacant, ignorant, abashed, disconcerted, blown away by some event, apparition, predicament.

Becoming a thinker or becoming a writer—already misleading expres-sions—let us say being thoughtful, trying to write with integrity and sincer-ity—are not striving to become whole; are not the Nietzschean most spiritual forms of the will to power, those that will one to possess the universe with one's own mind. They are the continual experience of emptying oneself out, be-coming more and more impoverished, striving to find ignorance and perplex-ity, with no guarantees whatever that one will. Trafficking in thoughts is so like trafficking with prostitutes, a matter of throwing good money after bad, losing one's self-esteem, one's good sense, being the first to jeer at one's reputation, never knowing if one is a romantic or a fool, addicted to this dispossession, this expropriation.

This strange path the life of thought finds itself taking can illuminate the life of action. How rare it is that one manages to do good deeds, brave deeds! I think the further one goes the more one is struck by how hard it really is. Some-times people seem to have found the formula early in life and they apply it with equanimity until they die: they are genial, affable, helpful. Others find it is good sense: before any problem, their own or those of others, they apply good sense, appraise the issue, survey the alternatives, select the best one, do not worry over it if, as often happens, the best available decision did not work. I think that if we look about us, the majority of people fall into those categories—the kind ones and the sensible ones. The majority of people are vaguely repugnant: Trivializing, levelling, shallow, self-justifying. If we would stop, one afternoon, and ask when last we managed to do a good deed, a brave deed, probably we would have to search back over months, maybe over years. Most of the things we do, routinely, that the people around us find praiseworthy and make them think of us as a good man or a good woman are behavioral patterns that are there, are known, that the situation itself calls for, that we do more or less automatically and which in fact it would be harder for us not to do. We stay overtime so that a colleague can take off early to pick someone up at the airport, visit a friend in the hospital, give blood for a neighbor who was in a car accident, lend the kid who cuts our lawn $500 for bail for his buddy who got busted for dope. A good deed, a brave deed is something else, and when we manage it we know it. Maybe nothing spectacular, but it is like a piece of thinking that is really our own, something that engages our own powers, that we really devote ourselves to, that we somehow manage to work on and compose until it is right, coherent and consistent, closed in itself. When we ourselves are the recipients of such good deeds, brave deeds, we know it, and remember them always. I was eighteen, flunking out of college, in a fucked-up relationship with a woman, parents declaring that this was it, when the semester was over you go get yourself a job and pay rent, and he came along and said a few things or maybe said nothing but made it clear he believed in me and made me believe in myself and loaned me the money to go to the conservatory and study dance . . .

We really weren't friends, we just used to go to the same health club, and have a plate of fruit together after, sometimes, and I don't know how it started, I started telling her about my marriage and my herpes and the depression I'd been in for months and all the doctors I'd gone to, and then it got worse and went on and on and she just kept with me, sometimes she'd come over and spend the whole night with me, she'd cancel dinner dates, even birthdays and anniversaries . . .

These things leave you empty when you do them. You happened to be there at the right time, somehow said the right thing to the kid, were able to pass him on the money for the tuition in such a way that he would take it. Well, it's something out now, it needed to be done with a lot of tact and secrecy to be done right now, and any lifting of that veil of secrecy would spoil it now. Nietzsche understood that so profoundly, and once he wrote that there are good deeds that one does that one better grab a stick and give a sound thrashing to any bystander who happened to see them, to muddle his memory. Well, prostitutes understand that. There are some, Nietzsche went on, who know how to grab a stick and muddle their own memory . . . Or whack it with that stick, break off a segment that will wriggle off by itself. You can't anchor its diagram in yourself, make it a paradigm, and from then on be on the lookout for cases when you can recycle it. What is a friend for, we say, if not to help? Yet it really is very hard to really help, and many of us have been able to help a friend maybe once in a lifetime, and we cherish that time as one of the best things about having lived. The most abominable people in literature are people who know the formula, who do nothing but help, who make naive virgins into good wives and mothers, who make children decent contributors to society. I have a good friend who, after drifting a bit after graduating, started to work in state institutions for the retarded. A fine, positive, generous work when everyone else in his generation went off to exploit the market and see how far how fast they could get up on the pile. He quit after a few years, and told me you have to. It does weird things to the soul, he said, to be the sugar daddy, the Santa Claus, the Jesus Christ to a group of people. He told me of those who didn't quit, the Big Nurse ones, every last one of them. Being there when the situation needed you, some third eye finding the right thing to do somehow, that, like coming up with an idea when thinking, sticks to the bones like a paradigm, and then the hard thing is to be ignorant and concerned and afraid the next time. Out of that ignorance and concern and fear alone the good deed, the brave deed could come. One might well have to learn wickedness before one could do a good deed again.

Aristotle put courage first in the list of the virtues; it is not only the first in the list but the transcendental virtue, the virtue that makes all other possible. No one can be wise or just or magnanimous or even witty in conversation without bravery. Aristotle, like Socrates, thereby composed an essentially military ethics, arguing that there is no courage when one confronts death by drowning or by disease but only in battle, for in battle one goes to face death of one's own will. Aristotle, like Socrates, went on to argue that it is philosophers who are truly and properly courageous, because their knowledge of the eternity of ideas makes them not fear death and be totally fearless, while soldiers do not fear death because they fear something more—dishonor or the massacre of their family and kinsmen. Aristotle, however, unlike Socrates, did not set out to personally prove this when the time came, saying that he did not want Athens to sin twice against philosophy.

Yet really the purest courage is the courage to deal with death from disease or drowning or industrial accidents, death without glory, death without the admiration of disciples, death that does not leave the will intact and resolute, death whose sting the intellect that thinks of eternity cannot remove. Perhaps for us the first example of a good deed, a brave deed, that comes to our minds is the neighbor who goes each day to be with the young man who has to die of AIDS.

To have managed a good deed, a brave deed is a little like that kind of courage: one is left the next day emptied, one's own good deed more a burden than a glory, the glory of it surely a burden, not left with strengthened powers but with harnessed powers, not knowing if new powers, the right powers, will be there when the time comes.

PART THREE

# Exteriority, Life in the World

# CHAPTER 11

# Envisioning the Other

## LACAN AND MERLEAU-PONTY ON INTERSUBJECTIVITY

### HELEN A. FIELDING

After having read the final work of his contemporary, Jacques Lacan re-
sponded to Merleau-Ponty's *The Visible and the Invisible*[1] in four seminars published under the title, "Of the Gaze As Objet Petit a."[2] In these seminars, Lacan
cites several fruitful points of departure. He concludes, however, that while
there are a "few whiffs of the unconscious to be detected in his notes [which]
might have led him to pass" into psychoanalysis, Merleau-Ponty's phenomenology is ultimately dependent upon a Cartesian ego and an abstract eye, and
is, accordingly, incompatible with psychoanalysis (Lacan 1981, 119). While
Merleau-Ponty does not take up specifically the processes of signfication in the
unconscious, Lacan's assessment of the incompatibility of Merleau-Ponty's
work with his own may have more to do with his *méconnaissance* of the
philosopher or perhaps with his own need for recognition and resistance to citing (sighting) his influences.[3] However, as Lacan himself initially observed,
there are indeed points where their work intersects. Crucial to this intersection
is their mutual emphasis on the social. Indeed, it is this concern with the social, and not the solipsistic Cartesian cogito, where they most closely come together and most greatly diverge.

Ironically, while Merleau-Ponty's theory of perception constitutes the
focus for Lacan's critique, we can also turn to this theme in order to explore

Lacan's psychoanalytic account; ultimately, this account excludes the possibility of intersubjective relations. Lacan's critique of Merleau-Ponty's intuition of vision is a caricature; he also criticizes Merleau-Ponty for not providing an adequate explanation of the unconscious, one that would account for signification and a language of desire. However, if we investigate Lacan's critique from the perspective of Merleau-Ponty's phenomenology, it becomes apparent that Lacan's own psychoanalytic perspective does not account for intersubjective and intercorporeal relations that go beyond the intrapsychic. Given the importance Lacan's work has assumed for theories of subjectivity, particularly for feminist theory, such an account is vital if psychoanalysis is to have anything to offer in terms of theorizing both change and community. While Lacan does offer a theory of the social that he defines within the category of the symbolic order, in many ways it is static or explanatory, and thus does not allow for change. In this chapter I would like to think through the connection between Lacanian psychoanalysis and Merleau-Ponty's phenomenology for explanations of subjectivity that aspire to be more than merely descriptive.[4]

Clearly, vision is important to both theorists in terms of exploring our relations with others. What distinguishes the two approaches, however, is that while Lacan relies on vision, for Merleau-Ponty, vision is taken up as significant through its intertwining with motility and touch—an intertwining that grounds us in the lived world. Accordingly, in Lacan's account, our vision does not leave us open to new vistas, to new experiences; rather, our sight only leads us to alienation and *méconnaissance*.[5] It is in "The Mirror Stage" that Lacan outlines how the infant first comes into a sense of self but only through an alienation of her corporeal body.[6] In his account, the infant experiences, through viewing her own image in the mirror, an initial awareness of her body as it is seen by others. This image provides a projection of unity upon her disordered perceptions. At the same time, the infant observes in the mirror an image of her body as elsewhere from her interoceptive or felt self. This leads her to experience, according to Lacan, a fundamental schism between the outer body, which provides the illusion of unity, and the lived self, which is, for the child in her immature state, necessarily fragmented. That is, the mirror image is an anticipatory projection of future capacities. After the mirror stage, the child will experience alienation in that she will now be aware of her outer, corporeally visible, and apparently unified self, which is not the self she lives. The child is caught up by the spatial image of this fictitious identity that she will now identify as her self. Even more alienating is that others will relate to this external image, drawing the child even more surely away from her lived experience.[7] With this introduction to otherness, the child's future intersubjective relations will be marked or re-marked by the psychic processes, such as castration anxiety and the emergence of desire, that are etched upon her and through her during the pre-oedipal and oedipal stages of her life; notably, these psychic processes that generate the symbolic rely heavily upon vision.

In his writings on the eye and the gaze, Lacan returns over and over again to Freud's case history of "The Wolf Man."[8] It seems that this case history holds Lacan's attention because the analysis draws us back each time to the intertwining of signification and the eye. The signification itself centers around the analysand's memory of being witness to the primal scene as a young boy, that is, his parents engaged in coitus. Significantly, as we shall see, the act is described by Freud as "coitus *a tergo* [from behind]" (Freud 1979, 269). While Freud at first assumes that this event indeed took place, he later concludes that the primal scene is not actually witnessed by the young child but is produced by psychic affects. The veracity of the event is not important but the existence of the event in the unconscious, in the symbolic, is important (Freud 1979, 293).[9] However, this original signification is derived through a connection to actual events.

In this particular case, Freud assumed that the child, after having witnessed white dogs copulating, projected this act upon his parents whom he did see in their white bedclothes but did not see engaged in the act. In observing the dogs copulating, the boy concludes that his "Nanya's" warnings of castration, if he were to continue to masturbate, were indeed true as copulation required the "passivity" of a vagina, which could only be a castrated penis. In Freud's interpretation, this was the boy's discovery of the biological significance of the masculine and feminine, and accordingly active and passive sexuality. As the boy's own sexual aim was passive, he was faced with the paradox that he would have to lose his pleasure-giving organ in order to take the passive position. In repressing this psychic dilemma, his desire for his father is turned into a phobia. Thus, from the drama enacted in the "other" scene, in the unconscious, the boy derived his phobia of the wolf standing on its hind legs, the wolf symbolizing for him his father who took the active position in the drama. Correspondingly, he falls in love with women he first sees engaged in such activities as washing floors which require the position his mother was to have taken. Indeed, one of his lovers, a peasant woman, was even named Matrona. According to Freud, the primal scene as a psychic event, removed from considerations of actual time and space, repeatedly affects the Wolf Man's sexual relations.

Lacan returns to Freud's case study in order to show that intersubjective relations can only be understood in terms of an analysis of the "symbolic value of the different moments of the drama."[10] Intersubjective relations cannot be considered outside both the symbolic and the imaginary. The Wolf Man's case history shows, for Lacan, that "it is in relation to the real that the level of phantasy functions. The real supports the phantasy, the phantasy protects the real" (Lacan 1981, 41).

An analysis of the symbolic in the analysand's discourse is the only way the analyst can make the subject aware of her unconscious desires. And this is all the Lacanian analyst can hope to accomplish. In order to understand how the symbolic choreographs our relations with others we are once again directed, apparently, to sight, or more specifically, to the gaze. While it seems that Lacan's gaze (*le regard*) was heavily influenced by Sartre's look (*le regard*), there are differences. For Lacan, it is not an actual gaze or the gaze of an other that brings me to shame, but rather the gaze that is fixed as the other in my unconscious. That is, the gaze becomes the object itself that is bound up in the splitting that the subject initially experiences during the mirror stage and which recurs throughout the subject's life. As the "privileged object" (*the objet a*), the gaze emerges "from some primal separation, from some self-mutilation induced by the very approach of the real" (Lacan 1981, 83).[11]

Significantly, the other of the gaze is not an other body subject but rather the other as my own projected intrapsychic experience. Lacan employs an example from *Being and Nothingness* in order to illustrate this point. In Sartre's story, the subject, who is looking at others through a keyhole, is suddenly interrupted by the gaze of an other. It is not the identity of this other that matters. Indeed, the subject does not even see the other's gaze but rather senses it in the sound of approaching footsteps.[12] He[13] is "literally caught in the act, which is not an act, that is, in its role as voyeur or support of desire."[14] Under this gaze the subject experiences the central lack, which is the Lacanian understanding of castration.[15] It is in the vortex of this void, of this lack, that the desire to sustain desire and to always defer satisfaction is found through sustaining absence. Although for Sartre, the look can entail a reversibility between observer and observed, for Lacan, it is being gazed at by the internalized other that is always primary (Grosz 1990, 78–79). The gaze "is not a seen gaze, but a gaze imagined by me in the field of the [o]ther" (Lacan 1981, 84). Thus, the gaze in its relation to castration is, for Lacan, fundamental to all desire (Lacan 1981, 118). And the primal scene, as is, for example, recounted in the "Wolf Man," is the setting where castration anxiety begins.

> In the Wolf Man's case history, the primal scene is followed by a recurring dream: I dreamt that it was night and that I was lying in my bed. . . . Suddenly the window opened of its own accord, and I was terrified to see that some white wolves were sitting on the big walnut tree in front of the window. There were six or seven of them. The wolves were quite white, and looked more like foxes or sheep-dogs, for they had big tails like foxes and they had their ears

pricked like dogs when they pay attention to something. In great
terror, evidently of being eaten up the wolves, I screamed and woke
up. (Freud 1979, 259)

In Freud's analysis of this dream we encounter the gaze as reversal. This dream
comes from the analysand's own psychic observance of the primal scene. In accordance with Freud's dream theory, the dream is structured so as to disguise
its origins. Thus, the gaze is reversed. In the dream the boy is watched. The
wolves have big tails or penises and are white, which is the color of his parents'
bedclothes. The child also connects this dream to a fairy tale he was often told
in which a wolf has its tail pulled off and so is, in effect, castrated.

I have recounted these threads of the analysis in order to emphasize not
only the importance and significatory implications of the primal scene to the
emergence of desire in the subject, but also how Lacan links the gaze to castration anxiety. In Lacan's account, the gaze has the power to arrest movement,
to kill life. After recognition of the gaze, "at the moment [that] the subject
stops, suspending his gesture, he is mortified." The reversed gaze in its connection to castration anxiety can only be "maleficent," the "evil eye" (Lacan
1981, 118). Thus, the gaze is linked through the threat of castration to desire;[16]
and it is through this gaze that all of our adult sexual relations are filtered.[17]

What is at stake, then, for Lacan, is the eye and its relation to knowledge.
According to Lacan, that which we see and represent geometrically[18] refers more
to flat optics or mapped-out space than to what he calls sight. He distinguishes
between what the eye takes in according to the laws of physics and sight, which
must incorporate the symbolic in the form of the gaze (Lacan 1981, 86). The
gaze cannot be represented through perspectival optics. To illustrate this point
in his seminar, Lacan refers to a replication of the Hans Holbein painting, *The
Ambassadors*. This painting is a richly detailed representation of two figures,
"frozen, stiffened in their showy adornments" (Lacan 1981, 88), surrounded by
objects symbolic of the sciences and arts. What is remarkable about this picture
is a ghostly object that seems "to be flying through the air." If the viewer stands
at a certain angle, this mysterious figure shows itself to be a skull or the death's
head and, as an elongated form, it is, for Lacan, "obviously" phallic. With this
picture Lacan illustrates the split between the conscious and the unconscious,
geometral optics and the gaze.[19] That is, in this anamorphic representation one
can never see both illustrations at the same time. It is only when one stands to
the side that the death's head takes shape as the "imaged embodiment of . . . castration," of "the subject as annihilated" (Lacan 1981, 89, 88).

This split between geometral optics and the gaze is what Lacan cannot
identify in Merleau-Ponty's account of perception. Lacan does concede that in

*The Visible and the Invisible* Merleau-Ponty begins to move beyond that which we can see geometrically by contemplating that which is not directly visible but intertwines with sight (Lacan 1981, 93). But Lacan ultimately chooses to understand Merleau-Ponty's work as dealing with the visible and the invisible in relation to geometral optics as well as phenomenological intentionality. While he acknowledges Merleau-Ponty's critiques of rationalist optics and discussions of lived perception, phenomenological vision does not help to expose the distinction between "an itself" and the mimetic surface activity behind which it lies.[20] For Lacan, the split between an itself and a mimetic camouflage illustrates the split between the eye and the gaze, that "strange contingency" that disrupts the unity of the subject (Lacan 1981, 72–73).[21] Thus, argues Lacan, Merleau-Ponty's supposedly alternative account of perception is doomed to failure. Ultimately it engages nothing other than the Cartesian eye as an "extension with its correlative of a subject."[22] According to Lacan, the phenomenologist's eye is an eye that sees according to the laws of physics and light, registers the flat optics, and transmits this message back to the subject. Such vision is not particular to the subject but is abstract and universal (Lacan 1982–83, 74). Of course, Lacan's reading of Merleau-Ponty is self-servingly simplistic.

Despite Lacan's interpretation of the philosopher's work, a challenge to the Cartesian ego is central to Merleau-Ponty's phenomenology. Significant to his critique is his rejection of the concept of the isolated thinker who can never do more than speculate upon what the other is thinking; this speculation would amount to the introjection of her own thoughts upon the other's body. Rather, Merleau-Ponty, in moving away from a solipsistic concept of the ego as well as a mind/body split, concludes that because he can see the other seeing the same things he sees, he cannot doubt that we share the same world. When he looks at a landscape and speaks about it with someone else, he observes that, "through the concordant operation of his body and my own, what I see passes into him, this individual green of the meadow under my eyes invades his vision without quitting my own, I recognize in my green his green" (Merleau-Ponty 1968, 142). Through her relations with the other the subject is brought out of herself and into the world. And her relations with the other are played out not only in her conscious interactions but also throughout her body and through the other's body in "an anonymous visibility [that] inhabits both" subjects (Merleau-Ponty 1968, 142). According to Merleau-Ponty, because we are embodied, because we live in and encounter the same world, the primacy of the ego can be dismissed and the problem of solipsism is not a problem. This does not mean, however, that he envisions a unified and transparent subject. Like Lacan, Merleau-Ponty asserts that the subject experiences disunity, but he intuits this disunity as a bodily experience rather than an intrapsychic one. As he explains, otherness exists within us. When I touch one hand with the other hand, my two hands do not share the same tactile experience. But this does not mean that these tactile expressions are not connected. Indeed, they are not connected in one sole consciousness that produces a juxtaposition between worlds, rather, each touch "is bound in such a way as to make up with them the experience of one sole body before one sole world, through a possibility for reversion, reconversion . . . transfer, and reversal . . ." (Merleau-Ponty 1968, 142). There is no juxtaposition of sensations but rather a surrounding, a "levying" off from, an "interweaving," a fitting together of "sensibilities." Similarly, our activities, our moods, and our passions intertwine and flow into one another. Because as corporeal beings our bodies are both sensed and sentient, visible and invisible, our perceptions arise from the midst of our relations and not from the periphery as is suggested by the image of Lacan's voyeur. Merleau-Ponty thus adds another dimension to our understanding of intersubjectivity and that is the dimension of our intercorporeal relations. At this level he opens up a concept of perception that is not experienced at the conscious level but is rather defined in terms of latency, "a relation of simultaneity between the visible and the invisible"[23] that pervades our being. Lacan's critique of Merleau-Ponty's vision as one that is ultimately tied to rationalist optics only further indicates Lacan's own gaps in conceptualizing an embodied subject. Vision is not just visual signification but is also bodily experience intrinsically tied to touch and to motility. Indeed, we only understand what we see as subjects who move in and engage with the world; the eye itself moves as the object of vision shifts. While Lacan's theories of subjectivity rely on our intersubjective relations in the formation of the intrapsychic and the imaginary ego, he does not have a developed theory of the body that would resolve this dualistic split between the intrapsychic and intersubjective. It is true that Lacan moves beyond representation of the body in terms of visual imagery as exemplified by the mirror stage to an interpretation of words as corporeal imagery and finally, to the body in terms of drives. But the body as lived in daily and often mundane experience escapes his theoretical posture. In a parallel to Cartesian thought and in conjunction with postmodern theorists, Lacan would assert that we can never know what the other is thinking; such thoughts would always be our own projections, and sight lends itself to these misconceptions. For Merleau-Ponty, however, vision helps to confirm for us that we live in the same world.

In his development of the overlapping between phenomenology and psychoanalysis, Merleau-Ponty does not develop, as does Lacan, an account of the signification processes of the unconscious. Although Merleau-Ponty, following Freud, intuits an unconscious, he does not understand signification in terms of a chain of causality.[24] In two brief discussions we can see how he comes both closer to and diverges more widely from the classical psychoanalytic account. This "hinge" of which I speak is observable in two notes in *The Visible and the Invisible* that Lacan alludes to as worthy of his praise. In the first note, Merleau-Ponty clearly acknowledge's Freud's unconscious and the play of signification that takes place in language and thought. Addressing Freud's case history, Merleau-Ponty refers to overdetermination in the Wolf Man's "dreams of an Espe whose wings are torn out" (Merleau-Ponty 1968, 241). In short, the Wolf Man dreams of a wasp, a *Wespe*, but in his analysis he alludes to an *Espe*. In cutting off the 'W,' he both symbolically castrates the word *Wespe*, as well as himself as his own initials are 'S. P.' pronounced *espe* in German. But Merleau-Ponty recounts this dream in the cryptic brevity of his note, apparently, in order to point out once again that although one's thoughts are overdetermined, these plays of signification are not in themselves thought. At the same time, because they manifest in language, these significations are expressed on the level of the cognitive and not that of the ideality of the lived body. Overdetermination is part of our being in the world. There will always be that which does not find its way into words but nevertheless pervades our being as a generality that structures our existence in the world. Indeed, the body, which correlates more closely with the Freudian preconscious, can never be made fully conscious or brought to a conscious reflective level; that can only take place through language. Merleau-Ponty, in seeking to move away from an interpretation of the body as text, uses words such as *tissue* and *fabric* in referring to our corporeal being;[25] the body as lived, as an existential site of possibility, cannot be reduced to a flat surface of representation. Significantly, it is in the body that repressions are actualized.[27]

Thus, for Merleau-Ponty, signification enters the scene in terms of a memory screen, as "'rays' of time and of the world" that can produce an overdetermination of meaning (Merleau-Ponty 1968, 240). These significations accompany the subject; they pervade her thoughts and her actions. At the same time, they pervade her thoughts as she encounters the world. There is still a possibility for rebirth and for change. And this is perhaps the most significant difference between the two thinkers. While Merleau-Ponty does acknowledge signification in our intrapsychic relations, in general he takes up the Freudian Unconscious as a "depth or horizon" to our conscious and intended existence (Olkowski 1982–83, 114). In other words, the overdetermination that is particular to the ideality of the body cannot be represented through the signification processes of language. It is, rather, an overdetermination that is a modulation or a reverberation of simultaneous but often mutually contradictory meanings that nevertheless intertwine as the subject's depth. In the subject's encountering of the world, specific meanings will become articulated or take on significance against the relief of the subject's own bodily being (Merleau-

Ponty 1968, 270). This approach allows for Merleau-Ponty's notion of the unconscious, which does not characterize it as a closed system that directs our relations. For Lacan, however, analysis is a process of catching sight of the unconscious, of hearing it speak, though the content of the unconscious cannot be changed.

Despite the differences in Merleau-Ponty's and Lacan's understanding of the unconscious, there is an intertwining of the two approaches to perception. Specifically, Lacan's gaze and Merleau-Ponty's perception are similar in that both have a sense of reversibility in terms of subject-object relations, the seer and the seen, the visible and the invisible. Indeed, it is in the relation of the visible to the invisible, the sentient to the sensed that Merleau-Ponty's vision emerges as one that takes in both more than and less than what is optically visible. This reversibility is most eloquently articulated in his discussions of painting. In Cézanne's work, Merleau-Ponty explains that the painting not only expresses the painter's own vision but Cézanne himself also becomes the "consciousness" of the landscape that speaks through him: "Essence and existence, imaginary and real, visible and invisible—a painting mixes up all our categories in laying out its oneiric universe of carnal essences, of effective likenesses, of mute meanings."[27] In Merleau-Ponty's discussions of painting Lacan finds, as he admits, that the philosopher, in his "vacillations between object and being," along with his discussions of the invisible, "moves forward here to a field different from that of perception." Lacan finds in the discussions of the "'little blues' and 'little chestnuts' . . . [an understanding of the] subtle weight of the corporeality of light that the eye of the painter tries to capture with all its eros" (Lacan 1982–83, 79–80). But the painting, which is the moment produced through the termination of the painter's brushstroke, captures the desire of the gaze as the phallic desire of castration. The eye is once again the evil eye (Lacan 1981, 114–115). Thus, for Lacan, the invisible is that which is charted through the psychic in the form of the childhood memories, fixations, and repressions that constitute desire, and castration anxiety is pivotal to these. Accordingly, his gaze, as exemplified in the Wolf Man's dream, entails a repetition of the same, an unconscious written in the pre-oedipal and oedipal dramas, and is not open to change. In contrast, for Merleau-Ponty, the invisible has a corporeal and fleshy weight that interweaves with the visible; vision entails a "continual rebirth of existence . . . a reciprocal insertion and intertwining of one in the other" (Merleau-Ponty 1968, 138).

In considering the second note from *The Visible and the Invisible* that Lacan praises, a note that deals specifically with reversibility, it begins to become more apparent that Lacan's simplistic reading of Merleau-Ponty could, in fact, be the screen for a far more sophisticated adaptation of one of Merleau-Ponty's central themes. In this note Merleau-Ponty writes of the finger of the glove which has two sides: "There is no need of a spectator who would be on each side. It suffices that from one side I see the wrong side of the glove that is applied to the right side, that I touch the one through the other . . ." (Merleau-Ponty 1968, 263). However, what is an illustration of reversibility for Merleau-Ponty is, for Lacan, the doubling up or the split, the disunity that comprises the subject. After all, it is through reversibility that the subject is not only the subject for itself, but also for the other. And this is, for Lacan, the "inside-out structure of the gaze" (Lacan 1981, 82). According to his interpretation, at the point where the two sides of the glove meet "the end of the finger of the glove is nothingness—but a nothingness one can turn over, and where then one sees things" (Merleau-Ponty 1968, 263). This point of negativity is subjectivity, which is the point where the subject sees but she cannot see herself. The subject herself is not in the picture. Because she is not in the picture she must imagine herself there, and this can only be done through her reflection in the gaze of the other (Lacan 1981, 80).[28] But the other does not actually see her; the other's gaze is formed by his own psychic experiences, which cut him off from a recognition of her. However, the gaze as mediation cannot be avoided. When the subject views herself in the mirror, because the gaze cannot be seen, it is momentarily elided. This is illustrated in Merleau-Ponty's note, Lacan claims, in "the way in which the leather envelops the fur in a winter glove— that consciousness, [is] in its illusion of 'seeing itself seeing itself'" (Lacan 1981, 82). Elision of the gaze is the illusion of the Cartesian subject who apprehends himself[29] as thought.

While, for Lacan, the significance of reversibility is that subjectivity is a negativity structured by the gaze of the other turned in on myself, for Merleau-Ponty, the zero point is not a turning inward but a turning outward. The subject only perceives herself and the world through her movement in the world: "*Wahrnehmen* [perception] and *Sich bewegen* [self-movement] are synonymous" (Merleau-Ponty 1968, 255). Thus, the subject is directed toward the world and others through her actions, which also govern her perceptions. In Merleau-Ponty's understanding of reversibility, there could never be a fusing together of sensibilities but nor is there an absolute isolation from others. Rather, our relations with others involve a reciprocity and mirroring that demand not a possession of the other but a dispossession (Merleau-Ponty 1968, 266). Although there is a "surface of separation" between the self and the other, this is also the place where people come together—it is the "geometrical locus of the projections and introjections." The negativity to which they both refer is, then, for Merleau-Ponty, the hinge or the *écart* that separates the senses, that allows our lives to "rock into one another" while remaining distinct (Merleau-Ponty 1968, 234). Thus this negative is a positive:

> For if these experiences never exactly overlap, if they slip away at the very moment they are about to rejoin, if there is always a "shift," a "spread," between them, this is precisely because my two hands are part of the same body, because it moves itself in the world, because I hear myself both from within and from without . . . [but this hinge] is not an ontological void, a non-being. (Merleau-Ponty 1968, 148)

This is the negative point at which, in Lacan, the subject is found but which for Merleau-Ponty is one of the "joints where the multiple entries of the world cross" (Merleau-Ponty 1968, 260). The coming together in difference, and the overlapping without fusing that are inherent to our intersubjective and intercorporeal relations mark the joints where philosophy must direct its inquiries. A focus on the *for Itself* or the *in Itself* apart from these hinges leaves philosophy at the risk of "being unintelligible."[30]

This emphasis on encountering the world, implicit in Merleau-Ponty's concept of intersubjectivity, is exemplified in his reading of Hegel's master/slave dialectic where only for adults are intersubjective relations problematic (Merleau-Ponty 1962, 355).[31] In the *Phenomenology of Perception*, Merleau-Ponty points out that the child is not yet fully a subject in that she does not yet grasp herself or others as "private subjectivities" nor understand points of view. Thus, before the struggle between consciousnesses that Hegel describes, the child has already experienced being with others. According to Merleau-Ponty: "For the struggle ever to begin, and for each consciousness to be capable of suspecting the alien presences which it negates, all must necessarily have some common ground and be mindful of their peaceful co-existence in the world of childhood" (Merleau-Ponty 1962, 355). Prior knowledge of peaceful coexistence leads to a vision of intersubjectivity that does not necessarily involve a violent outcome, as in Kojève's reading of Hegel, a reading that the French, including Lacan, have relied upon. Whereas Lacan sees the original schism or alienation in our relations with others first generated by the mirror stage as impossible to overcome, Merleau-Ponty, while agreeing that the body is never fully united with the "ghostlike" image that the subject sees in the mirror or projects as her seen self (Merleau-Ponty 1964, 168), does not intuit this alienation to be insurmountable. Once the other's gaze has fixed the subject as an object, robbed her of being, and she in turn has posited the other as object, this alienation can only be overcome but it can be overcome through establishing relations with the other (Merleau-Ponty 1962, 357). In the *Phenomenology*, Merleau-Ponty uses the example of a young woman who has lost her ability to speak because her relations with a young man have been cut off by her parents. The loss of voice is connected to a childhood trauma; but in this case, regaining speech is the effect of both therapy and reconstituted relations with the young man. Clearly, in this situation the intersubjective relations with the other are essential to her recovery (Merleau-Ponty 1962, 161). In my bodily encounter with the other, as Merleau-Ponty explains, "the seeing that I am is for me really visible . . . I appear to myself completely turned inside out under my own eyes" (Merleau-Ponty 1968, 143). Certainly, according to Lacan, the analytic relation is structurally an intersubjective relation, that is, a relation between two subjects. But, in effect, it is intrapsychic, not intersubjective.

Lacan's fascination with the phallus, using it as a symbolic pivot, a phallic eye, is, as Elizabeth Grosz suggests, useful as an explanatory theory for current social relations in Western society. At the same time, theory is problematic if we view it in universal terms, as is suggested by such a theory of the unconscious, or if we consider the static nature of a universal approach (Grosz 1990, 188–92). How does society change when neither the individual's oedipal nor the wider social significations can be affected? If, following Merleau-Ponty, we understand significations as existentials that, "like all structures [are] between our acts and our aims and not behind them" (Merleau-Ponty 1968, 232), then change is still possible. Accordingly, we would understand our actions to be shaped but not determined by the psychic; moreover, the reverse would also hold true, that our interactions in the world would shape these structures. Lacan once claimed that "I do not eliminate [intersubjectivity]. I take a case in which it may be subtracted. Of course, it can't be eliminated" (Lacan 1988, 188). Perhaps the problem for Lacan is then that while acknowledging our intersubjective relations, he is neither interested in nor able to explore them within the framework he has established. But as Merleau-Ponty illustrates, a theory of the intrapsychic that is divorced from our intersubjective relations with others does not allow for change nor for the possibility of community. If it is to be of any value as an emancipatory theory of social relations, Lacan's work needs an understanding of corporeal intersubjectivity. Merleau-Ponty, however, understands subjectivity to be both embedded in the world, and at the same time open to change and rebirth because his subject is a subject that sees and is affected by vision.[32]

## NOTES

I would like to acknowledge the helpful comments I received on an earlier version of this chapter from both Samuel Mallin and Geoffrey Miles of York University. Acknowledgment is also due to the Social Sciences and Humanities Research Council of Canada for a scholarship that enabled me to both write and read this paper at the Seventeenth International Conference of the Merleau-Ponty Circle.

1. Maurice Merleau-Ponty, *The Visible and the Invisible*, trans. Alphonso Lingis (Evanston: Northwestern University Press, 1968).

2. Jacques Lacan, "Of the Gaze As Objet Petit a," in *The Four Fundamental Concepts of Psycho-Analysis*, ed. Jacques-Alain Miller, trans. Alan Sheridan (New York: W.W. Norton & Company Inc., 1981), pp. 67–119.

3. Elisabeth Roudinesco, in her book *Jacques Lacan & Co.*, claims that Lacan often took ideas from other sources without citing his influences. At the same time, she claims, he would always teach in public spaces because he "could not do without public recognition." It seems he needed to be under the eye of his contemporaries (Chicago: University of Chicago Press, 1990), p. 390.

4. John O'Neill has also explored other aspects of the intersection of the work of Lacan and Merleau-Ponty. See "The Specular Body: Merleau-Ponty and Lacan on Infant Self and Other," *Synthese* 66 (Fall 1986), pp. 201–17, and "The Mother-Tongue: The Infant's Search for Meaning," *Revue de l'Université d'Ottawa* 55 (1985): pp. 59–71.

5. According to Lacan, consciousness is regarded as a principal of idealization and of *méconnaissance*, "as—using a term that takes on new value by being referred to a visible domain—*scotoma*" (Lacan, 1981, 83).

6. Lacan, "The mirror stage as formative of the function of the I," in *Écrits: A Selection*, trans. Alan Sheridan (New York: W.W. Norton & Company, 1977), pp. 1–7.

7. Merleau-Ponty, "The Child's Relations with Others," in *The Primacy of Perception*, trans. William Cobb (Evanston: Northwestern University Press, 1964), p. 136, and Lacan, 1977, p. 4.

8. Sigmund Freud, "From The History of an Infantile Neurosis (The Wolf Man)," in *Freud: Case Histories II*, trans. James Strachey (Hammondsworth: Penguin Books, 1979).

9. Lacan himself writes of the primal drama that "[t]he primary process . . . must, once again, be apprehended in its experience of rupture, between perception and consciousness, in that nontemporal locus, . . . which forces us to posit what Freud calls, in homage to Fechner, *die Idee einer anderer Lokalität*, the idea of another locality, another space, another scene, the 'between perception and consciousness'" ("The Unconscious and Repetition," in Lacan 1981, 56).

10. Lacan, *The Seminar of Jacques Lacan: Book II*, ed. Jacques-Alain Miller, trans., Sylvana Tomaselli (New York: W.W. Norton & Company, 1988), p. 187.

11. Elizabeth Grosz describes the Real as "the order preceding the ego and the organization of the drives. It is an anatomical, 'natural' order (nature in the sense of resistance rather than positive substance . . ." *Jacques Lacan: A Feminist Introduction* (London: Routledge, 1990), p. 34.

12. Jean-Paul Sartre, *Being and Nothingness*, trans. Hazel E. Barnes (New York: Washington Square Press, 1966), pp. 347–50.

13. Although I am using female pronouns for the subject, in certain situations the subject is clearly male. The male pronoun is also used if necessary for clarity.

14. Jacqueline Rose, "The Imaginary," in *Sexuality in the Field of Vision* (London: Verso, 1986), p. 194. Rose writes further that "the voyeur is not, therefore, in a position of

pure manipulation of an object, albeit distant, but is always threatened by the potential exteriorisation of his own function. That function is challenged three times over: first, by the fact that the subject cannot see what it wants to see . . . ; secondly, by the fact that it is not the only one looking; thirdly, that the reciprocity implied in this is immediately challenged, since the subject can never see its look from the point at which the other is looking at it. These three moments can be seen to correspond to the three moments of privation, frustration and castration."

15. Lacan takes the significance of the castration complex to the level of the symbolic. For Freud, a boy's fear of castration emerges with a fear of his father who he imagines as threatening to cut off the child's penis as a warning against desiring the mother; the girl in turn realizes that she is castrated like her mother and thus can never have the phallus. She can only be the phallus. For Lacan, however, the phallus is the "privileged signifier" which emerges with desire in its relation to language. As the signifier of the desire of the Other that the subject seeks, Lacan asserts, the phallus is not "the organ, penis or clitoris, that it symbolizes." To be castrated, which is fundamental to entry into the symbolic order, is to be deprived of the phallus, which means that the subject will never be able to satisfy desire (see note no. 16) (Lacan 1977, 285–88). Although Lacan claims that the phallus does not represent the penis, Jane Gallop points out that the cultural association of the one with the other lends itself to this association. Moreover, in one of Lacan's own descriptions of the phallus he asserts that, "by virtue of its turgidity, it is the image of the vital flow as it is transmitted in generation"; his imagery clearly evokes the association of the phallus with the penis (Lacan 1977, 287; Jane Gallop, *Reading Lacan* [Ithaca: Cornell University Press, 1985], pp. 136, 156).

16. What is crucial to this link is that desire cannot be articulated. It is barred or repressed from consciousness, although it is structured like a language. Linking desire to the symbolic and the subject's entry into language and, following Hegel, Lacan describes desire as representing for the subject a "fundamental lack, a hole in being that can be satisfied only by one 'thing'—another('s) desire." But this desire must necessarily remain insatiable. Because desire is regulated in the symbolic, it is "always an effect of the Other, [but it is] an 'other' with whom [desire] cannot engage, in so far as the Other is not a person but a place, the locus of law, language and the symbolic" (Grosz 1990, 66–67).

17. Lacan writes: "When, in love, I solicit a look, what is profoundly unsatisfying and always missing is that—You never look at me from the place from which I see you" (Lacan 1981, 103).

18. Lacan uses the word *geometral* in reference to geometrical optics.

19. Although as Lacan himself points out, the Holbein painting illustrates how the "geometral dimension of vision" can also be used in "order to capture the subject" in relation to desire (Lacan 1981, 92).

20. In this context Lacan writes: "The effect of mimicry is camouflage, in the strictly technical sense. It is not a question of harmonizing with the background but, against a mottled background, of becoming mottled—exactly like the technique of camouflage practised in human warfare" (Lacan 1981, 99).

21. Ellie Ragland-Sullivan supports Lacan in this interpretation of Merleau-Ponty although she gives no indication that she has actually read the philosopher's work. See *Jacques Lacan and the Philosophy of Psychoanalysis* (Chicago: University of Illinois Press, 1986), p. 45.

22. Lacan, "Merleau-Ponty: In Memoriam," trans. Wilfried Ver Eecke and Dirk de Schutter, *The Review of Existential Psychology and Psychiatry* 18, nos. 1,2,&3 (1982–1983): p. 74. This piece was written several years before the seminars were written and before Lacan had read *The Visible and the Invisible*. While in the seminars he seems more willing to explore the insights of the philosopher, he ultimately claims that his views have not changed (Lacan 1981, 119).

23. J. B. Pontalis, "The Problem of the Unconscious in Merleau-Ponty's Thought," *The Review of Existential Psychology & Psychiatry*, trans. Wilfried Ver Eecke and Michael Greer, trans., 18, nos. 1,2,&3 (1982–1983): p. 92.

24. For a development of this theme, see Dorothea E. Olkowski, "Merleau-Ponty's Freudianism: From the Body of Consciousness to the Body of Flesh," *Review of Existential Psychology and Psychiatry* 18, nos. 1, 2, & 3 (1982–1983): pp. 97–116.

25. Lacan reverses this emphasis by describing speech itself as a body. Thus, "[w]ords are trapped in all the corporeal images that captivate the subject . . . [making, for example,] the hysteric "pregnant.'" Conversely, "speech may become an imaginary, or even real object in the subject" giving us the 'Espe' as the sign of the castrated subject ("The function and field of speech and language in psychoanalysis," in Lacan 1977, 87–88).

26. Merleau-Ponty, *Phenomenology of Perception*, trans. Colin Smith (London: Routledge & Kegan Paul, 1962), p. 164.

27. "Eye and Mind," in Merleau-Ponty 1964, 169.

28. Lacan explains this concept by referring to an incident in his youth when, on a fishing boat, Petit-Jean, one of the local fishers, pointed to a small sardine can floating in the sunlit water, "witness to the canning industry, which we, in fact, were supposed to supply. It glittered in the sun. And Petit-Jean said to me—'You see that can? Do you see it? Well, it doesn't see you!'" (Lacan 1981, 95). This story explains how the picture is in the subject's eye but the subject is not in the picture. The eye comes at the geometral point where perspective starts. It is this point illuminated by a "gleam of light" which is the screen, which is where subjectivity is found.

29. The Cartesian subject is male.

30. James Schmidt, *Maurice Merleau-Ponty: Between Phenomenology and Structuralism* (New York: St. Martin's Press, 1985), p. 92.

31. Martin J. Matustik also discusses this issue in his article "Merleau-Ponty on Taking the Attitude of the Other," *Journal of the British Society for Phenomenology* 22, no. 1 (January 1991): pp. 47–48.

32. Merleau-Ponty writes: "Two things are certain about freedom: that we are never determined and yet that we never change, since, looking back on what we were, we can always find hints of what we have become. It is up to us to understand both these things simultaneously, as well as the way freedom dawns in us without breaking our bonds with the world." See, "Cézanne's Doubt," in *Sense and Non-Sense*, trans. Hubert Dreyfus and Patricia Allen Dreyfus (Evanston: Northwestern University Press, 1964), p. 21.

CHAPTER 12

# wildly — other — than — being

## WILHELM S. WURZER

There are so many different worlds, so many different songs . . .
We live in different worlds . . .

—Dire Straits

I would like to learn to live finally . . . Not *without* Marx, no future
without Marx. Read me, will you ever be able to do so . . .

—Jacques Derrida

Alienated from truth, God, and nature—digressing from the very
essence of western mimetology—philosophy is suddenly thrown
into a world it can no longer understand. Such hermeneutic dete-
rioration is clearly linked to an inevitable renunciation of the theoretical, i. e., of the dialectic of theory and practice. Merleau-Ponty
responds to this problem by exploring philosophy's "unhappy consciousness" in the face of an unprecedented form of world in which
a techno-tele discourse spectralizes our time. (*SM*, 51).[1]

From time to time a man lifts his head, sniffs, listens, considers,
recognizes his position: he thinks, he sighs, and drawing his watch
from the pocket lodged against his chest, looks at the time. *Where
am I*? and, *What time is it*? Such is the inexhaustible question
turning from us to the world. (*VI*, 103)[2]

Pursuing this question passionately, Merleau-Ponty is relentlessly confronted by the crisis of Marxism, by the rift of thinking and dwelling. Heidegger and Derrida, too, challenge and resist the unresponsiveness to Marx's 11th thesis on Feuerbach. The thesis reads: "The philosophers have only *interpreted* the world, in various ways: the point, however, is to change it." A certain responsibility on the part of philosophers today helps to bring together the names of Heidegger, Merleau-Ponty, and, particularly, Derrida who respond to Marx's thesis by deconstructing the hermeneutic legacy.[3] I will show how their philosophical discourse subverts the overdetermination of pure textuality in the history of philosophy, thereby opening thinking beyond mere philosophemes.

What fascinates in Merleau-Ponty's later philosophy is not only his rigorous reading of Heidegger's logic of *Differenz* but also his ability to relate this reading to the experience of our world. This does not mean interpreting the world again as Merleau-Ponty indicates by his desire to challenge Marx's 11th thesis on Feuerbach: "What I want to do is restore the world as a meaning of Being absolutely different from the 'represented,' that is, as the vertical Being which none of 'the representations' exhaust and which all 'reach,' the wild Being" (*VI*, 253). His deconstruction of the Marxian thesis is intriguingly Heideggerian.[4] Being is now redefined out of a concern for difference. "This thing called difference," Heidegger writes, "we encounter it everywhere and always in the matter of thinking, in beings as such—we encounter it so unquestionably that we do not even notice (it)" (*ID*, 63).[5] For Merleau-Ponty, this very encounter marks the flesh of world, not as a unified body of interpretations with common interests but, more intriguingly, as a new disturbance in time, an undeconstructible community. Difference here is not a matter of political accomplishment or representation. Indeed, "(history) is neither mind nor man, neither liberty nor necessity, neither one Idea nor another . . ." (*BP*, 158).[6] Merleau-Ponty's subversion of Hegel's historical idealism allows for a singular existence of spirit which is no longer essence or subject but rather nonessential presentation of history in which past and present are "*Ineinander*, each enveloping-enveloped, that is flesh" (*VI*, 268). Without yielding to speculation, Merleau-Ponty's rewriting of spirit recognizes that *we* are exposed to and belong to community, quite plainly, that "we live in the world and in Being" (*VI*, 109).[7]

To dare the impossible, then, I will read the signature of our *Zeit/Geist* as economy of the uncanny, wildly different from being—*la chaire* marking the in-visible in the visible. This signature begins to surface in a threefold naming of *Differenz* (Heidegger), *écart* (Merleau-Ponty), and *différance* (Derrida). Clearly they are not the same. We are merely recalling one to another. Irreducible dispersions, *Differenz*, *écart*, and *différance*, very much markings of our time, provide a curious echo of the subject, giving freely of the double—world/flesh. Between these two "graphic" dimensions, a split occurs (*kommt*)—" the event of capital,"coming-to-be the madness beyond the clearest reference of all ready-to-hand beings. Now, taking to heart this "higher split," the textual threefold of *Differenz, écart, différance* play (out) the ends of textuality in "a philosophy of wild being and not of docile being which would have us believe the world can be fully explained" (*TD*, 12).[8]

These ends (of textuality) begin with virtual flesh, once again speaking in the ontological difference, the unachieved gap which Merleau-Ponty names *écart*. Decentering the subject, this *Selbsterscheinung* points to presence, the new carnality or invisible incarnation of capital. "Here is the common tissue of which we are made" (*VI*, 203). A postmodern divergence is given precisely as pure auto-apparition. No longer nature, nor the beauty thereof, no longer subject, nor its object, capital signifies the anonymous divergence of all beings, always at a distance from "the *Selbstgegebenheit* of the exterior thing" (*VI*, 191).

A free emblem, capital is no longer simply a concept but rather what Derrida calls "the other heading" of presence, the possibility of a postmodern *Urerlebnis*, always other than a primal referent. Derrida elucidates:

> From this paradox of the paradox, through the propagation of a fission reaction, all the propositions and injunctions are divided, the heading splits, the capital is deidentified: it is related to itself not only in gathering itself in the difference *with itself* and with the other heading, with the other shore of the heading, but in opening itself without being able any longer to gather itself.[9]

Beyond a Marxian reading, capital marks a certain renunciation of presence. Diverging from the left and the right, capital indicates the site of the impossible. A rhythmic alterity, a specular libido, an invisible flesh, capital blurs the thematics of Being. In Derrida's words: "To say it all too quickly, I am thinking about the necessity for a new culture, one that would invent another way of reading and analyzing *Capital*, both Marx's book and capital in general" (*OH*, 56).[10]

Capital is linked to our threefold theme precisely in what Merleau-Ponty calls "wild being" (*VI*, 204). *Wild because being is capital rather than concept, historical rather than transcendental.* Wild being, then, is the milieu without which nothing is thinkable. Without always naming capital per se, Merleau-Ponty proposes the question of *le capital* from the perspectives of "a wild perception," a desire to see philosophy advance toward *écart*, a certain separation from textuality, a *Vorhabe* of Being, in short, a meta-textual, post-textual, exceedingly out-of-textual, untraversable, in-visible *échappement* (leakage). There is no textual immanence in *écart/*capital so that, as Merleau-Ponty writes, "the conception of history one will come to, will be nowise *ethical* like that of Sartre" (*VI*, 275).

> It will be much closer to that of Marx: Capital as a *thing* (not as a partial object of a partial empirical inquiry as Sartre presents it), as "mystery" of history, expressing the "speculative mysteries" of the Hegelian logic. . . . Worked-over-matter-men=*chiasm.* (*VI*, 275)

For Heidegger, this "mystery" of history is played out in his refusal to repeat the historical mimesis of Western ideologies. A differentiated space of community is intimately linked to his reading of time, a space named—*Übermacht*.[11] An incomparable power, temporalizing (*Zeitigung*) captures an apparitional deepening, interpreting, and rewriting of Nietzsche's critique of historicism. What draws Heidegger irresistibly to Nietzsche's early work, *The Use and Abuse of History*, is a post-Cartesian eye glancing at the unhistorical and the superhistorical. The unhistorical signifies the necessary forgetting of the past as simple textual presence. It also signifies the touch of the moment, animality at a single glance, an ontologic naturality. So, when Heidegger unfolds *Da-sein* as primarily historical, there is something unhistorical about this. More sublimely, there is something superhistorical here, namely *Ereignis*. Thus, less and more of the historical, less and more of the textual, the ontologically historical happens without disregarding the event. Thus, we are no longer consumed by the weight of the *culture of textuality*.

What is set in place in *Being and Time*, the site Merleau-Ponty is wondering about, without drifting aimlessly, is the region (*Gegend*) that holds a unique temporalizing in so historical a manner that nothing present-at-hand may surface. What happens, then, when we look at the textual terrain of philosophical towns and cities? The site we regard, the place that opens up allows for textualities, indecidables indeed, which suddenly fascinate in their peculiar coming from the future.

A certain erasure of the philosophical letter and the presumption to dispense with it by other means will be necessary: for Merleau-Ponty, obliteration, therefore, of both reduction and expansion of textuality. Beyond recent textual invocations, how does Merleau-Ponty cull the most crucial themes from Heidegger's out-of-textual temporalizing? Here, we meet a more radical off-centering, specifically, an ex-centric posttextualizing which Merleau-Ponty regards as belonging very much to the ambiguity of philosophy's *farewell*.[12] The erasure of historical presence engenders the proliferation of certain textual economies. One may, however, as Nietzsche urges, break textuality's windows and leap into freedom or, as Blake might say, drive our carts and plows over the bones of dead philosophers. *We still have the how, we no longer have the what.*

Merleau-Ponty repeats the soundings of Heidegger's *Dasein*-analysis, which signifies resistance of the what, first of all. Invariably, an operation of the how, philosophy opens up world in its most proper historical performance. *Dasein* is not present; it shows itself in the unique temporalizing of an unparalled play (*ID*, 66). Thinking philosophy's farewell is *now* linked to time, singularly to *Zeitigung*, temporalizing, expressing the very becoming of difference. The ambiguity of becoming lies in how time temporalizes itself, in how it goes beyond itself and gives itself up. Obliterating the what, time is primarily futural. It always already erases the past and present in its distinctive coming (*Zukunft*) toward the undeconstructible (*SM*, 59). A performative strategy, thinking with and beyond Heidegger, determines the very possibility of world as time and capital coming together. In these times, *Zeitkapital* marks an unprecedented difference. Heidegger might say: "(It) speaks transitively, in transition. (That is to say) Being here becomes present in the (wild) manner of a transition to beings" (*ID*, 64).

Not a mere joining of words (*Wortgefüge*), nor a delightful textual interweaving, *Zeitkapital* is an oblique naming of a certain farewell to *what* philosophy *thinks*, if it claims to belong inseparably to philosophical textuality. Attempts to distinguish philosophy from the philosophical language of textuality, whether old or new, arise out of a desire not to let philosophy become the subject again.[13] *Philosophy is not the subject.* Philosophy is merely *how* we regard the subject. *The subject is time, our time—now—*our finite history, the "I" within the "we," a metamorphosis of capital in time, "the *écart*" that set itself up in more than one speech, the difference of community beyond communities. Indeed, (as we will see) the subject is a nonidentical comma, the *écart* between "we, now."[14]

Understanding *écart* nonidentically, Merleau-Ponty rewrites being in a more diverse historiality than Heidegger. Being arrives wildly as *le Capital comme chose*. Because of this vertical, historical dislocation of being, capital cannot be merely theorized. Nor, if taken other than "carnal, figure and ground," can it be merely inscribed into *différance* (*VI*, 265). Merleau-Ponty is still working with *histoire*, namely, the way things are with the body. "My body is to the greatest extent what everything is" (*VI*, 260). Accordingly, my body touches the universal thing, wild being/capital, the *visible comme in-visible* (*VI*, 295). Flesh of the world, while distinct from my flesh, touches me as intracorporeal capital. This historical touching does not install another architecture of *noeses-noemata* but opens up *écart* in multiple possibilities of being, wildly enveloped in the visible. The touch-divergences that Merleau-Ponty introduces are to be understood as "a community of verbal *Wesen*," "*eine Art der Reflexion*" (*VI*, 256). To touch oneself is to touch the wild thing, the unpresentable, a decentering of the body. This is not a question of narcissism but rather a communal mirroring, a self-showing of capital as intercorporeality, ontological in the Heideggerian sense. Philosophy, therefore, is still a question of *phainesthai*, not of the flesh per se, but of a wilder presence: multiple intercorporealities, consistently indifferent to a phenomenology of narcissism.[15] Beyond a new form of subjectivity, supplementing Heidegger's narrative of *Differenz*, capital exceeds philosophy-writing-about-its-textual-ends. It is a wild phenomenon in the sense that its origin "can no longer be thought of within the scope of metaphysics" (*ID*, 71). Thus, Merleau-Ponty does not slide into the void of a new dimension but opens philosophy to nonphilosophy. This does not reduce history to the visible but it touches philosophy on both sides—the visible *and* the invisible: "Meaning," Merleau-Ponty says, "is *invisible*, but the invisible is not the contradictory of the visible: the visible itself has an invisible inner framework, and the in-visible is the secret counterpart of the visible, it appears only within it, it is the *Nichturpräsentierbare* present to me as such within the world . . ." (*VI*, 215).

Derrida recognizes the historical intimacy of the visible and the invisible. He supplements Merleau-Ponty's reading of the unpresentable by suggesting that it ought to mark the call for interminable textual resistance, advising that there is still a neo-capitalist exploitation.

> The world is going badly, the picture is bleak, one could say almost black (*SM*, 78).

> Electoral representativity or parliamentary life is not only distorted, as was always the case, by a great number of socio-economic mechanisms, but it is exercised with more and more difficulty in a public space profoundly upset by techno-tele-media apparatuses and by new rhythms of information and communication, by the devices and the speed of forces represented by the latter, but also and consequently by the new modes of appropriation they put to work, by the new structure of the event and of its spectrality. (*SM*, 79)

> (There is) the inability to master the contradictions in the concept, norms, and reality of the free market . . . (*SM*, 81)

Regardless how valid this reading, Derrida views the divergences from the standpoint of a fidelity to a certain spirit of Marxism. He disregards the exemplary power of capital in its heterogenous spectralities, with notable disruptions and disturbances in its worked-over matter. Merleau-Ponty, however, responds to this chiasm: (of) "carnal relations, from below, no less than from above and the fine point . . . entwining" (*VI*, 269)—wild capital/vertical being, doubtlessly, the *Horizonthaftigkeit* of inevitable differences. Today one may regard his notion of carnality as radically transforming Spinoza's 15th proposition in book one of the *Ethics*. Suddenly, it reads: "Whatever is, is in capital, and nothing can be or be conceived without it." Still, "we cannot identify (capital) in all certainty" (*SM*, 7). Its historical spectralities are "quite different from the simple simulacrum of something in general" (*SM*, 7). Derrida is aware of the essential contamination of substance by capital, of spirit (*Geist*) by specter (*Gespenst*). He proceeds from Text to texts, beyond metaphysics to a grammatological "time." There are discontinuities, a postfigurable *écart*, a textual homelessness, a *glissement* indifferent to history as well as to the concrete philosophy of wild being. Regarding being as a nostalgic preference, Derrida exceeds the Heideggerian configurations of *Denken* as well as Merleau-Ponty's ontological presencing.

Haunted by the spirit of Heidegger, Merleau-Ponty listens not to only to Marx's identifiable source of alienation but also to Diotima's discursive *Gelassenheit*, which, more pointedly, unfolds the erotic stillness in work, a demonic in-between, an erotic shift from philosophy to nonphilosophy back to a certain figurability in philosophy: "After all, everything that is responsible for creating something out of nothing is a kind of poetry; and so all the creations of every craft and profession are themselves a kind of poetry."[16]

Between philosophy and nonphilosophy lies capital's symposium, a commemorative gathering of scenes from life, descending to a concrete, dynamic work world (*Werkwelt*). Such is the fictioning power of world—*poiesis*, tracing the invisible to the visible. Here, there is still too much figurability for Derrida precisely because he regards *différance*, as if she were beyond being wild. Wild being, then, presents a distinct nonimaginal tracing of the invisible to the visible. Still, writing and capital are not one and the same. There is always an intershadowing of references, which does not proceed from an assimilation of textuality to history. In a continuous dissimulation, capital as *écart* is more wildly differential than Heidegger's *Differenz*, more primordially free (and open), more and less spectral, than Derrida's *écriture*.

Regarding this, the relationship between Heidegger, Merleau-Ponty, and Derrida is quite complex. While *écart* reveals a certain alliance with *Differenz/différance*, Merleau-Ponty's irreversible desire for historical presence, more clearly, for the figurability of work, more strenuously the worked-over-matter-men=chiasm=capital, makes this alliance undecisive. *Écart* abandons the "sunny places of thought,"[17] desisting any typography beyond historical presence. Straying from the *jouissance* of the general text, philosophy is destined to clarify the intimacy of pain and thought. Regarding this, Merleau-Ponty quotes Nietzsche:

> We are not thinking frogs, nor are we objective and registering mechanisms with their innards in refrigeration. We constantly give birth to our thoughts out of pain, and, like mothers, endow them with all we have of blood, heart, ardor, joy, passion, agony, conscience, fatality. For us, life consists in continually transforming all that we are into clarity and flame, just as it transforms everything that we touch.[18]

Philosophy, in turn, presupposes a necessary world thesis (*Weltthesis*) of work/pain/history. Such a dynamically concrete filiation is not merely another heading for being but is organized around the historical work-to-be—a new naturality, in Nietzsche's words, "a new enlightenment," in Derrida's, "a new international." Nonetheless, philosophy's alliance with this economy of work/pain/history is simultaneously a separation from it. And this *écart* too signifies wild being, now regarded beyond capital infrastructures as the chiasm, the intertwining of visible and invisible, of flesh and *phainesthai*. Thus, *écart* signifies "a deployment of our relation to being" (*TD*, 10), an ontological history rooted in a phenomenological *how*, a mysterious *who*, as in Heidegger saying: "*Der Mensch ist und ist doch nicht.*"[19] Capital, too, looks like being and then again, it does not. So it is with *écart*. At once, pretextual, textual, posttextual, it occurs notably in the conversation we are, in our articulation of the world as it turns.

Derrida is aware of this *écart*, which he records under the heading of "signature," more precisely, *signature événement*.[20] This means that presence yields to historical styles rather than to figurability. "Style," he writes, "uses its spur as a means of protection against the terrifying, blinding, mortal threat [of that] which *presents* itself, which obstinately thrusts itself into view."[21] Clearly, this shows that Derrida proceeds from a rather refined grammatological view of protection, an academic guarding, if you will, "against presence." *Différance* serves as an "unintended" shield for the chiasmatic presence of "the worked-over-matter." It appears, then, that he does not speak to "the global conversation," notably, to the current information revolution, precisely, another heading for capital.[22] Nor does he seem to address the urgent question regarding the relation of *différance* and the "electronic text," in particular "digitization."[23] Instead, on his view, style becomes a protective event by means of graphic effacement, leaving behind a mark, a trace, a signature, to be sure, a presentation of beings, beyond the event of presence. Which means—if we sharpen the contours of *différance*—that philosophy is more or less a matter of styles, a dispersed network of signatures. Merely exposed to these markings, philosophy is essentially no longer concerned with capital in its "worked-over-matter." It is therefore not humans we encounter but signatures, perhaps, a wilder capitalism than even Merleau-Ponty imagined, *différance* marking the marking.

Derrida's implacable fidelity to the spectralities of *différance* presents philosophy as virtual incorporations of an economy of metaphilosophy, differentially more philosophical, less metaphysical, yet undoubtedly also more professorial. While Merleau-Ponty understands philosophy as providing a global, primordial temporalizing, conceding historical presence without installing it into a supplementary scriptive textuality, Derrida finds it to be a matter of the advent of styles, futural specters. Must one not think that the loss of work can affect these specters? "To the point that it is then impossible to discern between the specter and the specter of the specter, the specter searching for proper content and living effectivity?" (*SM*, 101).

While Heidegger, Merleau-Ponty, and Derrida manifest openings reflecting the untimely collision of capital and spirit, they do not explore capital's trajectories, its rhythmic renunciations of presence, its obliteration of cultures and metaphysical closures. It is important here to see that we are not merely talking about a monetary sign.[24] Straying from political images and the commodified metaphysics of technology, capital disrupts the former alliance of dialectics and hermeneutics in its eccentric electronic "presencing." Not merely a postmodern image-system, capital is more than a cursory glance at the ecstatic obscenity of capitalism. No longer mirroring a particular cultural/textual space, it sketches time straying from presence *and* simulation, from the logocentric signal of spirit to disseminal experimentations. *Timecapital*, therefore, is neither solely the they-time (*das Man*) nor authentic time. Both time and capital are no longer regarded authentically or inauthentically. Inscribed into wild being, they are one without being the same.

In its oblique play, capital separates time (*Zeit*) from spirit (*Geist*). Destabilizing culture, while disturbing the politics that follows from capitalism, wild being/power/capital begin to obliterate the West's sovereignty of an exclusive *logos*. There is no awakening of the feeling of the supersensible here: only the uncanny play of a tangible intangibility with digressions that have yet to be studied. Most notable in these digressions is the separation of culture from a wild working-over-the matter of the West. In view of the collapse of presence, capital persists in free "interactive" relations. This new eccentricity demands more than the standard interpretation of world. With regard to this, Merleau-Ponty already raised the issue of a "hyperreflection," (*sur-flection*),[25] a more rigorous redefining of world, taking into account what the human experience of capitalism and Marxism has revealed after Marx" (*TD*, 57). Such a hyperreflection inserts the ontological problem into the very rewriting of our time, revealing operations within *écart* that raise capital beyond the speculum of *Zeitgeist*, forward to a wild aspecificity that effaces the universal while dispersing the particular.

More pointedly, Merleau-Ponty's hyperreflection evades neither the accomplishments of Marxism nor those of a late capitalist world. In part, it makes it possible for us to engage in a rigorous and critical study of *Zeitkapital* out of a concern for the unlimited possibilities revealed by a postaesthetic convergence of satellites, television, fax, cellular telephones, and global computer networks. A new mood sets in motion the collision of this "ecstatic" economy founded above all on "the propagation of information and knowledge" (*TD*, 13).[26] As being-in-wild-play, capital turns from a commodified presence into an immense field of postaesthetic experimentations. Without vanishing, it withdraws from the aesthetics of the political, drawn "onto-electronically" into the "worked-over-matter" of *écart*. This experience of *écart* comes to be a narrative, to be sure, a discourse (*discurrere*, Lat. "to run about") regarding the posttextual twilight of our time. Replete with diverse operational dispositions, it echoes a baffling economy, swaying ever so openly from "book to screen," from text to filming, from capitalism to the spectralities of wild being: time and capital.

Although intertwined, they are not the same. Arguably, time may even resist capital's doing (*Handeln*). More concretely, this resistance happens in new narratives of sending/receiving, in a hyperreflection that points neither to the other nor to the self. Nor does it signify a triumph of privatization. Instead, it indicates a *disappropriation*, properly anonymous, yet frequently open to "visible-invisible" reversibilities. In short, the thoughts of both Merleau-Ponty and Derrida regarding the paradox of *écart/différance* necessitate a certain transformation of Heidegger's account of readiness-to-hand. In Merleau-Ponty's words: "Everything will have to begin from scratch, in politics as well as in philosophy" (*TD*, 13). However we begin, we cannot separate *écart* from a world that allows us to understand what no thinker today can deny: the unassignable assignment beyond the mimesis of ready-to-hand beings—the extraordinary convergences, quite simply, capital transforming world electrotechnically. Within these operations, the question of being-wild gets immediately underway.[27] Hence, it is not abusive to suggest that capital is more than the sovereignty of a certain textuality. It is the sovereignty of all textualities inasmuch as we, now understand sovereignty as "more than one/No more one" [*plus d'un*], as Derrida might say. In effect, capital may turn out to be the twilight of all sovereignties beyond pure textual surging. Or, more hopefully, perhaps, it may illustrate being less wildly by letting *disappropriation* be. "It would (then) be the absolute disappearance of the property relation; it would continue a change in our relations, not only to one another but to the animals and things that constitute our environment."[28]

With regard to this possible *disappropriation*, we, now, "are no longer able to understand ourselves as a determined step within a determined process"

(*BP*, 166). We, now are nonidentical. We do not have centers. We no longer address one another by way of substance or subject. Ours is a complicated world beyond a dominant discourse.[29] The electro-economic systems change more rapidly than we do. "The now" becomes a paradox. "The we" itself collapses, fading into the "now," beneath our streets, into the power lines and cables inside our walls . . . Farewell to us . . . The nonidentical comma remains a pause, between the we and now. Still, *now* is always different from "the now" we know, the centerless whole. Hence, the nonidentical comma may still be *promesse du bonheur*, a flash of the unexchangeable, flesh anew.[30] Is this another heading for *Zeitkapital*—the unexchangeable, the nonidentical, the undeconstructible we, no doubt, beyond "the now"?

Are we able to separate the nonidentical from new bits of data, from the domain of the techno-media? When the economic unit is the globe, where is the subject? Who are we, now? Now, that the gods have fled and dubious models of telecommunication shine without wanting to become phenomena? Speculation has become very light indeed. It belongs to the madness of economic apparitions.[31] Merleau-Ponty writes: "The philosopher does not have the right to enclose himself in an inner life. The philosopher strives to think the world of everyone" (*TD*, 3). So, how are we? "It is no mere coincidence that along with the integration of the world's economy into a seamless electronic whole, there is an upturn in ethnic rivalries and violence and civil unrest."[32] With the electronic rise of "the now," what is happening to "the we"? Will the "we" become *one* "now"?

For many we's, a world that is rapidly integrating, becoming one with a different spirit than Hegel's, is quite frightening in the face of a threatening "now." What is going on *now*? How/where do *we* fit in? Are these questions merely a matter of replicating Romanticism's desire to blend the real and ideal. It might be good to understand the *we* as belonging to *now* without letting the *now* become another belonging. A certain nonidentical invitation still holds. *We* are invited to join the *now*, "*to turn ourselves over to the future*" (*SM*, 29). To affect the now. To permeate the links. To give ourselves to the now without ever letting the now become a mere present. Merleau-Ponty agrees with Heidegger, that the essence of technology, the now we are and are not, is not, by itself, anything technical. Inclined toward a bizarre content, who/how are we, now?

After nature, the new political imaginary exceeds the modern/postmodern aesthetics of law and politics. "However," Merleau-Ponty claims, "this does not mean that philosophy has nothing more to say or that it is destined to disappear. On the contrary, what paralyzes or renders philosophy mute is that it cannot, by traditional means, express what the world is now living through" (*TD*, 9.) We, now belong to how we will be. We, now means, according to

Nancy, that we are prepared to think, "to leave behind what 'thinking' usually means. But, first of all, to think this, that there is something to think" (*BP*, 174): to think community beyond Hölderlin's melancholy, beyond Gottfried Benn's aesthetic nihilism, and Peter Handke's lyrical cynicism; beyond nature, in particular, even beyond Adorno's *Naturschöne*. Now, one may very well wish to think community within and beyond our electro-economic experience under a new spacing of time—*Zeitkapital*. That which bears such a name is not unrelated to what Heidegger speaks of when he directs our thinking to a realm in which the key words of metaphysics—"Being and beings, the ground and what is grounded—are no longer adequate to utter" (*ID*, 71).

Another heading for philosophy's concern today, *Zeitkapital* marks the *revenant* of spirit beyond the West, a futural flux of discursive (electronic) *Gelassenheit*. Marking the postaesthetic site of spirit (*FJ*, 86), capital signals how time ought to be in a world beyond fear. Spectralizing *Capital*, capital withdraws from narrow infrastructures. Ahead of its time, it is already ahead of capitalism. In advance of it, beyond it, it marks the twilight of the "best investments." For time in *Zeitkapital* is a spectral coming, a "not-yet," "the possible." But it is also something that has come back, a genuine *revenant* in the nonidentical sense of a dynamic critique of capital. Accordingly, time comes to resist how things are. So, time is resistance of the living present, first of all. And then, a *revenant*, a coming back of something we have always hoped for in the West, a "*post-scriptum*"—a becoming-of-world, writing without fear, becoming justice, perhaps, an undeconstructible.

In short, then, there is always an *écart* between time and capital. Time is first understood as resistance of the what, the status quo, capitalist sovereignty in all its forms. Secondly, this resistance is inspired by a possible *revenant*, a historical *promesse du bonheur*. For capital, here, is neither Marx's capital nor that of capitalism. Instead, it is the specter of philosophy's fading spirit as well as the anticipatory trace of a radically different spirit. Capital is always ahead of the game, whether this game be philosophical or infrastructural, theoretical or practical. Necessarily relating to the nonpresent, the nonidentical, capital is "the most formidable difference," as Derrida might say. It is a fading and falling from the principle of Western consciousness, *das Sein* (*FJ*, 104), now becoming critique without repeating the old criticisms.

How, then, are we really to understand the difference between *Zeit* and *Kapital*. Time is always already capital's other heading, a continuous declinging, eventually letting capital come back differently. In this regard, capital is the very spectrality of the "essence" of time, an electronic linking that does not turn into a technovisual clinging.[33] Clearly, the two cannot be without the other. They flow into each other. They embrace each other, yet they are always other than themselves.

Having fallen from being's mimetic ground, capital is "carried away" to a time beyond ground, an open theater beyond being, beyond the scene of *Dasein* even. A nonidentical event, capital is the "shattered instant" (*zerbrochene Augenblick*—the *kairos*) of imagination's hypertextual mood, the electronic erosion of dialectic anchoring. It is truly a futural *Gesamtkunstwerk*, uniquely, irreducibly dispositional, non-Wagnerian, a matter of a speculum beyond specula, what Derrida might call "an irreducible singularity." As such, capital is time's abyss (*Abgrund*), an unexchangeable exchange. Far from a methodical technique, *Zeitkapital* is the philosophical art of differentiating between our time and time. This very differentiation is capital. It is the head (or *head-land* in our time) beyond the heads that determine and plan what is going on today. It is the mirrorless mirror of the given economy, a spectral writing desisting identification. How we relate to it is not determined by a subject but by time. Time determines the way we relate to our time. Time appeals to its own heading. Hence, capital resists *our* time, indeed, runs ahead of it. Yet, it cannot run ahead of time. Because it is always already its own spectral time, the *revenant*, time coming back in a new and different relation to world. Ahead of its historical temporality, capital is time heading into the future, into an unknown *revenant*, a certain coming back of spirit . . . taking on time, or, the exordium of learning to live, finally, to let electronic visibilities be.

In summary, then, a few more remarks about this. Timecapital signals a post-Hegelian *Zeitgeist*, not of comprehension but, what Merleau-Ponty calls, "a *Zeitgeist* of extension." Quite plainly, an obliteration of *Geist*-in-time, allowing for diverse spirits to transpose us into our time, not into a mere representation of time. Here, our time is no longer regarded as "spirit" in the singular but as a multiplicity of specters marking *capital/flesh* within and beyond the inevitable paradox of a ready-to-hand world with its electronic technologies. Such a new relation to vertical being is not built by politicians, economists, central bankers, or finance ministers. No high-level international conference will provide a new master plan. But as Merleau-Ponty points out, "Existing society is not transparent, and to that extent, philosophical expression remains necessary" (*TD*, 7). The contemporary disarray of history makes possible a new time-structure that "is no longer the natural surge that comes from before we were" (*TD*, 127). This change in time is related to what Merleau-Ponty describes as "a discovery of history that is not a discovery of a thing, force, or destiny but rather a discovery of a questioning, and, you might say, a kind of anguish" (*TD*, 128).

Beyond the natural and traditional historical time structure, *Zeitkapital* marks a new kind of being, a novel relation to humans. In its spontaneous hypertextuality, *Zeitkapital* is not a postmodern interpretation of time instrumental to commercial enterprises. From an empirical perspective, one might be tempted to regard it as another version of "the mechanical clock invented in Benedictine monasteries of the 12th and 13th centuries to provide regularity to their routines: seven periods of devotion during the course of the day."[34] As Postman notes, "the paradox, the surprise, and the wonder are that the clock was invented by men who wanted to devote themselves more rigorously to God." "It ended as the technology of greatest use to men who wished to devote themselves to the accumulation of money. In the eternal struggle between God and Mammon, the clock quite unpredictably favored the latter" (*T*, 15).[35] More specifically, "the transformation of the mechanical clock in the 14th century from an instrument of religious observance to an instrument of commercial enterprise is given a specific date—1370—when King Charles V ordered all citizens of Paris to regulate their private, commercial, and industrial life by the bells of the Royal Palace clock, which struck every sixty minutes" (*T*, 27). If *Zeitkapital* were to be assigned a concrete origin in our time, and, if it were to be regarded as primarily transforming the contemporary time structure, it would only be significant as a ready-to-hand being. For us, however, timecapital signifies the twilight of being, in short, a fading of being into capital. This is the question that needs to be raised today. Not the question of being itself but rather the question of its complex itinerary in our time. It is not sufficient to regard this itinerary from the standpoint of the history of technology. It is more fruitful to see the disappearance of being in capital from the standpoint of futural comings, that is to say, from the global electronic twilight of idols. Here, you will note our desire to begin with Heidegger again. That is, to take Merleau-Ponty seriously in his continual turn to Heidegger. Yet, beyond this, it becomes worthwhile to desist a Heideggerian textuality that merely serves to strengthen the Heideggerian project. We want to begin where Heidegger ends *Being and Time*. According to Merleau-Ponty, it is not up to us to accept or reject Heidegger's idea of temporality. It is thrust upon us. From the moment we begin discussing this temporality, we are inclined to destabilize its specific ontology. Indeed, Merleau-Ponty's phenomenology helps us to move from Heidegger's rhetoric of ecstatic temporalizing to the margins of a radically different textualizing, noticeably an uncanny capitalizing. This new temporalizing needs a distinct language of reading, interpreting, and rewriting capital. The possibilities related to this rereading/rewriting together with the ready-to-hand global integration of marketing, financing, digitization, and research measure today's great upheaval.

Beyond a new source of wealth, beyond the instantaneous information standard, beyond the end of sovereignties, *Zeitkapital* does not merely "blink and sparkle behind the proper names of Marx, Freud, and Heidegger" (*SM*, 174), instead, it is inextricably linked to "where we stand," to "how we are" in our time and beyond it.

More clearly, perhaps, timecapital comes into being out of a certain tearing apart of our time and their (namely, the old philosopher's) spirit. Spirit, however, is not abandoned. It lingers in a wild alliance of many different spectralities. Now, the question of spirit becomes a question regarding the relation of time and capital. This brings us back to what Derrida calls "a certain spirit of Marxism, to at least one of its spirits for, and this can never be repeated too often, there is *more than one* of them and they are heterogenous" (*SM*, 75). A new arrival (re-turn/future/*Zu-kunft*) of spectropoetics signifies multiple rewritings of Being, which show that capital is neither simply out there in "reality," nor is it confined to philosophical textuality. Effacing the spirit of essentiality, capital demands to be dynamically redefined. Perhaps, one may read it as "spontaneous sociability."[36] Challenging the orthodoxies of both left and right, Fukuyama reads capital as unspoken, an unwritten bond between fellow citizens, a spontaneous, posthistorical trust in the intriguing contemporary play of hypertextual signifiers. Beyond Heidegger and Merleau-Ponty, we are now exposed to a communal future which transmits new textualities by means of a revolution of (dis)continuous relations, setting in motion a collision of diverse electronic conversations, indicating the twilight of old communities. Suddenly, philosophy is placed before its strangest, most disconcerting truth (*EF*, 150): the possibility that no aspect of human life is philosophically intelligible.[37] Inevitably, then, the question arises: whether this new community has anything to do with what we, now think we were yesterday.

## NOTES

1. See Jacques Derrida, *Specters of Marx*, trans. Peggy Kamuf (New York and London: Routledge, 1994). Henceforth cited as *SM*.

2. Merleau-Ponty, *The Visible and the Invisible*, trans. A. Lingis (Evanston: Northwestern University Press, 1968), p. 190. Henceforth cited as *VI*.

3. Derrida believes that the project of deconstructing hermeneutical philosophy has already begun with Marx. He writes: "Deconstruction is already in Marx, already in *The German Ideology*, and not just in a 'practical state' but named as such . . ." (*Points . . .*, trans. Peggy Kamuf [Stanford: Stanford University Press, 1995], p. 74).

4. Without referring to Merleau-Ponty, Derrida claims that a Heideggerian (Nietzschean) deconstruction has not been "*effectively* read and *situated* . . . by today's Marxist discourse." See *Points . . .*, p. 75.

5. *Identity and Difference*, trans. Joan Stambaugh (New York: Harper & Row, 1969). Henceforth cited as *ID*.

6. Jean-Luc Nancy, *The Birth to Presence*, trans. B. Holmes (Stanford: Stanford University Press, 1993). Henceforth cited as *BP*.

7. Here I am limiting my remarks mostly to Merleau-Ponty's *Texts and Dialogues*, *The Visible and the Invisible*, Heidegger's *Identity and Difference*, and Derrida's *The Other Heading* and *Specters of Marx*. My task is not to analyze these texts but rather to operate within the freedom that is given by them with its inevitable risks.

8. Maurice Merleau-Ponty, *Texts and Dialogues*, ed. H. Silverman and J. Barry (Atlantic Highlands, N.J.; Humanities Press International, 1992). Henceforth cited as *TD*.

9. *The Other Heading: Reflections on Today's Europe*, trans. Pascale-Anne Brault and M. B. Naas (Bloomington: Indiana University Press, 1992), p. 75. Henceforth cited as *OH*.

10. "Beyond appearance and essence, capital is seen as a 'postmodern' roaming of filming, an evanescent, ruptured movement of spirit without originary unity or purpose, inevitably disrupting the smooth surface of the dialectic as well as the ontologic interplay of presence and absence. Breaking out of its former metaphysical appearance, capital emerges as apparition, a sublime epistemic explosion of discontinuous images that shatters any ideological critique of capital. Withdrawn from historic teleology with political vestiges of representation, capital exceeds concepts of profit or labor as shown in conventional readings, and undergoes a radical transformation. The metaphysical idea of capital is inadequate for clarifying the filmic economy of the sublime. Precisely because it is not regarded as source and goal of production, capital is no longer solely aligned to the commodity structure of production." W. S. Wurzer, *Filming and Judgment: Between Heidegger and Adorno* (Atlantic Highlands, N.J.: Humanities Press International, 1990), p. 88.

11. See *Sein und Zeit* (Tübingen: Max Niemeyer Verlag, 1967).

12. See Jacques Derrida's *On the Name* (Stanford: Stanford University Press, 1995). Henceforth cited as *N*.

13. See my "Heidegger und die Enden der Textualität," in *Textualität der Philosophie*, ed. Ludwig Nagl and Hugh J. Silverman (Wien/München: R. Oldenbourg Verlag, 1994).

14. See "Finite History" in Nancy's *BP*. The idiom "we,now" is crucial to Nancy's thought.

15. Here, we encounter an ineluctable return to a carnal assignment, a presence on the verge of depresencing, perhaps, even multiple attempts to exit the textual logic of *Differenz*. In his later work, Merleau-Ponty does not show, as D. M. Levin claims, that he was as much an enemy of the "metaphysics of presence" as Derrida has been (*MPV*, 67). Philosophy is not ever a question of being an enemy of metaphysics. If anything, it is a sad friend after a certain separation (*écart*), wild as it may seem.

16. Plato, *Symposium*, trans. A. Nehamas and P. Woodruff (Indianapolis/Cambridge: Hackett Publishing Co., 1989), p. 51.

17. See J. R. Watson, *Between Auschwitz and Tradition* (Amsterdam: Rodopi B. V., 1994).

18. *Philosophy and Non-Philosophy Since Merleau-Ponty*, ed. Hugh J. Silverman (New York and London: Routledge, 1988), p. 10.

19. "Man is, yet he is not. It looks like being and it is not. And so it is with poetry." *Hölderlin Hymen "Germanien" und "der Rhein"* (Frankfurt am Main: Klostermann, 1980), p. 36.

20. See H. J. Silverman's "Writing on Writing: Merleau-Ponty/Derrida," in his *Textualities: Between Hermeneutics and Deconstruction* (New York and London: Routledge, 1994), p. 189.

21. *Spurs, Nietzsche's Styles*, trans. Barbara Harlow (Chicago: University of Chicago, 1979), p. 39.

22. See Walter B. Wriston's *The Twilight of Sovereignty* (New York: Charles Scribner's Sons, 1998).

23. "For the deepest implication of electronic text for the teaching of literature is that literature can no longer be taught in isolation from the other arts. Digitization has made the arts interchangeable. You can change a visual signal into a musical one. You can zoom in on a letter until it changes from an alphabetic sign to an abstract pixel-painting. The digital equivalence of the arts has provided a genuinely theoretical basis for comparing the arts and for teaching them together. The new theory of prose style proves to be a general theory of style for the arts altogether." See Richard A. Lanham, *The Electronic Word* (Chicago: University of Chicago Press, 1993), p. 130.

24. That capital is more than an infrastructural phenomenon is brilliantly elaborated in Georg Simmel's *The Philosophy of Money* , trans. T. Bottomore and D. Frisby (London and New York: Routledge, 1978).

25. See also my *Filming and Judgment*, ch. 8, "Surflectants—Strife of Filmic Surfaces," p. 92.

26. See Stuart Moulthrop's "Rhizome and Resistance: Hypertext and the Dreams of a New Culture," in *Hyper/Text/Theory*, ed. G. P. Landow (London: Johns Hopkins University Press), p. 299.

27. "Finally the cold truth was revealed: I had simply died,
    And the terrible dawn enveloped me. Could this be all there is?
    The curtain was up, and I was waiting still."

Baudelaire, *Les Fleurs du Mal*, trans. R. Howard (Boston: David R. Godine, 1983), p. 151. Regarding being, be-coming wild, and being-wild see my "Velazquez's Glance, Foucault's Smile," ch. 3 in *Filming and Judgment*.

28. Graeme Nicholson, *Illustrations of Being: Drawing Upon Heidegger and Upon Metaphysics* (Atlantic Highlands. N.J.: Humanities Press International, Inc., 1992) 278–79.

29. Derrida's claim that there is "today in the world a *dominant* discourse" (*SM*, 51) is questionable, especially in light of the emerging "ecstasy machine," the "Internet" with its explosive possibilities.

30. See Theodor Adorno, *Ästhetische Theorie* (Frankfurt am Main: Suhrkamp, 1970).

31. Jacques Derrida, *Given Time: 1. Counterfeit Money*, trans. P. Kamuf (Chicago: The University of Chicago Press, 1992), pp. 34–70.

32. See Joel Kurtzman's illuminating reading of our time in *The Death of Money* (New York: Simon and Schuster, 1993), p. 205. Henceforth, *DM*.

33. Derrida speaks of a "*cramponnement*" (the clinging instinct) and "*dé-crampon-nement*" (declinging) in *Points* . . . , p. 6.

34. Neil Postman, *Technopolis* (New York: The Free Press, 1990), p. 14. Henceforth cited as *T.*

35. Angelus Silesius might say: "*I muss noch über Gott in ein Wüste ziehn*" (*N*, 53).

36. See Francis Fukuyama's *Trust* (New York: The Free Press, 1955).

37. See Jean-Luc Nancy, *The Experience of Freedom*, trans. B. McDonald (Stanford: Stanford University Press, 1993), p. 150.

CHAPTER 13

# Chaos Theory and Merleau-Ponty's Ontology

## BEYOND THE DEAD FATHER'S PARALYSIS TOWARD A DYNAMIC AND FRAGILE MATERIALITY

### GLEN A. MAZIS

The Dead Father's head. The main thing is, his eyes are open.
Staring up at the sky. The eyes are a two-valued blue, the blues of
the Gitanes cigarette pack. The head never moves. Decades of
staring. The brow is noble, Good Christ, what else? Broad and
noble. And serene, of course, he's dead, what else if not serene? . . .
Dead, but still with us, still with us, but dead.

—Donald Barthelme, *The Dead Father*

## OVERCOMING THE "TWO CULTURE" DICHOTOMY

Merleau-Ponty's ontology and the diverse developments in recent science
that have been called "chaos theory" can be used to bring about a new encounter between philosophical and scientific thinking. It is my contention that
Merleau-Ponty's philosophy allows for a way of thinking about both humans
and the materiality of the world that would overcome the split between the
human and the so-called natural world in such a way as to also create a renewed sense of resonance between science and philosophy—between science

219

and the humanities in general. This rejoining does not take place through what has been called "philosophy of science," which, in fact, reiterates the oppositions of "human reality" to "physical reality," of subject to object, and of mind to matter, and seeks to solve this conflict through recourse to a reductive foundation that would systematize both. Instead, the analysis of Merleau-Ponty's philosophy of perception and ambiguity, along with the developments in science that are addressed by chaos theory, articulate an ontology that reconfigures time, materiality, identity, and other traditional categories of analytical thought as used both in the sciences and humanities—and in such a way that the human and the natural can be seen as intertwining or in a chiasmatic relationship. Instead of being either competing oppositional orders or orders competing within a hierarchy, the phenomenology of the self-in-the-world and the science of the complexity of the world pivot around one another in ways both irreducible and inseparable.[1]

However, to heal the "two culture" split between science and the humanities requires that we delve into the underlying resistances to considering this possibility. It is passed off as an obvious conceptual matter that "we" as humans cannot be comprehended in the same manner as the "stuff of the world." This has been our "common sense" for centuries—an insight understood to have been part of Western culture's emergence out of the "dark ages" of the Medieval world into the Enlightenment of the scientific and humanistic revolution. This seemingly obvious epistemological disjunction is a corollary of seeing the world as grasped in the "book of numbers"—the Galilean vision of quantitative and mechanical terms grasping the truth. In this vision, if human reality were ever to be properly understood, it would be by reducing its apparent qualitative disparities and complexities into merely quantifiable terms—into Cartesian "simples." Until this century, it was considered to be a matter of scientific method to remove the observer from the system observed in order to preserve objectivity and truth. However, not only has this disjunction been called into question by a science determined to deal with matters of greater complexity (and now having the tools to do so), instead of remaining with artificially simplified laboratory or methodologically idealized settings, but additionally, this removal of the observer is now to be questioned as a gendered response. The motivation to insist on such disjunction and simplification in a reductive science or philosophy now appears in a context that raises the question of whether this epistemological narrowness is tied to patriarchy and the construction of masculine gendered responses.

After looking at the parallel and complementary articulations of Merleau-Ponty's ontology and chaos theory, this essay will explore how the ongoing opposition between science and philosophy may be an artifact of a gendered retreat from the significance of death, and how this death-denying retreat has been a key to very disparate aspects of patriarchal thinking. For this reason, not only do disciplinary universes have to be mixed in a way that threatens their perceived purity, but also in a way that introduces and questions what seem to be different orders. So I will bring together questions concerning interpretations of the meaning of death and the dominance of the logic of linear causality, as well as juxtapose queries concerning differences in gender identity with notions of the nature of materiality.

I would like to start to weave these themes together by invoking the scientific and philosophical narratives that we can draw from chaos theory and Merleau-Ponty's ontology to help make sense of two images. The first image is drawn from the world of "natural events" and introduces the kind of concerns that chaos theories have brought to modern scientific thinking. The second image is from the world of literature and raises concerns about the contingency of existence that Merleau-Ponty's ontology has addressed by enlarging the scope of philosophical thinking. Both images can be interpreted in such a way as to bring us to the intersection of differing logics of change and identity: science and phenomenology. These images and the explanatory narratives of chaos theory and Merleau-Ponty's ontology will allow us to consider the body as interwoven in the flesh of the world, to see the logic of personal and material identity emerging from a dynamic unfolding of a fragile endurance, and to encounter the patriarchal fears of death that haunt the seemingly distant considerations of method. Hopefully, a third image can serve as focal point for the concluding speculations regarding how fear of death can kill the inherent life of materiality and its representation in science and philosophy.

## CHAOS THEORY AND OVERCOMING THE DEAD FATHER'S MECHANISM

Present-day research leads us farther and farther away from the opposition between man and the natural world.

—Ilya Prigogine, *Order out of Chaos*

Chaos theory helps us to think of the causality of events in a different way. From within its discourse, the first image for us to consider appears: a DC-9 jet takes off, lumbering toward the sky, but quickly is transformed from a way to soar above the earth into a gateway to sudden death. Chaos principles help us understand the plight of a DC-9 that took off in a snowstorm in Denver, stalled, and flipped over, killing twenty-eight people. After investigating the incident, it became apparent that this tragedy and its physical events of rather considerable magnitude were actually the consequence of the formation of a few grains of ice and the role they then played in a complex interaction.[2] These few grains of ice formed on the wing of the plane. However, rather than seeing the wing as a mere self-subsistent entity, it is important to realize the wing is a dynamic player in an ongoing complex event that comprises the flight of the DC-9. The grains of ice had set up another flow of air that doubled back upon itself within the larger flow of air over and under the wing as part of the aircraft's flight. In setting up a divergent flow that kept feeding back into itself, the impact of a seemingly trivial event became more significant as it gained force.

The instabilities of air flow fed back into movement patterns in such a way as to self-amplify: airflow vortices contributed to further vortical dispersions such that a rhythm of dissipation and turbulence disrupted the previous rhythmic flow and burst forth in the air. Chaos theory has described how turbulence springs from a seed of irregularity, a tuft of resistance, that creates a rift in the linear order of unfolding events. Suddenly, an emergent rhythm of change can engulf the entire system (Briggs and Peate 1990, 24). Through the interconnection of entities—that are more properly seen as events—having a place in larger events which are comprised by the interplay of many aspects of their field-identity, an entity or occurrence that by itself seems to have minimal impact and importance can suddenly bring forth overwhelming change. Most of us still think of science as dealing with changes that are incremental, strictly proportionate to their antecedents, and predictable, at least ideally. To understand how science can now comprehend sudden, disproportionate change and unpredictable transformation, it is important to grasp how the notion of feedback has displaced linear causality insofar as science has begun to look at the world in terms of "open systems."

In an open system, an entity functions and unfolds only within the interrelated functioning and unfolding of its environment. Thus, whatever one tries to designate as a discrete entity is probably an interrelation of its constituents. The environment is likewise an interrelation of various of its constituents, including the so-called discrete entity. I use the word *interrelated* to designate the case in which the current state between these two entities is fed back into the identity of each and each is transformed by it. This is in contrast to the old mechanistic view of parts affecting each other through a series of impacts whose identity is separable from their relatedness: a cog is a cog or a spring is a spring, no matter what other parts of the machine it is connected to at the moment.

As scientists focused on both more complex phenomena, like the weather, and on living systems, they discovered there were so many high-energy flows occurring that they were "self-organizing": their processes became interwoven in order to maintain their identity, using the flux of the total environment to facilitate their own unfolding. From the point of view of the mechanical metaphor with its atomistic assumptions, this sounds anthropomorphic, yet myriad phenomena demonstrate openness to the whole as well as this self-organizing characteristic. However, before discussing this, it may be helpful to hesitate for a moment to consider the other term used above in introducing the notion of open systems: *feedback.*

Feedback phenomena designate the way in which different entities are in a relationship such that the action of the one is factored back into the action of the other. In a "negative" feedback loop, the action of one entity is triggered by the other which in turns regulates the action that triggered it. For example, the rise in the thermostat of my heater is what causes the heater to momentarily stop regulating the very activity that caused the thermostat's thermometer to rise. Each works as a function of the other. In a "positive" feedback loop, an entity, in relation to the activity of a first entity, augments that original activity, is "fed back" into it in such a way that self-amplification is created. For example, when a public address system produces an ear-splitting screech, the output from the amplifier has been picked up by the microphone, fed back into the amplifier and emitted from the speakers as a chaotic burst of sound where each stage of output has become input for new output. These self-regulating and self-amplifying cycles among parts of a system exist as a tension between order and chaos (Briggs and Peate 1990, 25–26). Represented mathematically, feedback gives rise to iterations, to terms repeatedly multiplied by themselves. This aspect of self-ordering allows for both sudden change or turbulence and for maintaining a certain rhythm in a process.

When most people think of factors that are multiplied by themselves, they tend to think this in a linear way, as a value growing in predictable and regular patterns, such that it can even be graphically represented in a progressive and orderly fashion. However, for the complexly interwoven phenomena scientists have turned to exploring, nonlinear equations have proven to be better representations of the interactions involved. In nonlinear equations a small change in one variable can have a catastrophic impact on other variables, correlations that were relatively constant can suddenly demonstrate wildly different behaviors, values that were close together can soar apart, and solutions to nonlinear equations are not generalizable to other nonlinear equations (Briggs and Peate 1990, 24). Unlike the smooth curves made by plotting linear equations, nonlinear plots show breaks, loops, recursions, and various forms of turbulence. The power of iteration—the feedback that involves the continual reabsorption or enfolding of what has come before—mathematically represented, also creates a sensitivity to initial conditions that seem to get lost in the process of unfolding but then can suddenly reappear again. Even in its mathematical representation, self-amplifying open systems demonstrate an alternation, a tension, of order and chaos.

Without this new paradigm, sudden transformations in the realm of human action were at odds with logic of change within the material world, since its changes were thought to be predictably, incrementally, and mechanically ordered. Given that dominant view, human unpredictability has been explained by recourse to concepts that set the human in opposition to the material world. The sudden transformation in the behavior of a person or a group has often been explained as the result of a faculty transcendent to the plane of earthly life or a result of mystical intervention of a supernatural power or the upsurge of unconscious drives or some sort of demonic possession. However, rather than interpreting the sudden transformability and fragility of human life as designating a realm contradictory to the natural, material realm, a more responsible approach is to include ourselves as part of this turbulently ordered, self-regulating or autopoietic realm of earth, its matter, and its creatures. Here, we can only note the parallel with how air flow bursts out of a flight-enabling trajectory into turbulence whose sudden engulfing power is strong enough to flip a DC-9 into the netherworld of a lumbering bird of death. Kali[3] can and does dance in feedback loops, and these changes are awe inspiring enough within the interactions of the material planet of which we are part to preclude having to seek awe in another realm.

Returning to chaos theory, we see that, scientifically, any movement or change can be represented by designating a dimension of space to represent the variables of motion or development. Tracing the pattern of movement creates a "phase space" composed of as many dimensions as are needed to describe a system's movement. Most people are familiar with graphs that trace a movement pattern's unfolding with two variables—or what is called "two degrees of freedom." For example, the unfolding path of vertical versus horizontal distance against the time elapsed is plotted in order to yield a represented trajectory. However, when one starts to trace movements in a more open system, more complex patterns emerge.

Instead of the change being additive, orderly, and external, forging a linear path, the movements of the system shift through patterns of transformations that embody a certain rhythm. Tracings of these changes become loops. Within phase space, in these open systems, one finds not a homogeneous expanse, but a pull toward a certain sector within phase space, a site of returning rhythms of change, a so-called "attractor." Rather than laying out movements indifferent to one another, a "limit cycle" emerges, a way of moving or changing that is self-directing, learning from its past, and making the path into which it has strayed through the complex interaction its ongoing self-maintaining path. By absorbing itself, it amplifies itself to maintain dynamic equilibrium. Rather than all phenomena returning to near equilibrium states, "far-from-equilibrium" systems (as Prigogine called them)—where energy flows remain hot but dynamically ordering—are prevalent in the complex world.

If existence is a becoming and a folding back on itself, as Merleau-Ponty articulated in his ontology, then the chaos theorists' notion that all iterates itself in a dance of self-reference in which a thing returns to itself as a way of being itself is an appropriate way to express this scientifically. Prigogine called systems that maintained their identity only by remaining continually open to the flux and flow of their environment "dissipative structures," He saw them "emerging everywhere—in biology, in vortices, in the growth of cities and political movements, in the evolution of stars" (Briggs and Peate 1990, 139). Phase space represents dissipative structures and is resonant with a vision within science that discards the notion of self-subsisting and atomistic entities.

For example, the pancreas replaces most of its cells every twenty-four hours, the stomach lining every three days, 98 percent of the brain protein is recycled every month (68). Rather than seeing the so-called "organ" as some sort of given being, Prigogine's sensibility and rationality allows us to see that the organ is a self-amplifying flow, a meeting of variant forces, whose pattern we mistakenly took to be a static being, something substantial. The deepest ramifications of this notion, and a parallel articulation by a modern poet can be seen in the wonderful line written by W. H. Auden in praise of W. B. Yeats: Auden wrote that when Yeats died "a way of happening" ceased. If all entities are events (including human being), ways of self-amplifying themselves within the interplay of open systems, then we are merely "ways of happening," fragile, yet enduring.[4]

It is interesting that the Tao's symbol is the flow of water, a favorite example of ordered chaos. If one throws a rock into the flowing brook, the flow returns to its path after being disturbed. In phase space, the constant velocity of the flow is marked by a single point, a point attractor. In a fast-flowing brook, the smooth flow is warped by oscillation in which stable vortices form. The flow, however, returns to this same basic oscillation, the same vortex, and can be represented by a single limit cycle, a circular path. With increases in speed or disturbances on the flow of the system caused by temperature differentials in the water, further turbulence is generated. The turbulence fits a doughnut-shaped attractor—a torus—in three dimensions. Further increases in flow and turbulence move the tori on to further dimensions of representation. However, instead of the jump from a two- to a three-dimensional system, the surface of the representation of the movement can get caught between two and three dimensions. The current wanders in byways of "indecision" known as a "strange attractor," which has a traceable path in its unpredictable transformations, in its turbulence. Resting in its becoming, turbulence finds a place in the maps of science as recurring rhythms of instability.

When, at the end of the nineteenth century, thermodynamics led Boltzmann to propose that physics speak of probabilities rather than entities, the Cartesian-inspired layperson assumed that there were certain factors unknown to the scientist in the phenomena being described and that the use of probabilities signalled an approximation based on this incomplete information: an indeterminacy of knowing that now plagued modern science. However, this is a superficial interpretation of a more profound shift in ontology. The turn to probability signalled a new way of thinking about identity and difference. Probabilities function as explanatory principles, a way of representing the notion that entities are processes rather than substances, irregular in their unfolding, open to other events, fluctuating in identity: a knowing of indeterminacy. Such entities are never really anywhere, as discrete, self-founding beings, and the probabilities represent the gaps in their substantiality and in the Cartesian world, rather than designate a paucity of knowledge about the system described.

It is also an emerging belief of chaos theorists that matter might be better represented as a Chinese box in which different levels of magnitude are repetitions of larger structures on different scales. The different levels of structures within other structures would then be yet another kind of self-amplification, but this one an "internal" reiteration on differing scales. Such repetition, multiplied in a diminishing magnitude but a repeated ratio, was called, by Mandelbrot, a "fractal." If a structure is continually iterated at continually diminishing scales, then not only is there a self-similarity between its different levels of structure, but it is one that continues infinitely. However, if the observer can decide that a certain magnitude of detail is the measure, this means that fractals resemble other phenomena of modern science in that the kind of question the observer poses to the observed is part of the outcome. At any rate, with the insight that changes of scale are fractal cosmoi identified in their self-similar configurations by nonlinear iterations, then the core of matter is not to be imagined as a constant, a substratum, but rather as spiralling, proliferating galaxies of intermittent identities, self-improvising and organizing as identities-within-difference.

The Greeks, for example, discovered history's most famous scale, the "golden mean," which is created by dividing a line such that the two segments are in the same ratio as that of the larger segment to the whole line. The proportion that is generated is the irrational number 1.618... It has been found that for up to ten generations, lungs branching into bronchial tubes follow this scaling until suddenly, they may dramatically change, which is what happens when irrational numbers are reiterated, they suddenly take discontinuous, irregular turns (Briggs and Peate 1990, 107).

The fractal dimension also operates in the realm of time. Life's most central rhythm is the heart's beat. The Cartesian might dream of a beat that is regular and mechanical, and condemn irregular variations as pathological. However, while each beat of the heart is similar to the last, it is fractally iterated, thus never quite the same. If the heartbeat and respiration were to become highly regular, to assume a constant period in their cycle, the heart rejoins the fate of the machine: death; it ceases in "congestive heart failure." However, if the rhythm becomes too aperiodic, loses the self-similarity of family resemblance or style, then it disintegrates into the aperiodic defibrillation of a "heart attack." As Briggs and Peate phrase it, "the normal 'time' of the heart oscillates in the borderland between order and chaos" (Briggs and Peate 1990, 108).

In general, whether looking at white blood cell levels or other rhythms of change in the body, it is the fractal rhythms that are the norm, and as West and Goldberger conclude, "a loss of physiological variability in a variety of systems appears to be characteristic of the aging process," the loss of spontaneous variation is the running out of life. Or as Briggs and Peate put it, "To be healthy is to be composed of shimmering cycles of fractal time" (Briggs and Peate 1990, 108). It would seem that as an unfolding event, life is an attractor that self-amplifies according to not one, constant, fractal generating factor, but differing, random, fractal generators in the self-iterating processes that allow for a richness of organic rhythms and configurations.

The evolution of complex systems cannot be traced in a linear, causal fashion, because "everything affects everything else," which generates nonlinear change. As much as turbulence or chaos, order may spontaneously burst forth in an open system. Most waves in a body of water dissipate in turbulence. Yet, as the Scottish engineer John Russell noticed in 1834 when, on horseback, he chased a wave that maintained its configuration for a few miles along the Union canal near Edinburgh, the wave continued on its path with a constant shape, not falling into foam nor into smaller wavelets, not losing its energy but rolling off into the horizon. This is an example of a wave phenomenon called a "soliton" that occurs whenever the energy of the wave is not so great that it breaks into turbulence or so little that it dissipates. Instead, in a soliton, nonlinear component waves, rather than fragmenting one another, feed back into one another, coupling the motion of any waves that might otherwise speed up and escape from the soliton. We do notice such waves in water when they aug-

ment into tidal waves. However, whether one points to the atmospheric soliton known as the Great Red Spot of Jupiter, which has been observed for hundreds of years, or to the candle flame that fascinates as its seemingly ethereal
form persists, or to the electrical pulses that pass down the human nerves at a
constant speed without changing shape, the phenomenon of the soliton is pervasive in the spontaneous emergence of order in the material and biological
world about us.

Whether thinking about superconductors, nuclear fusion, automobile
traffic, or waves in the ocean, scientists have seen that there is a need to go beyond thinking of atomized parts coming into conflict or collision, and remaining external to one another. For example, intense laser light passing right
through an opaque solid can do so because, along the wavefront, a complex
nonlinear collective entity is formed that is no longer light nor matter, but a
"polariton." Or, cell structure emerges when oxygen using rod-shaped bacte-
ria invade cynobacteria that are unable to use the oxygen, and feedback loops
emerge linking their chemical systems. These linked processes are now identified as mitochondria of the cell.

Probably, the most culturally influential scientific theory of the nineteenth century was Darwin's theory of evolution, which still carries linear,
atomistic, and dualistic modes of thinking to the threshold of dealing with a
world of becoming. Darwin saw that instead of systems running down into
homogeneity, their interactions could token dawning complexity. However,
the notion of the "survival of the fittest"—an interaction within the environment created through each species' linear, random proliferations, and resolved
through insular, external relations represented by the metaphor of competition—serves as a good symbol of the classical way of thinking, the code of the
old fathers. However, by taking nonlinear processes as their paradigm, scientists can now see more cases of emergent symbiosis, changes that occurred
within the evolution of systems linking into other systems, achieving feedback
and self-regulation, so they might continue. In general, competition can usually be circumvented through an openness to the environment that allows systems variability in their unfolding.

Scientists such as Ilya Prigogine and Isabelle Stengers have declared that
the science of the past centuries is no longer their science:

> Not because we are concerned today with new, unimaginable ob-
> jects, closer to magic than to logic, but because as scientists we are
> now beginning to find our way toward the complex processes
> forming the world with which we are most familiar, the natural
> world in which living creatures and their societies develop. Indeed,

> today we are beginning to go beyond what Koyre called "the world
> of quantity" into the world of "qualities" and this of "becoming."
> (Prigogine and Stengers 1984, 36)

Identities understood as dynamic and complex processes unfolding require another logic.

Another way of looking at this shift is to appreciate that science is beginning to take time into account in a far more radical manner than classical science. In nonlinear systems in which there is constant transformation, there is no "going back," because there is true "becoming" in the sense of transforming identity. Entities that are processes enfolded within other processes and entering into turbulences have transformed in time, in a way unlike entities comprised of external parts. The latter, at least ideally, could be put into "reverse gear" to reverse their mechanical interaction. However, the complexity of processes means there is no underlying "x" with which to defeat temporal flow as merely illusory. Scientists call this the "infinite entropy barrier."

The paradox of this insight is that in accepting the reality of temporal flow, scientists have discovered that the sudden nonlinear shifts that bring systems back to their past are still present in ongoing reiteration. Systems most open to their environment feed back into themselves and can create an order of autopoiesis and maintain their identity. These same systems may arrive at points in which so many possibilities of feedback loops emerge that the smallest fluctuation in an interacting factor, perhaps as small as a single photon of energy, can be iterated so drastically that the system will sweep into a totally new and unpredictable direction. These are called "bifurcation" points and they represent both the way in which, through iteration and amplification, one future was chosen and others vanished, and also how, through these loops, the past is continually recycled and stabilized through feedback so that the system embodies the exact conditions of the environment at the moment in which the bifurcation occurred.

So, for example, rather than the ocean being a disordered mass, the ocean's surface is so highly modulated in its flow patterns that it, in a very real sense, contains remembrances of its earlier structures, and the giant waves that occur are not brought about by chance but are "a self-focusing or surfacing of the ocean's memory in the form of a soliton" (Briggs and Peate 1990, 127). As Briggs and Peate conclude, "Thus the dynamics of bifurcations reveal that time is irreversible yet recapitulant" (Briggs and Peate 1990, 145). This sense of the world as made of open systems interacting as self-ordering phenomena within a temporal flow brings science to an ontology like that articulated by Merleau-Ponty.

## MERLEAU-PONTY AS PHILOSOPHER OF
## DISSIPATIVE STRUCTURES

> The very pulp of the sensible, what is indefinable in it, is nothing
> else than the union in it of the "inside" with the "outside," the
> contact in thickness of self with self—The absolute of the "sensi-
> ble" is this stabilized explosion, i.e. involving return. The relation
> between the circularities (my body-the sensible) does not present
> the difficulties that the relation between "layers" or linear orders
> presents.
>
> —Merleau-Ponty, "working note," November 1960

Merleau-Ponty's last written sentence in his unfinished manuscript
about the nature of truth (published posthumously as *The Visible and the Invisible*) asks the question whether the present terms and contexts of explanation were not "insufficient to define our openness upon 'something'" (Merleau-Ponty 1968, 162). Merleau-Ponty's question highlights the fact that both
the nature of the relationship of self and world and the identities of both terms
of the relationship have not been properly formulated in the intellectual tradition he inherits. Throughout his life, Merleau-Ponty sought to articulate the
same sense of existence that can be summed up by Saint-Exupéry's statement
that "man is but a network of relationships"—the statement with which Merleau-Ponty ended the *Phenomenology of Perception.*[5] Many treatments of Merleau-Ponty's thought seem to emphasize the positive resonance he delineated
between the dynamic unfolding of the environment, history, and the affairs of
people, that leaves us always at "the first day"—the effulgence of new sense
from our intertwining with the world. Nonetheless, Merleau-Ponty's vision of
human being "helixed" with the world, in a "chiasm" with the world, as he put
it at the end of his life, has a dark side too.

Virginia Woolf's writings, I believe, articulate much of the same sense of
embodiment and perception, as well as a nontraditional ontology that parallels
Merleau-Ponty's work. Passages from *To the Lighthouse*, for example, provide
images of the positive sense of the resources for new meaning in Merleau-
Ponty's idea of "reversibility."[6] However, Woolf's text also provides images of
the sense of the intertwining of the unfolding relationship between the perceiver and world that captures the darker aspect of Merleau-Ponty's analysis in
its resonance with chaos theory. In the text, Virginia Woolf has just described
how sitting down to the candle-lit table has managed to give a sense of soli-
darity to the group around the table that is facing the large window overlook-
ing the ocean-night:

> [F]or the night was now shut off by panes of glass, which, far
> from giving any accurate view of the outside world, rippled so
> strangely that here, inside the room,seemed to be order and dry
> land; there, outside, a reflection in which things wavered and
> vanished, waterily.
>
> Some change at once went through them all, as if this had
> really happened, and they were all conscious of making a party to-
> gether in a hollow, on an island; had their common cause against
> the fluidity out there.[7]

The reversibility of this moment is apparent. In looking out at the night pressing against the pane of glass, the assembled group sees itself from the perspective that the night would have on them, mere waverings of existence within an encompassing fluidity that is dark, engulfing, and ongoing. This scene expresses the fragility of being a seer only because, as Merleau-Ponty repeatedly states, each seer is caught up in the seen.[8] As one of the characters, Lily Briscoe, ponders in the next sentences, one can feel connection, meaning, and exhilaration, only as the reverse side, as part of the same movement that also allows solidity to vanish, vast spaces to lay between partners, and the painful weight of destruction to be felt.

This other side of reversibility, the asymmetry, turbulence, loosening of relations, and the breakdown of rhythms where there had been a functioning intertwining or awareness is brilliantly articulated by Woolf in the middle section of the novel, titled "Time Passes." There she writes in the whisperings of the wind, the night, the material shiftings of the world, the rhythms of the seasons, in which the deaths of protagonists of the novel are mentioned in brief parenthetical asides. It seems more than coincidental that this section makes time, in its flow and unfolding (which enfolds surprising phenomena), both the protagonist and title of the section. This emphasis echoes both chaos theorists' assertion that time's flow and its historicity are finally being taken into account by science,[9] and Merleau-Ponty's initial assertion in *Phenomenology of Perception* that instead of a discrete "subject" of experience, "we must understand time as the subject and the subject as time" (Merleau-Ponty 1962, 422).

For Merleau-Ponty, both terms of the human-world relationship are time: "I myself am time" (Merleau-Ponty 1962, 421) and "time and significance are but one thing" (Merleau-Ponty 1962, 426). Accordingly, he later develops the sense of reversibility and the chiasmaic intertwining in terms of temporal unfolding: "one understands time as chiasm" (Merleau-Ponty 1968, 267).[10] It is only within temporal unfolding that there is the intertwining interplay and generation of overlapping significance designated as "reversibility."

The tradition had maintained its dichotomies between distorting oppositional terms, such as subject versus object or mind versus matter, by taking the instant removed from time as the defining moment.

Woolf writes, at the beginning of the stunning twenty-five-page interlude that details time's passing, that "a downpouring of immense darkness began. Nothing, it seemed, could survive the flood, the profusion of darkness . . . there was scarcely anything left of the body or mind by which one could say, 'This is he' or 'this is she.'"[11] It is because each person is only a rhythm in the beating of these forces, a way in which they come into a certain rhythm for a time, known as Mrs. Ramsey or Lily Briscoe, that suddenly, by some absurd little occurence that rhythm can cease to be.

However, it is in the same sense of precarious reversibility, what Merleau-Ponty called a "thread" in the "fabric of the world," that one is also part of a resonating, circulating, and cooperative articulating—dialogically—with the world in perception, in speech, in love, in art, in thought. The illumination and the darkness are inseparable moments of a fragile process, which transforms in differing moments of its shimmering rhythms. Reversibility not only means that both sides of the relationship make each other be what each is in its discrete identity, but also that this relationship is itself double-sided: both comprising the illumination of "this Visibility, this generality of the Sensible" as a shared power of the human world, but also yielding darkness, disintegration, and recalcitrance (Merleau-Ponty 1968, 139). This sense of the world, made of open systems interacting as self-ordering phenomena within a temporal flow, brings science to an ontology like that articulated by Merleau-Ponty.

In the introduction to the *Phenomenology of Perception*, many points take on a different resonance when one keeps the principles of chaos theory in mind. Merleau-Ponty begins by asserting that the individual's identity is a function of a constant retrieval from being caught up within the inexhaustibility of the unfolding world—understood as a weave "incorporating the most surprising phenomena" (Merleau-Ponty 1962, x)—in which "some local circumstance or other seems to have been decisive" (Merleau-Ponty 1962, xxviii), and whose massive indeterminate identity only emerges through a faith that is actually a peculiar iteration: "'There is the world'; I can never completely account for this ever-reiterated assertion in my life" (Merleau-Ponty 1962, xvii). This assertion, the ever-reiterated factor of perceptual faith, is like the strange attractors that chaos theorists have discovered in the unfolding of complex material interrelations in a far-from-equilibrium flow: a so-named "irrational" value repeating itself within the dynamic interplay of the relations of the open system that causes an indeterminate, intermittent, cycling back of order within chaos, of identity within difference. The reiteration of the world is the incompleteness—the openness—of human being that makes it always a coming back to itself from its ecstatic being in the phenomena.

In Merleau-Ponty's description of how one is absent from oneself as taken up in an ongoing becoming, the coming back to itself of human being is most tellingly articulated as a "deflagration"[12] or turbulence, in which one is returned to oneself[13] as a fold in the enfolding-unfolding of the "flesh of the world." This seems to make us, the human—as perceiver, as artist, as scientist—in our perceptual faith and ability to take up the sense of the world in meeting it, in active-passive dialogue or interplay, a constantly recurring dissipative structure.

The human as dissipative structure is echoed even in the way the *Phenomenology*'s introduction continues to describe the power of the body pulling seemingly disparate moments into a relatedness in which "chance happenings offset each other, and facts in their multiplicity coalesce and show up as a certain way of taking a stand in relation to the human situation, reveal in fact an event which has its definite outline" (Merleau-Ponty 1962, xviii–xix). From the perspective of chaos theory, perceptual faith is a strange attractor in the circulation of sense, in the interweaving of perceptual and material systems. Intentionality, here, is the means of feeding back the unfolding of itself and the world into its further becoming: the autopoiesis, as scientists call it (Briggs and Peate 1990, 154–55), or the self-organizing aspect of phenomena, as Merleau-Ponty characterizes it.

Merleau-Ponty describes the nature of perception as an intertwining process as early as the chapter "The Thing and the Natural World" in *Phenomenology of Perception*, when he calls the interplay of human and world "certain kinds of symbiosis, certain ways the outside has of invading us and certain ways we have of meeting this invasion" (Merleau-Ponty 1962, 317) which is "a coition of our body with things" (Merleau-Ponty 1962, 320). What emerges from this interplay is a continual becoming whose every fragment "satisfies an infinite number of conditions" and whose temporality is "to compress into each of its instants an infinity of relations" (Merleau-Ponty 1962, 323) as "a single temporal wave" (Merleau-Ponty 1962, 331). As in the flow phenomena described by chaos theory—even the literal flow of water in a stream with its turbulence but also limit cycles—perception emerges as an open system allowing differing rhythms to play into each other but also keeping alive the reiterating factors that were part of its unfolding.

The shift in scientific thinking from substance to event, embracing probabilities as a way of representing presumptive identities within interrelated processes is parallel to Merleau-Ponty's shift away from traditional ideas of substance to a notion in the *Phenomenology* that "the perceptual synthesis is a temporal synthesis, and subjectivity, at the level of perception is nothing but temporality." In trying to articulate what he means by the perceptual "field" that we are, Merleau-Ponty moves to an understanding of process that contains the same paradox as the idea of "dissipative structure": "The world, which is the nucleus of time, subsists only by virtue of that unique action which both separates and brings together" (Merleau-Ponty 1962, 332). The idea of feeding back the world into itself, so that it never literally recapitulates the past but is a novelty that draws on the past, was articulated in Merleau-Ponty's reinterpretation of Husserl's phenomenological notion of "sedimentation" or *Fundierung*. For Merleau-Ponty, sedimentation came to signify the way in which, through the iteration of perceptual faith, novel unfoldings developed previous rhythms in such a way that "a past which has never been a present" (Merleau-Ponty 1962, 242) was "realized" in the present. For Merleau-Ponty, it was a matter of coming to articulate a truer sense of "becoming" than Western philosophy had allowed by positing a Being or consciousness or sense of time and/or space outside the interplay of the sensible-sensing dialogical unfolding. This is precisely the direction in which Prigogine and Stengers see chaos theory leading science: toward a recognition of becoming (Prigogine and Stengers 1984, 310). For Merleau-Ponty, the indirect articulation of the sense of becoming will take him beyond traditional categories of philosophy but, even in the *Phenomenology of Perception*, he is moving in this direction: "under these circumstances one may say, if one wishes, that nothing exists absolutely, and it would, indeed, be more accurate to say that nothing exists and that everything is 'temporalized' (Merleau-Ponty 1962, 332).[14]

In *The Visible and the Invisible*, Merleau-Ponty understands the perceiver as perceiving "by dehiscence or fission of its own mass" (Merleau-Ponty 1968, 146), so that the perceived "is not a chunk of absolutely hard, indivisible being . . . but is rather a sort of straits between exterior horizons and interior horizons ever gaping open" (Merleau-Ponty 1968, 132). The perceiver and perceived are "two vortexes . . . the one slightly decentered with respect to the other" (Merleau-Ponty 1968, 138). Like Merleau-Ponty's image of the strands of the chromosome that constitute the chromosome's being in their encircling chiasm in order to represent this perceptual, intellectual, imaginative, emotional, etc., witnessing of the world, his sense of the relationship of the human and world as one in which they are "turning about one another" (Merleau-Ponty 1968, 264) has moved him far from the substance philosophies of the Western tradition.

Merleau-Ponty, in articulating this notion of embodiment as part of the flesh of the world—as part of an event of dynamic intertwining of open systems—has decentered the traditional sense of the subject. Criticizing Husserl's still progressive sense of the unfolding of time, Merleau-Ponty anticipates his own later movement to a view of time lodged within the world in its "wild" being, a "barbaric time," one that is "without fictitious "support" in the psyche" (Merleau-Ponty 1968, 267). Without its traditional foundation within itself as self-subsistent consciousness, there is no more subject as discrete being, but rather, as Merleau-Ponty stated in the passage cited as epigraph to this section, a "relation between circularities," one that is part of the "return" in "this stabilizing explosion" that is "my body-the sensible" (Merleau-Ponty 1968, 268). In other words—the words of chaos theory—my body in the world is a way of interacting in an open and chaotic system to achieve self-organizing continuance.

Having articulated human being as part of a turbulent but self-organizing event or open system, Merleau-Ponty's later ontology has succeeded in describing how "there is no freedom without a field" (Merleau-Ponty 1962, 439) for human being, as he had claimed almost two decades before. Merleau-Ponty has undermined the materiality-mind split by showing that we are of the same stuff as the world, and that this "stuff" is an intertwining or enlacing open system of transformation:

> That means that my body is made of the same flesh as the world (it is a perceived), and moreover that this flesh of my body is shared by the world, the world *reflects* it, encroaches upon it and it encroaches upon the world (the felt [*senti*] at the same time the culmination of subjectivity and the culmination of materiality), they are in a relation of transgression or of overlapping. (Merleau-Ponty 1968, 248)

Merleau-Ponty has replaced the 2,500-year-old Platonic insistence that we are self-moving creatures of will grounded in transcendent reason by human beings moved within the world like flows of energies—some represented as material, some as mental—so that we are a part and a distinctive self-asserting factor, but no more. Our freedom in maintaining ourselves and in transforming ourselves is only possible because we belong to the flux of the open system of which we are an active constituent.

The notion of intertwining means that Merleau-Ponty has conceived human being to be a fragile being, a vulnerable being. As a dissipative structure, reiterating its faith in recapitulating its rhythmic becoming with others, the human being is always on the brink of being lost in larger cycles and turbulences. This is a philosophy that recognizes our mortality, our fragility, and our openness in a way that is opposed to a long tradition of patriarchal thought.[15] It is one thing to determine that lives are processes, parts of chaotic systems, but another kind of recognition is needed to take to heart the transitory, fragile, and unpredictable nature of our existence.

The ramifications of Merleau-Ponty's ontology and chaos theory's deli-
nation of systems have been embraced by Susan Griffin in a painstaking examination of hundreds of key texts in the Western scientific and philosophical tradition. Griffin draws the conclusion that the dualistic philosophical and
scientific tradition was an effort to separate the "spirit from matter . . . the
clean from the unclean. The decaying, the putrid, the polluted, the fetid, the
eroded, waste, defecation, from the unchanging."[16] The motivation she finds
as a subtext recurring throughout the texts of this tradition is that "the thought
of their death terrifies them" (Griffin 1978, 121). The tradition holds philosophy and science apart from the question of facing mortality, as discrete endeavors, but given the way in which each relationship to self and world inter-
plays with all others, can we honestly maintain this separation?[17]

## EMBRACING INTERWEAVING, FRAGILITY, AND MORTALITY

If, for the moment, we accept that in articulating an ontology and epistemology that places humans in an interplaying flow with the rest of the
planet—as a dynamic, material being—then we must also face the conclusion
that we are facing the inherent instability of human existence, its contingency
within the vectors of the open system, and our inevitable dissipation. For many
contemporary thinkers, this means facing the overflow from the masculine-
heroic ideal of overcoming or denying the power of death that has shaped our
philosophical and scientific tradition. In her work, *Woman and Nature: The
Roaring Within*, Griffin details patriarchy's march of classical rationalistic philosophy and science as a war of denial against matter in its enveloping, cyclic
nature, in its promise of interaction with the world and others. If, in a warrior
mentality, a vulnerability to death, the devourer, meant defeat, then matter itself becomes an enemy, as well as something from which one must separate—
even though this presents an impossible project. The war against matter was
also a war against whatever was identified with women, since woman was identified by this same tradition with nature and matter:

> He says that woman speaks with nature. That she hears voices
> from under the earth. That wind blows in her ears and trees whis-
> per to her. That the dead sing through her mouth and the cries of
> the infants are clear to her. But for him this dialogue is over. He
> says he is not part of this world, that he was set on this world as a
> stranger. He sets himself apart from woman and nature. (Griffin
> 1978, 1)

To see matter as distinct from mind and then to identify mind as the human essence is a *motivated* assertion: it serves the purpose of hiding from mortality. Both Merleau-Ponty's ontology and chaos theory not only face the implications of mortality that undoing the dualistic retreat from matter entails, but both conceive of matter as itself part of a dynamic, unfolding open system of forces. Thus, they reveal, for the first time, the authentic fragility of both human and nonhuman existence. Yet, at the same time, such a system does not consign existence—human and nonhuman—on this planet to an utter foundationlessness nor to a sense of chaos in its oppositional dualism as mere randomness. Rather, in chaos as we have described it in this chapter, there is a self-ordering that promotes both meaning and vitality, but it is precarious.

As "outcasts" from the insulating power structures of patriarchy, Griffin maintains that many women been have consigned by the weight of history to enter what she calls "the room of the undressing." This is a recognition of vulnerabilty and interconnectedness with the rest of the planet—its creatures and material beings. Marked by the dualisms of the scientific and philosophical tradition, women have been targets of exploitation and devaluation in ways parallel to aspects of the material environment. However, like Woolf and Merleau-Ponty in the passages quoted above, Griffin recognizes that in being forced—even coerced—to face the vulnerability of our material being in kin with other entities on the planet, there is also a wisdom gained that had been ignored by the tradition: "Where we go in darkness. Where we embrace darkness. . . . The shape of this cave, our bodies, this darkness. This darkness which sits so close to us we cannot see, so close that we move away in fear. We turn into ourselves. But here we find the same darkness, we find we are shaped around an emptiness, that we are a void that we do not know" (Briggs and Peate 1990, 157–59 ). Although obtained at the cost of oppression, the insight is valuable. The freedom from a substantialist view of reality, the return to indeterminacy and interweavement, betokens a vulnerability that Griffin sees emerging by different avenues in modern science. Ironically, Western science, as one of the systems that helped to devalue both the status of materiality and women has been forced by its own conceptual impasses to move toward insights that closely parallel the journey that women's spirituality has had to make in dealing with its difficult history.

Then the fractal reiterations of chaos theory take on a different weight, the weightiness of being embodied without the guarantee of linear order and the eternity of substance. Dissipative structures and sudden catastrophic change suddenly take on a different sense when it is the rhythm of my heart that may be swept up suddenly in a vortex of turbulence and I will be no more. Philosophy since Plato has sought to create an infinite distance between our "true being" and nonbeing, in which realm we are temporarily residing. However, chaos theory, Merleau-Ponty's ontology, and Griffin's conviction that "We are nature seeing nature. We are nature with a concept of nature. Nature weeping. Nature speaking of nature to nature . . . and when I see the arc [of the bird's flight] . . . I fly with her . . . leave myself, die for an instant, live in the body of this bird whom I cannot live without, as part of the body of the bird will enter my daughter's body . . ." (Griffin 1990, 226–27) suggest that this gap does not exist: life is death in nonlinear iterations smiling through the face of time.

These reflections bring us back to the image with which this chapter began: the dead father. If traditional science and philosophy were part of an articulation of the human identity that sought to screen out the threat of uncontrollable, unpredictable change, and death, they also erected a barrier to embracing the source of dynamism and transformation which is the heart of vitality. In the denial of death, the father was creating what he feared:

> No one can remember when he was not here in our city positioned like a sleeper in troubled sleep, the whole expanse of him running from the Avenue Pommard to the Boulevard Grist. Overall length, 3,200 cubits. Half buried in the ground, half not.
>
> At work ceaselessly night and day through all the hours for the good of all. He controls the hussars. Controls the rise, fall, flutter of the market. Controls what Thomas is thinking, what Thomas has always thought, what Thomas will ever think, with exceptions. The left leg, entirely mechanical, said to be the administrative center of his operations, working ceaselessly night and day through all the hours, for the good of all. In the left leg, in sudden tucks or niches, we find things we need. . . .
>
> We want the Dead Father to be dead. We sit with tears in our eyes wanting the Dead Father to be dead—meanwhile doing amazing things with our hands.[18]

The corpse of the dead father kept blocking the avenues of thought: in science, philosophy, politics, economics, religion, and all avenues of human expression. This rule of a certain linear logic was often thought to be an enlightenment, a boon for the good of all, by those who proclaimed its universality. But this spirit of disconnection and inertness cast the only life left in his own image: a death in life.

Merleau-Ponty's last, unfinished manuscript was a long meditation on his frustration that notions of the thing, of the world, of psychology, and many of the key concepts of the Western tradition had been arrived at by a refusal to enter into the interrogative and involving nature of experience. The positivity, plentitude, and self-identity of concepts referring to things were the result of "threatening the things with our non-recognition of them": "The thing thus defined is not the thing of our experience, it is the image we obtain of it by projecting it into a universe . . . where the spectator would abandon the spectacle" (Merleau-Ponty 1968, 162). This is the detached stance of patriarchal philosophy and science—Barthelme's image of the dead father—that does not want to be implicated in a system that is contingent, interdependent, and unpredictable. Instead of maintaining this traditional distance, Merleau-Ponty called for facing up to the reality that "the thing, the pebble, the shell, we said do not have the power to exist in the face of and against everything; they are only mild forces that develop their implications on condition that favorable circumstances be assembled" (Merleau-Ponty 1968, 161). This vision of interplaying forces, even of the most "solid material objects," as radically open to the fluctuations of other forces, leaves us without the firm foundation of the tradition. So Merleau-Ponty notes of the recognition necessary to open this new vision: "we learn to know the fragility of the "real'" (Merleau-Ponty 1968, 40).

Merleau-Ponty struck a blow against the dead fathers when he claimed that "perceiving, speaking, even thinking" are experiences "both irrecusable and enigmatic" (Merleau-Ponty 1968, 130). The intellect and other modes of apprehension and articulation are not vehicles to remove us from being caught in interdependent and fluctuating processes, they only involve us more completely in a shared fragility with other beings. Thus, rather than certainty and security, Merleau-Ponty saw the fruit of inquiry to be "the insistent reminder of a mystery as familiar as it is unexplained, of a light which, illuminating the rest, remains at its source obscurity" (Merleau-Ponty 1968, 130). This is a different vision than that of an illumination that dispels doubt and allows for control of the planet and our existence.

The body, on Merleau-Ponty's account, is not separate, quantifiable, and ultimately mechanical, as is the corpse-body of the dead father. Instead, Merleau-Ponty postulates that "our own body is in the world as the heart is in the organism" (Merleau-Ponty 1962, 203). This metaphor can be seen as a sign that Merleau-Ponty was willing to let blood back into philosophy—its vitality—and think matter, not as inertness, but in the ensnaring pulsation of the "flesh of the world." Within the way of flesh in which selves and world entwine, he saw the chaos that is not the opposite of order, that is not blind randomness, the dead father's projection of fear, but rather, is a "winding," a "*serpentement*," the serpent, the ancient Goddess symbol of fecundity, of the risk of dissipation as part of ongoing cycles of creation and dissipation. The way to see this creative spiralling is not to pay attention to the stare of the dead father into the heavens, but to focus on our bodies within the matrix of the world, on how we are "meanwhile doing amazing things with our hands."

## NOTES

Author's Note: This essay is dedicated to the fond memory of Linda Singer. Her inspiration continues, and her thoughts helped form many thoughts in this essay (as she remains part of the process described here). However, the directly embodied presence of her shining spirit is sorely missed.

1. That is, in what Merleau-Ponty would call a chiasmatic relationship, as the two strands of chromosomal material entwine each other, neither two nor simply one.

2. John Briggs and F. David Peate, *The Turbulent Mirror* (New York: Harper and Row, 1990), p. 13.

3. Kali is the wild, erractic, dancing Hindu goddess of death and destruction.

4. If one looks at the supposed entity called a "lake," one finds various transformations interlocked in rhythmic patterns of ongoing transition or what Merleau-Ponty called "passage." One aspect of these fluxes is constituted by the population of pike preying on the population of trout. If one stocks the trout, the feasting pikes' numbers balloon. However, the now scarce trout spell the spiralling decrease of the pike. In turn, this ebb of pike only means the beginning of the curve upward of trout numbers in phase space. Yet, this spiral is a tale too simple to do justice to the complexity of the biosphere, to the fecund perceptual world. Frog-insect cycles also call for a meeting with pike-trout cycles and the representational spirals blossom into tori, doughnut shaped spaces of mapped rhythms. The movement within orders is fed into the movement among orders, the complicated cycles are not random, do not wobble off into sheer dissipation, but they too find a way, settle into a path of an "attractor." This bit of phase space seems to "pull" the system into patterns of change. The "pull" is a way of expressing that perturbations in the system that could have caused change or a new direction if merely added as external units, instead events are resisted from having this effect by the system feeding back into itself, allowing self-regulation or auto-ordering. What emerges in the represented change of the system is a circling on the surface of the sketched doughnut, a wavelike line that circles the doughnut without closing its path. This tracing a way in the phase space of events never quite links up with itself, and slinks unendingly around the surface of the torus chasing itself in a nonperiodic return: an identity of rhythm, which is not self-coincident (Briggs and Peate 1990, 37–40).

5. Maurice Merleau-Ponty, *Phenomenology of Perception*, trans. Colin Smith (New York: Humanities, 1962), p. 456.

6. See especially chapters 2 and 3 in Mazis, *Emotion and Embodiment: Fragile Ontology* (New York: Peter Lang, 1994).

7. Virginia Woolf, *To the Lighthouse* (New York: Harcourt, Brace, and World, Inc, 1927), p. 147.

8. "Thus since the seer is caught up in what he sees, it is still himself he sees: this is the fundamental narcissism of all vision. And thus, for the same reason, the vision he exercises, he also undergoes from things, such that, as many painters have said, I feel myself looked at by the things, my activity is equally passivity—which is the second and more profound sense of the narcissism . . . so that the seer and the visible reciprocate one another, and we no longer know which sees and which is seen" (Merleau-Ponty 1968, 139).

9. "The conceptual evolution we have described is itself embedded in a wider history, that of the progressive rediscovery of time. We have seen new aspects of time being progressively incorporated into physics, while the ambitions to omniscience inherent in classical science were progressively rejected" (Ilya Prigogine and Isabelle Stengers, *Order out of Chaos: Man's Dialogue with Nature* [New York: Bantam, 1984], p. 208).

10. For an extended treatment of how reversibility is about temporal intertwining see Mazis, "Merleau-Ponty and the 'Backward Flow' of Time: The Reversibility of Temporality and the Temporality of Reversibility," in *Merleau-Ponty: Hermeneutics and Postmodernism*, ed. Busch and Gallagher (Albany: State University of New York Press, 1992), pp. 53–68.

11. Woolf, pp. 189–90.

12. "Eye and Mind," trans. Carleton Dallery, collected in *The Primacy of Perception and Other Essays*, ed. James Edie (Evanston: Northwestern University Press, 1964), p. 180.

13. "Now perhaps we have a better sense of what is meant by that little verb 'to see.' Vision is not a certain mode of thought or presence to self; it is the means given me for being absent from myself, for being present at the fission of Being from the inside—the fission at whose termination, and not before, I come back to myself" (Merleau-Ponty 1964, 186).

14. "The ideal of objective thought is both based upon and ruined by temporality. The world, in the full sense of the word, is not an object, for though it has an envelope of objective and determinate attributes, it also has fissures and gaps . . ." (Merleau-Ponty 1962, 333).

15. See Mazis, *The Trickster, Magician, and Grieving Man: Reconnecting Men with Earth* (Santa Fe: Bear and Co., 1994), especially "Part One," which traces from Plato and the Greek reinterpretation of the "heroic," the genesis of a dualistic tradition that maximizes a sense of autonomy of self in order to negate the threatening sense of dispersion in mortality.

16. Susan Griffin, *Woman and Nature* (New York: Harper and Row, 1978), p. 95.

17. See also chapter one, Mazis, *Emotion and Embodiment: Fragile Ontology*.

18. Donald Barthelme, *The Dead Father* (New York: Simon and Schuster, 1975), pp. 10–11.

CHAPTER 14

# Afterword

## JAMES MORLEY

Inside and outside are inseparable. The world is wholly inside and
I am wholly outside of myself.

—Merleau-Ponty, *Phenomenology of Perception*

This volume has articulated an approach to the psychic that must become increasingly focal to philosophical inquiry, social theory, and psychological research. Recent advances in science and technology teach us, over and
again, that the mind is interwoven with the very fabric of nature, challenging
philosophers and psychologists to rethink the categories summarized by the
terms *interiority* and *exteriority*. As we learn of the complexity and intelligence
inherent in nature, the paradigm of inert matter and transcendental mind can
no longer sustain itself. We are forced to come to grips with mind as embedded in the external world and with matter, even nonorganic matter, as living,
patterned, and structured in a manner that can only be described as psychical.
The psychic, understood in terms of structure or system, supersedes interiority and exteriority; it joins them together.

The authors of this text have taken up that aspect of Merleau-Ponty's
thought that engages, and allows us to engage, with the psychic continuity of
cultural and physical existence. Merleau-Ponty's close reading of phenomenology, gestalt psychology, and psychoanalysis, led him to conclude that psychic

life and the world compose a totality that is not reducible to binary theoretical categories but is the ground from which all categories must arise.

The primacy of structure over both the physical and the ideal was taught to us by the gestalt psychologists. Yet despite the acceptance of certain aspects of gestalt thought by mainstream psychologists, it has proven difficult to escape the way of thinking that understands perceptual phenomena as *inside* a physical (external) brain. Merleau-Ponty is one of the very few thinkers who have taken up the bold metaphysical implications of a psychology of form. Merleau-Ponty realized that "pattern" is not a matter of brain function but that on a more fundamentally existential and ontological level, it is the underlying truth of how the world, itself, exists. By salvaging the fundamental insight of the gestalt school from psychology's perpetual collapse of the internal into the external, Merleau-Ponty shows us the possibility of cutting the Gordian knot of the dualism of subject and object.

The studies in this volume have successfully abstained from the dichotomization entailed by the categories of "subject" and "object," but, although they have rejected theoretical, and beyond it, ontological dichotomization, they have not collapsed internality and externality into one another. Rather, they have pursued Merleau-Ponty's project of inaugurating a discourse of continuity. Internality and externality are connected as much as they are distinguished, like the relations between figure and ground, or the imaginary and the real, or ourselves and other people and our cultural institutions. "Internal" and "external" comprise the multiple threads of a common fabric, sustaining its structure by their very divergence.

The continuity of interiority and exteriority has broad implications for the human sciences. The positing of continuity allows us to link the natural and social in a common stream of life and to acknowledge coexistence. What classical phenomenology called "intersubjectivity" Merleau-Ponty tightened into "intercorporeality" or the "flesh of the world"; in other words: the world as the common fabric, or flesh, out of which we arise as vantage points. Many of the essays in this volume have highlighted the lived body as the starting point of social inquiry. We are not isolated interiorities signalling to alien exteriorities across empty voids, but nodal points within a common system of relations. "Continuity" allows an integrative approach to the social and several of our authors have worked with the body image as the site where culture and flesh are most evidently interwoven.

By taking body schema out of the dualistic constraints of "interior" and "exterior," endemic to mainstream psychology, the understanding of body as the site of the psychic continuum offers psychology and psychiatry a fresh vantage point for future research and therapeutic applications. Allopathic medicine's commitment to external material causes for all bodily symptoms has stood in the way of a comprehensive understanding of imaginary bodily phenomena (so-called psychosomatic illnesses). The failure of allopathy to treat complex systemic illness will not be remedied by extending its mechanistic metaphysics into the psychosocial, but by a radical rethinking, such as that offered by Merleau-Ponty's ontology of structure, of this physio-psycho-social nexus. The recent neurological concept of "brain plasticity" indicates that our experience of the world structures our nervous system as much as our nervous system structures our experience of the world. One way of comprehending this circularity is the continuum model offered by this book. The end of a volume such as this one, if it has achieved its aims at all, can only be a beginning. We hope that this collection of essays has presented to scholars and practitioners in the human sciences, not conclusions, but an introduction to a general theoretical approach or attitude: a distinct and fruitful way of looking at the natural and human world.

# Contributors

DOROTHEA OLKOWSKI is Professor and Co-Chair of Philosophy at the University of Colorado, Colorado Springs, where she founded and directed the Program in Women's Studies until 1995. She is the author of *Gilles Deleuze and The Ruin of Representation* (University of California). She is the editor of *Feminist Enactments of French Philosophy* (Cornell).

JAMES MORLEY is Senior Lecturer, Department of Psychology, at Richmond College, The American International University in London, and former Chair of the Psychology Department at Saint Joseph College, Connecticut. His teaching and publications apply the thought of Merleau-Ponty to the psychology of imagination, human development, psychopathology, classical Indian yoga, and health studies. He is secretary to the Society for Phenomenology and Psychiatry and is currently co-editing a collection, with James Phillips, on philosophical psychopathology titled: *Imagination and its Pathologies.*

EDWARD S. CASEY is Professor and Chair of the Department of Philosophy at the State University of New York at Stony Brook. Casey's primary interests are in twentieth-century continental philosophy, especially phenomenology and deconstruction; aesthetics; and psychoanalysis. He has written a series of books: *Imagining, Remembering, Getting Back into Place* (all Indiana), and most recently, *The Fate of Place* (University of California).

HELEN A. FIELDING is Assistant Professor of Philosophy and Women's Studies at the University of Western Ontario. Her work brings together French philosophy and feminism. She is the author of "The Sum of What She is Saying: Bringing Essentials Back to the Body," and a bibliography of feminist essays on French philosophy (both in *Feminist Enactments of French Philosophy*, Cornell).

ELIZABETH GROSZ teaches in the Department of Comparative Literature at the State University of New York at Buffalo. She is the author of *Space, Time, and Perversions, The Politics of Bodies* (Routledge), *Volatile Bodies, Toward a Corporeal Feminism* (Indiana), and she is co-editor, with Elspeth Probyn, of *Sexy Bodies, The Strange Carnalities of Feminism* (Routledge).

LAWRENCE HASS is Associate Professor of Philosophy at Muhlenberg College. He is the author of articles on Merleau-Ponty and other themes in twentieth-century continental philosophy. He is co-editor, with Dorothea Olkowski, of *Rereading Merleau-Ponty; Essays Beyond the Continental-Analytic Divide* (Humanities) and, in progress, *Singing the World's Praises, Merleau-Ponty's Philosophy of Expression.*

GALEN A. JOHNSON is Professor of Philosophy and Director of the University Honors Program at the University of Rhode Island. His publications include numerous translations, more than thirty articles, and books, including, *Earth and Sky, History and Philosophy* (1989) and two edited collections, *Ontology and Alterity in Merleau-Ponty*, with Michael B. Smith (Northwestern), and *The Merleau-Ponty Aesthetics Reader* (Northwestern).

NOBUO KAZASHI teaches Contemporary Philosophy at Hiroshima City University. His publications focus on the intersection of the thought of Merleau-Ponty, James, and Nishida.

ALPHONSO LINGIS is Professor of Philosophy at Pennsylvania State University. He is a noted translator of Merleau-Ponty and the author of many books including, *Abuses* (University of California) and *The Community of Those Who Have Nothing in Common* (Indiana).

GLEN A. MAZIS is Associate Professor of Humanities and Philosophy at Pennsylvania State Harrisburg. Author of many essays on Merleau-Ponty, ontology, emotion, imagination, and aesthetics, he is the author of *The Trickster, Magician, and Grieving Mann: Reconnecting Men with Embodiment* (Bear Press) and a book on phenomenology, *Emotion and Embodiment: Fragile Ontology* (Lang).

DAVID E. PETTIGREW is Associate Professor of Philosophy at Southern Connecticut State University. Pettigrew is co-editor of *Disseminating Lacan* (SUNY) and has cotranslated four books on Jacques Lacan and Martin Heidegger including, Juan-David Nasio's *Five Lessons on the Psychoanalytic Theory of Jacques Lacan* (SUNY) and Françoise Dastur's *Heidegger and the Question of Time* (Humanities).

JAMES PHILLIPS is Associate Clinical Professor of Psychiatry at the Yale School of Medicine. His research emphasizes the interface between psychiatry and philosophy. He is the author of "Latency and the Unconscious in Merleau-Ponty" (Duquesne), "Hermeneutics in Psychoanalysis: Review and Reconsideration" (*Psychoanalysis and Contemporary Thought*), and "Lacan and Merleau-Ponty" (*Disseminating Lacan*, SUNY).

MICHAEL B. SMITH is Professor of French at Berry College. His translations include works by Michel de Certeau, Emmanuel Levinas, and Merleau-

Ponty. He has published on the work of Michel de Certeau, Emmanuel Levinas, Merleau-Ponty, Charles Peguy, and Catherine Chalier.

GAIL WEISS is Associate Professor of Philosophy graduate program in the Human Sciences at The George Washington University. She is the author of *Body Images: Embodiment as Intercorporeality* (Routledge) and co-editor of *Perspectives on Embodiment: The Intersection between Nature and Culture* (Routledge).

WILHELM S. WURZER is Professor of Philosophy at Duquesne University. He is the author of *Spinoza and Nietzsche* (Humanities) and *Judgment and Filming: Between Heidegger and Adorno* (Humanities), as well as numerous articles in postmodern aesthetics, hermeneutics, and deconstruction. He is founder of the International Philosophical Seminar (IPS) in Alto Adige, Italy.

# SELECTED BIBLIOGRAPHY

Allport, Gordon. "The Productive Paradoxes of William James." *On the Way toward a Phenomenological Psychology: Psychology of William James.* Ed. Hans Linschoten. Trans. Amedeo Girogi. Pittsburgh: Duquesne University Press, 1968.

Aristotle. *Poetics.* Trans. Ingram Bywater. *The Basic Works of Aristotle.* Ed. Richard McKeon. New York: Random House, 1947.

————. *Ethics.* Trans. W. D. Ross. *The Basic Works of Aristotle.* Ed. Richard McKeon. New York: Random House, 1947.

Artaud, Antonin. *Collected Works.* Volume One. Trans. Victor Corti. London: John Calder, 1978.

Barabas, Renaud. *De l'être du phénomène: Sur l'ontologie de Merleau-Ponty.* Paris: Jérôme Millon, 1991.

Barnes, Jonathan. *Early Greek Philosophy.* New York: Penguin Books 1987.

Barthelme, Donald. *The Dead Father.* New York: Simon and Schuster, 1975.

Bergson. *Time and Free Will.* Trans. F. L. Pogson. New York: The Macmillan Company, 1959.

Binswanger, Ludwig. "The Case of Ellen West." Trans. Werner M. Mendel and Joseph Lyons. *Existence: A New Dimension in Psychiatry and Psychology.* Ed. Rollo May, Ernest Angel, and Henri F. Ellenberger. New York: Basic Books, 1958.

Briggs, John, and F. David Peate. *The Turbulent Mirror.* New York: Harper and Row, 1990.

Butler, Judith. *Bodies that Matter: On the Discursive Limits of "Sex".* New York: Routledge, 1993.

Camus, Albert. *Lyrical and Critical Essays.* Trans. Ellen Conroy Kennedy. Ed. Philip Thody. New York: Vintage Books, 1968.

Charbonnier, Georges. "*Douze entretiens avec Maurice Merleau-Ponty.*" Recorded for *Radio-Télévision Française* May 22–August 8, 1958. Transcript. Paris: Institut National de l'Audiovisuel, 1958.

Collins, Patricia Hill. *Black Feminist Thought.* New York: Routledge, 1990.

Dastur, Françoise. "Merleau-Ponty and Thinking from Within." *Merleau-Ponty in Contemporary Perspective.* Ed. Patrick Burke and Jan Van der Veken. The Hague: Kluwer Academic Publishers, 1993.

Deleuze, Gilles. *Foucault.* Trans. Sean Hand. Minneapolis: University Press, 1986.

Derrida, Jacques. *Of Grammatology.* Trans. Gayatri Chakravorty Spivak. Baltimore: The Johns Hopkins University Press, 1976.

Dillard, Annie. *Pilgrim at Tinker Creek.* New York: Harper and Row, 1985.

Dillon, M. C., ed. *Merleau-Ponty's Ontology.* Indianapolis: Indiana University Press, 1988.

Dreyfus, Hubert L. *What Computers Can't Do.* Revised Edition. New York: Harper & Row, 1979.

Edie, James. *William James and Phenomenology.* Bloomington: Indiana University Press, 1987.

Fanon, Frantz. *Black Skin White Masks.* Trans. Charlem Lam Markmann. New York: Grove Weidenfeld, 1967.

Foucault, Michel. *Discipline and Punish: The Birth of the Prison.* Trans. Alan Sheridan. New York: Vintage Books, 1977.

———. *Maurice Blanchot, The Thought from the Outside,* Trans. Brian Massumi. New York: Zone Books, 1987.

Freud, Sigmund. "Creative Writers and Day Dreaming." *The Standard Edition of the Complete Psychological Works of Sigmund Freud.* Trans. James Strachey. London: Hogarth Press, 1986.

———. *Dora: An Analysis of a Case of Hysteria,* Trans. James Strachey, New York: Macmillan, 1963.

———. "On Narcissism: An Introduction." *A General Selection from the Works of Sigmund Freud.* Ed.. John Rickman. New York: Liveright Publishing Corp, 1957.

———. "The Ego and the Id." *The Freud Reader.* Ed. Peter Gay. New York: W.W. Norton, 1989.

———. *The Ego and the Id.* Trans. James Strachy. New York: W.W. Norton, 1962.

———. "The History of an Infantile Neurosis (The Wolf Man)." *Freud: Case Histories II.* Trans. James Strachey. Hammondsworth: Penguin Books, 1979.

———. *The Interpretation of Dreams.* Trans. James Strachey. New York: Avon Books, 1965.

Gallop, Jane. *Reading Lacan.* Ithaca: Cornell University Press, 1985.

Goldberg, David Theo. "Introduction" and "The Social Formation of Racist Discourse." *Anatomy of Racism.* Ed. David Theo Goldberg. Minneapolis: University of Minnesota Press, 1990.

Green, A. "*Du comportement à la chair: itineraire de Merleau-Ponty,*" *Critique,* no. 211 (1964).

Griffin, Susan. *Woman and Nature,* New York: Harper and Row, 1978.

Grosz, Elizabeth. *Jacques Lacan: A Feminist Introduction.* London: Routledge, 1990.

———. *Volatile Bodies: Toward a Corporeal Feminism.* Bloomington: Indiana University. Press, 1994.

Hass, Lawrence. "The Antinomy of Perception: Merleau-Ponty and Causal Representation Theory." *Man and World.* 24 (1991): 13–25.

Heidegger, Martin. "Logos." *Early Greek Thinking.* Trans. David Farrell Krell and Frank Capuzzi. San Francisco: Harper & Row, 1984.

———. *On Time and Being.* Trans. Joan Stambaugh. New York: Harper & Row, 1972.

———. "The Question Concerning Technology." *Basic Writings.* Ed. David Farrell Krell. New York: Harper and Row Publishers, 1977.

Henry, Michel. *The Essence of Manifestation.* Trans. G. Etzkorn. The Hague: Martinus Nijhoff, 1973.

Hesnard, A. *L'Oeuvre de Freud et son importance pour le monde moderne.* Paris: Payot, 1960.

hooks, bell. "Marginalization as Site of Resistance." *Out There: Marginalization and Contemporary Cultures.* Ed. Russell Ferguson, Martha Gever, Trinh T. Minh-ha, and Cornel West. New York: The New Museum of Contemporary Art & MIT, 1990.

Husserl, Edmund. *Cartesian Meditations.* Trans. Dorion Cairns. The Hague: Martinus Nijhoff, 1960.

———. *Ideas Pertaining to a Pure Phenomenology and to a Phenomenological Philosophy.* Trans. F. Kersten. Dordrecht: Kluwer Academic, 1982.

———. *The Crisis of European Sciences and Transcendental Phenomenology.* Trans. David Carr. Evanston: Northwestern University Press, 1970.

———. *The Idea of Phenomenology.* Trans. W. P. Alston and G. Nakhnikian. The Hague: Martinus Nijhoff, 1973.

James, William. *Essays in Radical Empiricism,* Ed. Ralph B. Perry. Gloucester: Peter Smith, 1967.

Johnson, Galen. "Introduction." *Ontology and Alterity in Merleau-Ponty.* Ed. Galen A. Johnson and Michael B. Smith. Evanston: Northwestern University Press, 1990.

Kristeva, Julia. *Powers of Horror: An Essay on Abjection.* Trans. Leon S. Roudiez. New York: Columbia University Press, 1982.

Lacan, Jacques. "Merleau-Ponty: In Memoriam." Trans. Wilfried Ver Eecke and Dirk de Schutter. *The Review of Existential Psychology and Psychiatry* 18. nos. 1,2,&3 (1982–1983).

———. "Of the Gaze As Objet Petit a." *The Four Fundamental Concepts of Psycho-Analysis* Ed. Jacques-Alain Miller. Trans. Alan Sheridan. New York: W.W. Norton, 1981.

———. "The Agency of the Letter in the Unconscious, or Reason Since Freud." *Écrits: A Selection.* Trans. Alan Sheridan. New York: Norton, 1977.

———. "The Mirror Stage as Formative of the Formation of the I." *Ecrits: A Selection.* Trans. Alan Sheridan. New York: W.W. Norton, 1977.

———. *The Seminar of Jacques Lacan: Book II.* Ed. Jacques-Alain Miller. Trans. Sylvana Tomasell. New York: W.W. Norton & Company, 1988.

Laplanche, J. *New Foundations for Psychoanalysis.* Trans. David Macey. Oxford: Basil Blackwell, 1989.

Lefort, Claude. "Flesh and Otherness." *Ontology and Alterity in Merleau-Ponty.* Galen Johnson and Michael B. Smith. Evanston: Northwestern University Press, 1990.

Levinas, Emmanuel. "Meaning and Sense." *Collected Philosophical Papers.* Trans. Alphonso Lingis. The Hague: Martinus Nijhoff, 1987.

———. *Totality and Infinity.* Trans. Alphonso Lingis. Pittsburgh: Duquesne University Press, 1969.

———. "Two Texts on Merleau-Ponty." Trans. Michael B. Smith. *Ontology and Alterity in Merleau-Ponty.* Ed. Galen A. Johnson and Michael B. Smith. Evanston: Northwestern University Press, 1990.

Lyotard, Jean-Francois. "Philosophy and Painting in the Age of Their Experimentation: Contribution to an Idea of Postmodernity." *The Merleau-Ponty Aesthetics Reader: Philosophy and Painting.* Ed. Galen A. Johnson. Evanston: Northwestern University Press, 1993.

Matustik, Martin J. "Merleau-Ponty on Taking the Attitude of the Other." *Journal of the British Society for Phenomenology* 22, no. 1 (January 1991).

Mazis, Glen. *Emotion and Embodiment: Fragile Ontology.* New York: Peter Lang, 1994.

———. "Merleau-Ponty and the 'Backward Flow' of Time: The Reversibility of Temporality and the Temporality of Reversibility." *Merleau-Ponty: Hermeneutics and Postmodernism.* Ed. Tom Busch and Shaun Gallagher. Albany: State University of New York Press, 1992.

———. *The Trickster, Magician, and Grieving Man: Reconnecting Men with Earth.* Santa Fe: Bear Press, 1994.

Mead, George Herbert. *Mind, Self, and Society from the Standpoint of a Social Behaviorist.* Ed. Charles W. Morris. Chicago: University of Chicago Press, 1962.

Merleau-Ponty, Maurice. "From Mauss to Claude Levi-Strauss." *Signs.* Trans. Richard C. McCleary. Evanston: Northwestern University Press, 1964.

———. "Merleau-Ponty in Person: An Interview with Madeleine Chapsal, 1960." *Texts and Dialogues.* Ed. Hugh J. Silverman and Jay Barry. Trans. Michael B. Smith. Atlantic Highlands: Humanities Press, 1992.

———. "Phenomenology and Psychoanalysis: Preface to Hesnard's *L'Oeuvre de Freud.*" Trans. Alden Fisher. *Review of Existential Psychology and Psychiatry, Merleau-Ponty and Psychology* XVIII, nos. 1,2,&3 (1982–1983).

———. *Phenomenology of Perception.* Trans. Colin. Smith. New York: Humanities Press, 1962. Revised edition. Ed. Forrest Williams. New York: Routledge Press, 1989. Originally published as *Phénoménologie de la perception.* Paris: Gallimard, 1945.

———. *Résumés de Cours: Collège de France, 1952–1960.* Paris: Éditions Gallimard, 1968.

———. *Sense and Non-Sense.* Trans. Hubert Dreyfus and Patricia Allen Dreyfus. Evanston: Northwestern University Press, 1964.

———. "The Child's Relations with Others." Trans. W. Cobb. *The Primacy of Perception.* Evanston: Northwestern University Press, 1964.

———. "The Indirect Language." *Prose of the World.* Trans. John O'Neill. Evanston: Northwestern University Press, 1973.

———. "The Philosopher and His Shadow." *Signs.* Trans. Richard C. McCleary. Evanston: Northwestern University Press, 1964. Originally published as "Le Philosophe et son ombre." *Signes.* Paris: Gallimard, 1960.

———. *The Prose of the World.* Trans. John O'Neill. Evanston: Northwestern University Press, 1973.

———. *The Structure of Behavior.* Trans. Alden L. Fisher. Pittsburgh: Duquesne University Press, 1983.

———. *The Visible and the Invisible.* Trans. Alphonso Lingis. Evanston: Northwestern University Press, 1968. Originally published as *Le Visible et l'invisible.* Paris: Gallimard, 1964.

Millay, Edna St. Vincent. "Dirge Without Music." *Selected Poems of Edna St. Vincent Millay: the Centenary Edition.* Ed. Colin Falck. New York: Harper, 1991.

Nishida, Kitaro. *An Inquiry into the Good.* Trans. Masao Abe and Christopher Ives. New Haven: Yale University Press, 1990.

————. *Fundamental Problems of Philosophy: The World of Action and the Dialectical World.* Trans. David Dilworth. Tokyo: Sophia University Press, 1970.

————. *Nishida Kitaro Tetsugaku Ronbunshuh: A Collection of Philosophical Articles by Kitaro Nishida.* 3 vols. Tokyo: Iwanami Shoten, 1989.

————. *The Complete Collection of Works by Nishida Kitaro.* 19 vols. Tokyo: Iwanami Shoten, 1953–55.

Nubuo, Kazashi. "The Musicality of the Other: Merleau-Ponty, Schutz, and Kimura." *The Prism of the Self.* Ed. Steven G. Crowell. Amsterdam: Kluwer Academic Publisher, 1995.

O'Neill, John. "The Mother-Tongue: The Infant's Search for Meaning." *Revue de l'Université d'Ottawa* 55 (1985).

————. "The Specular Body: Merleau-Ponty and Lacan on Infant, Self and Other." *Synthese* 66 (Fall 1986).

Olafson, Frederick A. *Heidegger and the Philosophy of Mind.* New Haven: Yale University Press, 1987.

Olkowski, Dorothea. "Merleau-Ponty's Freudianism: From the Body of Consciousness to the Body of Flesh." *Review of Existential Psychology and Psychiatry* 18, nos. 1, 2, & 3 (1982–83).

————. "Monstrous Reflection: Sade and Masoch—Rewriting the History of Reason." *Crises in Continental Philosophy.* Ed. Arlene B. Dallery and Charles E. Scott. New York: State University of New York Press, 1990.

Phillips, James. "Latency and the Unconscious in Merleau-Ponty." *Phenomenology and Psychoanalysis: The Sixth Annual Symposium of the Simon Silverman Phenomenology Center.* Pittsburgh: The Simon Silverman Phenomenogy Center, Duquesne University, 1988.

Pontalis, J. B. "*Presence, entre les signes, absence.*" *L'Arc*, no. 46 (1971).

————. "The Problem of the Unconscious in Merleau-Ponty's Thought." Trans. Wilfried Ver Eecke and Michael Greer. *The Review of Existential Psychology & Psychiatry* 18, nos. 1,2, & 3 (1982–1983).

Prigogine, Ilya, and Isabelle Stengers. *Order out of Chaos: Man's Dialogue with Nature.* New York: Bantam, 1984.

Ragland-Sullivan, Ellie. *Jacques Lacan and the Philosophy of Psychoanalysis.* Chicago: University of Illinois Press, 1986.

Ricoeur, Paul. *Freud and Philosophy.* Trans. D. Savage. New Haven: Yale University Press, 1970.

Ronbunshu, Nishida Kitaro Tetsugaku. *A Collection of Articles by Kitaro Nishida*, vol. II. Tokyo: Iwamani Shoten, 1988.

Rose, Jacqueline. "The Imaginary." *Sexuality in the Field of Vision.* London: Verso, 1986.

Roudinesco, Elisabeth. *Jacques Lacan & Co.* Chicago:University of Chicago Press, 1990.

Roviello, Anne-Marie. "*Les écarts du sens.*" *Merleau-Ponty, phénoménologie et expériences.* Ed. Marc Richir and Etienne Tassin. Paris: Jérôme Millon, 1992.

Sartre, Jean-Paul. *Being and Nothingness.* Trans. Hazel E. Barnes. New York: Washington Square Press, 1966.

Schelling. *System of Transcendental Idealism.* Trans. B. Rand. *Modern Classical Philosophers* Boston: Houghton Mifflin, 1908. Reprinted in *Romanticism and Evolution: The Nineteenth Century.* Ed. Bruce Wilshire. New York: Putnam, 1968.

———. *The Relation of Plastic Art to Nature* (1807). Trans. Bruce Wilshire. *Romanticism and Evolution: The Nineteenth Century.* Ed. Bruce Wilshire. New York: Putnam, 1968.

Schilder, Paul. *The Image and Appearance of the Human Body: Studies in the Constructive Energies of the Psyche.* New York: International Universities Press, 1950.

Schmidt, James. *Maurice Merleau-Ponty: Between Phenomenology and Structuralism.* New York: St. Martin's Press, 1985.

Silverman, Hugh. "Cezanne's Mirror Stage." *The Merleau-Ponty Aesthetics Reader.* Ed. Galen Johnson. Evanston: Northwestern University Press, 1993.

Spiegelberg, Herbert. *The Phenomenological Movement,* vol. I. The Hague: Martinus Nijhoff, 1978.

Stern, Daniel. *The Interpersonal World of the Infant.* New York: Basic Books, 1985.

Tetsgaku, Nishida. *Shinshiryoh to Kenkyuh no Tebiki* (*Nishida Philosophy: New Material and A Research Guide*). Ed. Yoshio Kayano and Ryosuke Ohashi. Kyoto: Minerva Shoboh, 1987.

Von Senden, Marius. *Space and Sight. The Perception of Space and Shape in the Congenitally Blind Before and After Operation.* Trans. Peter Heath. New York: The Free Press, 1960.

Whitehead, Alfred North. *Science and the Modern World.* New York: The Free Press, 1925.

Wilshire, Bruce. *William James and Phenomenology: A Study of "The Principles of Psychology."* Bloomington: Indiana University Press, 1968.

Woolf, Virginia. *To the Lighthouse.* New York: Harcourt, Brace, and World, 1927.

# Index

wonder, 66
Woolf, Virginia: chaos theory and, 20,
  232, 237; *To the Lighthouse*, 230–31
word: Lacan on, 199n. 25; ontology and,
  26, 29; the unconscious and, 59
work, 207–08
worked-over-matter, 206, 210; philosophy
  and, 208
*World as Will and Representation* (Schopenhauer), 177
world, the, 7, 80–82, 91, 93; ambiguity
  and, 110–11; art and, 60; Being and,
  67n. 7; the body and, 10, 58, 123, 136;
  body image and, 128; as capital, 205;
  change and, 202; chaos theory and, 219,
  230, 235, 239; chiasm and, 20; as
  community, 202; Descartes and, 9; existentials and, 59; experience and, 111;
  the feminist and, 153–54; as flesh, 31,
  43, 83, 113–15, 233–35, 244; freedom
  and, 199n. 32; intersubjectivity and,

190, 192, 195; nervous system and,
245; ontology and, 25; polymorphous
matrix and, 78; reflection and, 28;
reversibility and, 232; self-awareness
and, 56n. 21; Sorbonne Lectures and,
71, 75; the soul and, 65; spatiality and,
29
writer, the, 177, 179
writing, 177–78, 207, 212; spectral, 213
Wurzer, Wilhelm, 18–19

Yeats, William, 225
'yes' (initializing), 77
Young, Iris: the feminist and, 149, 150,
154, 156; Irigaray and, 155

*Zeit*, 212
*Zeitgeist*, 213
*Zeitgung*, 205
*Zeitkapital*, 205, 210–14
Zen, 108